DISHED!

DISHED!

The Rise and Fall of British Satellite Broadcasting

PETER CHIPPINDALE
& SUZANNE FRANKS

S I M O N   &   S C H U S T E R

LONDON·SYDNEY·NEW YORK·TOKYO·SINGAPORE·TORONTO

First published in Great Britain by
Simon & Schuster Ltd in 1991
A Paramount Communications Company

Simon & Schuster Ltd
West Garden Place
Kendal Street
London W2 2AQ

Simon & Schuster of Australia Pty Ltd
Sydney

A CIP catalogue record for this book is
available from the British Library
ISBN 0–671–71077–X

Typeset in Melior 11/14 by Falcon Typographic Art Ltd,
Edinburgh & London
Printed and bound in Great Britain by
Butler & Tanner Ltd, Frome

For our mums, Ruth and Hedy

Contents

Preface   page xi

Acknowledgements   xiii

Chronology   xv

Part One

Prologue   3

1 Pie in the Sky   5

2 Mr Marketing   18

3 The Empire Strikes Back   37

4 We're so Square   55

5 Film Wars   67

6 To Boldly Go . . .   87

Part Two

7 BSBBC   105

8 The Chips are Down   120

9 Mission Impossible   140

10 The Holes in the Mint   156

CONTENTS

11   X Certificate   176

12   Chicken Noodle   192

13   Cross Eyed   206

14   A Licence to Burn Money   219

Part Three

15   Midsummer Madness   235

16   Tie Me Kangaroo Down Sport   253

17   The Eagle is Landing   266

18   To BSkyB or not to BSkyB   280

19   Ninja Mutant Hero Television   295

20   Sky's the Limit   311

Index   320

'In the future everyone will be famous for fifteen minutes.'
– Andy Warhol, speaking on the subject of television in the 60s.

Preface

British Satellite Broadcasting was one of the greatest commercial disasters in British history, and certainly the greatest in the history of the British media. It came at a time when the country was poised on the cusp between regulation and free market forces, and its battle with Rupert Murdoch's Sky TV epitomised in many ways the two different approaches to business.

BSB was one of the great '80s roadshows, second only in size to the Channel Tunnel as a capital investment start-up, and a monument to the decade's prime industry of marketing. Few tears are likely to be shed for its demise as few people got to see any of its output. It will be remembered mostly for its squarial, an object second only to the Sinclair C5 as an 80s' absurdity.

Meantime the number of Sky-style satellite dishes redesigning the urban landscape bear mute testimony to the fact that the new merged company of BSkyB is 'bucking the brown goods trend'. Sales are continuing to climb despite recession and there is an underlying conviction both amongst the media and City analysts that eventually it will work. How much more money will disappear into the satellite black hole before that happens is still anyone's guess but analysts are confident that eventually it will be a money-spinner to exceed the track record of Rupert Murdoch's favourite and most profitable newspaper, The Sun.

Meantime the spin-off from BSkyB's American-style activity has been reflected in the aggressively commercial approach of the new ITV franchise applications, leading to fresh and correct agonising that British television is suddenly about to get much worse. BSkyB has emerged as the sharp end of the industry's pull towards America, just as the rest of the country goes into Europe.

But the story of the rise and fall of the old BSB itself is a peculiarly British one, which takes its place in a long and honourable tradition. Equally its battle with Sky reflects two very different attitudes, on which the authors have striven not to take sides.

The authors themselves have brought two very differing backgrounds to the book. One has worked most of his life in the printed word, whilst the other has always been in television. They hold differing views about the medium, but are united in their belief that it is an industry which tends to take itself too seriously. Nobody in the short but lively saga of BSB actually died. They also agree, as this book undeniably proves, that television is an industry which can gobble up extraordinarily large sums of money.

Peter Chippindale and Suzanne Franks
Wadebridge, North Cornwall and North London
August 1991

Acknowledgements

When researching this book on the News International side we made a number of enquiries via Jane Reed, the Director of Corporate Affairs, who refused us formal interviews with employees on the inaccurate grounds that we had 'sold the idea of the book on a particular angle'. All former Sky and BSB employees still with the merged BSkyB were then instructed not to talk to us. A substantial number at all levels however ignored this and were prepared to speak non-attributably. We would like to thank them both for being interviewed, generally helpful and for reading passages of the manuscript.

Former BSB shareholders exhibited mixed attitudes. A number were very helpful, including Robert Devereux of Virgin, David McCall of Anglia, Robert Rayne of LMS and David Plowright of Granada. Derek Lewis of Granada and Frank Barlow of Pearson went through various loops. Lewis first agreed to an interview but upon our arrival said he could not speak unless he was allowed to see and have right of veto over the manuscript. Barlow pulled out of his interview the day before it was scheduled without explanation and did not reply to subsequent letters and phone calls. Ian Irvine of Reed, whose time at BSkyB's helm was abruptly brought to a close earlier this year, did not reply to any letters or phone calls at all.

Their former employees were more forthcoming, although

several preferred to be non-attributable. We would particularly like to thank Anthony Simonds-Gooding for his patience and openness with us and others who agreed to be interviewed, sometimes at great length: John Gau, Peter Bell, Edward Bickham, Andy Coleman, Ellis Griffiths, Graham Grist, David Eglise, Chris McLaughlin, Andy Birchall, Hugh Williams, Chris Irwin, Susanna Capon and Nick Moncrieff.

Others who also consented to often lengthy interviews were Leighton Andrews, Bruce Todd and Peter Thornton at Crown-IRN, Ed Boyle, Adam Boulton, Ben Hawke, John Stapleton, Nick Carrington, Nigel Bogle, Steve Kershaw, Julian Aston, David Glencross of the ITC (formerly the IBA) and Chris Akers of Swiss Bank (formerly of Citicorp). A number of others on both the television and the political scene preferred not to be named.

Useful insights, suggestions and help were given by John Bowers, Eric Ellis, Barry Fox, the Channel 9 staff, Clive Wolman, Tricia McLernon, Leanne Klein, Andrew Croker, Variety staff, Angela Riley, Zoe Grimwood, Kerry Guswell, Amanda Glynn, Felix Franks, Tim Simmons, Mitchell Caller, Gunnar Rugheimer, Mitchell Symons, Paul Barry, Mike Taylor, Helen and the gang, the Whitbread Staff, Jeff and the team, Sarah Macdonald, Oxfam, Mike Poole and Sally Crawford. Special thanks to Nick Higham for help with the manuscript.

We are grateful to Roma Felstein for carrying out a number of the interviews, and Claudia Shaffer along with all at Simon and Schuster who put up with the strain of authors writing to a tight deadline.

Our thanks, as always, go to our agent, Mark Lucas, but most of all we would like to thank our editor, Brian Perman, for his belief in this project in the first place, and for his patience and support, along with Nick Webb for guiding it safely through its final stages.

Chronology

1977

Five DBS channels allocated to Britain at the World Administrative Radio Conference (WARC)

1979

Harold Wilson makes speech forecasting foreign cultural invasion

1980

Home Office investigates options for UK satellite broadcasting

1982

Two DBS Channels allocated exclusively to the BBC
Home Office recommendation D-MAC be adopted is accepted by Government
Launch of Sky Channel in Europe

1984

Government proposes joint DBS 'Club of 21' venture

1985

June: Club of 21 collapses

July: Home Secretary asks IBA to review prospects for commercial DBS

1986

December: BSB wins DBS contract

1987

March: Graham Grist appointed

July: Signing of contract between IBA and BSB and first round financing worth £222.5m

October: Stock market crashes on Black Monday. ASG starts as chief executive

1988

February: TV-am strikers sacked, three months after lock-out

March: Breakdown of BSB news negotiations with ITN

April: BSB meeting with Lord Young over fifth terrestrial channel

May: BSB moves from Old Park Lane to IBA building
Contracts with GI and ITT completed

June: Murdoch announces Sky

August: Presentation of BSB dummy squarial

September: Sky scraps ACTT agreement, announces will go non-union
BSB awards TWI sports contract, Daily Mail and YTV daytime contracts and Crown news contract
BSB announces plans for flotation in 1989
BSB complain to OFT and ASA re Sky ads

October: Sky announces movies will be encrypted. John Gau joins BSB

November: Andrew Neil joins Sky

December: BSB signs £200 million Paramount movies deal
Launch of Broadcasting White Paper
Virgin sells BSB stake to Bond
Disney Channel announced for Sky
BSB given permission to apply for Stock Exchange listing
Ariane rocket launch

1989

January: BSB's big investors raise another £131m for film purchases. Total investment now 353.5m
Austin Mitchell sacked from Labour front bench

February: Sky launches

May: BSB announces launch delay due to technical problems
Disney pulls out of Sky

June: BSB second round financing delayed

Sky sponsors *Carmen* at Earls Court
Australian Broadcasting Tribunal rules Bond unfit to control broadcasting interests
IBA awards two more channels to BSB
Graham Grist leaves

July: Sky 'relaunch'
BSB changes promotion from squarial to 'TV with Ears'

August: BSB completes move to Marcopolo House
Marcopolo I satellite launched from Cape Canaveral
Murdoch gives McTaggart lecture at Edinburgh Festival

September: Sky Project X launched

1990

January: BSB delays second round financing after Stock Exchange insists on shareholder approval
BSB mailshot to 10,000 'opinion-formers'

February: Murdoch takes over as Chief Executive of Sky
Robin Day signs up with BSB
West Indies Test on Sky 1
Sky starts to encrypt films
Whole Movie Channel encrypted by late February
BSB announces £900m of second round financing approved

March: BSB 'service' launch to cable homes

April: Official BSB launch

June: BSB misses banking target. Loan briefly in default

July: Cross-media amendment in House of Lords fails at Committee stage of Broadcasting Bill
Murdoch and Peter Davis of Reed meet at Claridge's
Bond diluted to 7.5% share, having failed to participate in second round financing

August: News International reports losses of £266m to June. Sky operating losses £95m, with £121m start-up costs

September: Sky announces 16,000 dishes removed in August because of bad debt
Second Marcopolo satellite launched
Sam Chisholm takes over as Chief Exec of Sky
BSB announces £50m marketing drive to Christmas
BSB achieves banking target

October: Cutbacks at BSB
10% cuts across the board at Sky
Peter Bell leaves BSB
Andy Birchall announces he is leaving

15/16:   Ian Irvine meets Murdoch in Australia

21–26:   Week of merger meetings at Lucknam Park

27:   Chairmen of shareholders and Murdoch meet at Reed

29:   Murdoch sees Thatcher

November:
1:   Broadcasting Bill becomes statute

2:   Merger completed. New company announced as BSkyB, trading as Sky

6:   IBA pronounces merger "serious breach" of BSB programme contract

20:   IBA announces BSB contract to terminate end of 1992

22:   Margaret Thatcher resigns

PART ONE

Prologue

On 5 December, 1979 Sir Harold Wilson, already the forgotten Prime Minister after the election of Mrs Thatcher earlier in the year, rose from his seat in the House of Commons to give his country a dramatic warning. Britain was about to be hit by 'a foreign cultural invasion through the satellite', he revealed. Television programmes beamed from the Continent in three languages were shortly to cover all of the country, and most homes would be receiving them by the simple use of a dish placed in the loft. TV PIRATES FROM SPACE, the *Daily Express* screamed from its front page the next morning, conveying to an unstartled public the latest message from the man famous for having introduced the 'white heat of technology'.

Sir Harold's credentials as a TV expert were currently being faintly boosted by hosting his own chat show, which turned out to be short-lived. But the evidence on which his prediction was based had come through official channels. It had been given to a committee he was chairing, and they had seen maps. 'The cultural invasion through the satellite', he now explained to MPs in his cultivated Northern accent, would bring 'Radio Luxembourg writ large'. Not only would 'the satellite' be a threat to the BBC, but it could put advertising revenue for the commercial companies in danger of shrinking to nothing. Satellites cost about £100 million to put up, he explained helpfully, but were expected to make a profit from advertising of £150 million in their first year alone.

'Broadcasting satellites will be a real force from 1983–4, building up during the 1980s to full saturation,' Sir Harold concluded. 'Ministers should be preparing for this very important development.'

At the Home Office they called another meeting.

CHAPTER ONE

Pie in the Sky

It was almost precisely seven years after Sir Harold's dire warning that a new company, proudly bearing the word 'British', was licensed to take up the mantle of 'the satellite'. Its mission was precisely the opposite of the foreign cultural invasion Sir Harold had predicted. Instead it was to beam down a celestial version of British television which, as everybody in the country had always been told, was the best in the world.

In the intervening years the satellite horror Sir Harold had predicted had notably failed to happen. In Europe there was Sky Channel, a little-watched service owned by the world's largest media-magnate, Rupert Murdoch, but Britain had remained immune from foreign contamination. Instead video had mushroomed as the alternative to conventional TV, to the extent that Britain had achieved the highest video penetration in the world, with machines in 67% of all households. The video market had got into gear at the beginning of 1980s, paralleling the new world of choice being ushered in by the Conservative Party under the thrusting leadership of Mrs Thatcher. For the first time TV viewers had been able to record programmes to watch whenever they felt like it, not just at the time they were broadcast. More importantly for most of them they could escape from TV entirely by renting films from the newly-emerging video rental shops, offering first hundreds and then thousands to choose from.

From the beginning video had been a downmarket-led industry, sucking in the traditional old working class which was now redefined in modern marketing-speak as social groups C2, D and

5

E. These had seized their freedom as an opportunity to pile into exactly the kind of material they had previously been denied on broadcast television. Soft porn had shot to the top of the rental charts alongside the new 'video nasties' – horrible, low-budget exploitation films with titles like Driller Killer, Nightmares in a Damaged Brain, and SS Experiment Camp. Uniformly these had nothing to recommend them except the nastiness which gave them their nickname, but the video audiences loved them, relishing the opportunity to study the goriest bits in close detail through the new gadgetry of freeze-frame and slow motion. And with the new freedom to watch at will some households were cheerfully ploughing through as many as four or five films a day.

After its initial cowboy days the video rental industry had since cleaned up its act and settled down to become respectable, with cinema-type regulation brought in via the British Board of Film Censors. The television industry had also adapted to living with the opposition, although there had been some graphic indicators of video's popularity as an alternative. When the 1983 election, which was to give Mrs Thatcher a landslide majority, was hailed in the media as the first real TV election, viewers responded to the saturation coverage by switching off in droves, and video shops reported a 40% increase in rentals during the campaign.

During the interim terrestrial television had also adapted to meet the new conditions with the introduction of breakfast television on both the BBC and ITV and the start-up of Channel 4. But the field of satellite, controlled by the government, had remained locked in the old world of the institutional past.

The government's direct interest sprang from WARC (World Administrative Radio Conference) in 1977 which, although this had not meant much at the time, had reallocated frequencies throughout the world, incidentally causing great traumas for Britain's highbrow radio listeners who had to retune their sets to continue listening to their beloved Radio Four.

The conference also allocated five Direct Broadcast by Satellite (DBS) channels to Britain, which the Home Office had then sought to exploit. The first attempt had been to foist two of them on to the BBC, but that idea foundered on cost grounds. The Home Office then came up with a muddled attempt at co-operation beween public and private enterprise by proposing a joint venture between the BBC, ITV and private companies. An attempt was made to drum up interest among the regional TV companies and others to form what became known as the Club of 21, but after many meetings, this collapsed in a welter of recriminations and lawsuits.

The Independent Broadcasting Authority, the regulatory authority for commercial television and radio, had then moved 'the satellite' into the straight commercial sector. Although its title stated it to be independent, the IBA was under the auspices of the Home Office, and in many ways mirrored the BBC's Board of Governors, awarding the franchises to all the regional ITV companies and then licensing and policing them. Now it moved to license satellite transmissions by offering a franchise on three of the five WARC-allocated channels. Proceeding in a suitably bureaucratic manner it first invited 'expressions of interest' in September 1985, reported 'strong interest' in January 1986, and then invited applications in April. It was greeted by a rush.

But the IBA had another iron in the fire apart from its regulatory duties. The Authority also had a substantial engineering side running its transmitters and carrying out research and development, which was where the quid pro quo of the franchise offer came in.

Since the advent of colour, television signals in the UK and in much of the rest of the world had been broadcast on the PAL system, which used 625 horizontal lines to build up the picture on the television screen. A rival, French-developed system known as SECAM, which also used 625 lines, was favoured by Francophone countries and the Eastern bloc. And a third system, the American-developed 525-line NTSC (unkindly translated as "Never twice the same colour" on account of the system's technical inferiority), held sway in the US and Japan.

By now these systems were universally acknowledged to be deficient and were appearing even poorer as the technology of other sound and vision improved. The Japanese, who had decimated the old British electrical industry, had developed a new High Definition Television (HDTV) system which offered a wider cinema-style screen and pictures even sharper than the 35mm film used in the cinema, thanks to an increase in the number of lines making up the picture to 1125. Work had started in 1979, at the time of the Harold warning, but development was still proceeding. The Japanese acknowledged they were working for the long-term as their system involved scrapping all existing sets. It was also suitable only for satellite television: so much picture information needed to be transmitted that the signals couldn't be squeezed into the narrow frequency bandwidth of existing terrestrial television transmissions.

But the IBA's engineers believed that they too had found a way to improve the quality of future television pictures out of all recognition. They had developed a system for transmitting 625 line pictures called MAC (which stood for Multiplexed Analogue Component) television. BBC engineers had then dreamt up a way of transmitting digital sound alongside the pictures, creating a hybrid system called C-MAC. But this proved difficult in practice to transmit, so two other variants of MAC were developed: D-MAC by the Germans, and D2-MAC by the French. Not only did picture quality improve with MAC, but it also made high definition television (or HD-MAC) possible, if the number of lines was doubled to 1250.

Apart from their technical similarity there were two common threads linking the different MAC systems and the blizzard of acronyms by which they were known. The first was that they all offered an "evolutionary route" to high definition television: MAC signals were easy to convert for reception on PAL or SECAM sets because the number of picture lines was the same or, in the case of HD-MAC, a simple multiple of 625. The second was that the IBA held many of the patents for MAC, and stood to benefit whichever variant was adopted in practice. And there was another advantage in European broadcasters switching from PAL and SECAM to MAC transmission for satellite television: it was a way for European electronics companies to acquire a new lease of life by developing and manufacturing their own receivers, rather than making Japanese high definition sets under licence.

What the IBA was offering applicants for the British satellite franchise was effectively a partnership between itself and private enterprise. The winner would get the satellite channels, but would also have to pay for the development of the MAC technology, as well as for the necessary satellites and their launch.

To those pitching for the contract the likely road ahead therefore appeared to be an overall franchise for 15 years on three of the satellite channels, and a monopoly for three years. The other two channels would then be released into the market. The incumbent satellite company, which would have had time to bed in, would be able to apply for them, although it would not automatically be awarded them.

The catalyst for the application that was to become British Satellite Broadcasting, forever to be known as BSB, was Chris Irwin, who had worked for the BBC and been heavily involved in its satellite exploration which had come to nothing. Irwin, realising he possibly knew more about the subject than anyone else, thought he might as well try to form a consortium. He first persuaded the blue chip company of Pearson to come in by telling it: 'This the last great monopoly.' Irwin knew a rival Astra satellite was to be launched from Luxembourg, presumably bent on bringing the 'foreign cultural invasion' Harold Wilson had warned of. But the IBA, keen to promote its D-MAC technology, said Astra was only a medium-powered satellite and so a dish of at least 1.2 metres across would be needed to pick up a decent signal. This was so large it was bound to be unacceptable, and would anyhow require individual planning permission for each installation.

Pearson, still controlled by the Cowdray family and chaired by Viscount Blakenham, was a disparate company with a wide range of interests from Royal Doulton china to Warwick Castle and Wookey Hole. In the media field it owned the Westminster Press group of local newspapers, the *Financial Times* and Penguin books, as well as having a stake in Yorkshire TV and a fund for new media developments which was headed by the tall and languid Mark Burrell, a family cousin and old Etonian, who now started taking an interest.

Another company which now became involved was Granada, which had previously dabbled in satellite through its membership of the Club of 21. The giant leisure company's interests, stretching from TV to motorway service stations, gave it a number of potential interests. There could be programming through Granada TV which held the ITV franchise for the North

West, and sales through the group's core business of TV rental. Rental of satellite equipment was seen as a possibly major part of the business, just as with the video market.

The first important meeting to get the franchise application together was held at Granada's offices in Golden Square, Soho, and also brought in Richard Branson's company of Virgin. Aggressive, expansionist and recently floated on the Stock Exchange, Virgin saw satellite as a major opportunity to branch out of the music and publishing sectors. The BSB application was being handled by the blond and dashing Robert Devereux, who was Richard Branson's brother-in-law. Devereux, a Cambridge graduate, had gone first to Amnesty International and then to Macmillans, the publishers, before running Virgin's publishing business, which concentrated on music books.

Whilst Burrell was representing Pearson, for Granada the business side was being seen to by Derek Lewis, a thrusting young accountant whose early days had been spent at Ford. Lewis did not know much about programming, so David Plowright, the respected and experienced programme-maker from Granada Television had been brought in to see to that end of the application. The mix worked well and they all felt they could pull together.

Trying to widen the basis for the application there were talks with Central Television, but they dropped out and their place was taken by Anglia, one of the smaller ITV companies, which took the view this was an opportunity to expand in the TV business. Looking around for more partners, the consortium then targeted Alan Sugar of Amstrad. The technology would be an important part of the initial bid and if they won, getting a supply of dishes into the market place would be critical. The involvement of a manufacturer of hardware like Amstrad would underpin that side of things.

Alan Sugar, Amstrad's boss, was one of the few British success stories in the brown goods market – the trade slang for consumer electronics which dated from the days products like radiograms had been encased in wood veneer to make them look like pieces of furniture. He was a rough diamond who had been brought up on a tough estate in Hackney, North London and started in business selling aerials out of the boot of his car. After successfully getting into the bottom end of the hi-fi market and briefly flirting with the early 80s craze of Citizens' Band radio, Amstrad had cashed in on the video boom by pioneering low-budget machines. Just as significantly, Sugar had demonstrated how a market could be broken open by revolutionising personal computers with his PCW 8512 word processor, cleverly marketed as a replacement for the typewriter and rightly hailed as the Model T of word processing.

Although his company had grown so phenomenally it had entered Britain's Top 100, Sugar had never really been accepted in the City which had remained suspicious of his 'barrow boy' image though it could hardly fail to be impressed by his sure touch. Amstrad did not make its own goods, but had them manufactured in the Far East, principally in Korea, and Sugar's success had been based on ferociously keen pricing, high volume which brought down unit costs, and intelligent marketing. Very little went on ostentatious premises, as Derek Lewis and Robert Devereux discovered when they trailed through the wastes of East London to meet him at his headquarters in downtown Brentwood, Essex. When the consortium had started talking to Amstrad on the phone they had encountered problems with staff obviously petrified of being locked in the building when it was closed promptly at 5pm by the security guards, as it housed all the company's stock. People would start getting edgy around 4.30 and by 4.45 it was usually impossible to hold their attention. Sugar's answer to this as a management problem was that if everybody knew they had to be out by 5, they would finish their work by then whatever.

Amstrad HQ was now revealed to be a nondescript nine-storey office block, a hundred yards from the railway station and next to The Railway Arms. To their astonishment the BSB representatives discovered Sugar did not even have his own office, but worked from a battered leather armchair and desk plonked in the middle of the open-plan top floor. The trio retired to the similarly unpretentious boardroom, where plasticky Amstrad products were arranged haphazardly on the shelves, for an hour-long meeting.

Sugar liked the satellite idea instinctively. He felt there was an appetite for more TV amongst the people who bought Amstrad products, who were labelled in the company 'the truck driver and his wife'. And he saw that however much money he might make out of his holding, there could be an equally neat spin off to the deal for him if he had the inside track on supplying the receiving dishes. He made an instant decision, telling them Amstrad was in and immediately assigning his operations' director to be Amstrad's representative on the BSB Board.

The various consortia coming together with their applications included a number of Britain's highest-flying companies, from John Gunn's conglomerate of British and Commonwealth to Cambridge Electronics, Ferranti, Hambros Bank, Dixon's, Saatchi and Saatchi and Trillion, a major publicly-quoted TV facilities company. From abroad, although non-EEC nationals were limited to a 20% holding, there were Sears, Alan Bond's Bond Corporation of Australia, which was in a consortium with Tiny Rowland's Lonrho, Columbia Pictures and Rupert Murdoch's News International bidding with John Jackson.

Nevertheless by the time the BSB consortium had been reasonably well cemented it realised it was the leading contender alongside DBS UK, headed by Michael Green, the chairman of Carlton Communications. Middle class and North London Jewish, Green had risen fast and was much admired by Mrs Thatcher. He had laid down a marker by making an unsuccessful franchise application for the Thames area ITV franchise in 1980, and then made a hostile takeover bid for the station, which had been beaten off. Now he was teamed up with London Weekend Television and BSB decided if they could bring him into its own bid they would be the clear winner. Green accordingly visited Robert Devereux at the Virgin office in seedy Ladbroke Grove for the two sides to compare notes.

It was immediately apparent that the differences between them were irreconcilable. Typically, Devereux thought, Green wanted either complete control or at least a leading role. That was unacceptable. Then Carlton did not believe that a subscription movie channel was viable, whereas it was an integral part of BSB's business plan.The two men parted on the basis that Green would talk to his partners at LWT, but the consultation did not take long. Green rang back within half an hour. The answer was no.

The BSB members, now knowing they had a fight on their

hands, spent two or three days rehearsing in Granada's Golden Square offices before going into the real thing at 70 Brompton Road, the IBA's large office block where its huge staff was located. Mark Burrell, chairing the BSB pitch alongside Devereux and Derek Lewis, introduced the application with a brief summary before the others gave a series of slide presentations on programming, finance, marketing, and revenue generation. The IBA questioning concentrated on the programming which was obviously the aspect it was most interested in. A particular question about whether BSB would be able to acquire its films gave Devereux the opportunity to lay out the philosophy which the BSB business plan was based on. The principle was earnings per viewer through subscription rather than advertising. This would mean BSB could afford to pay and the Hollywood studios would certainly sell if the price was right. The answer seemed to meet with approval, and the consortium members were extremely pleased with the way it had all gone – so much so that as they came out of the building David McCall of Anglia, who had some inkling of what might lie ahead, remarked to one of the others: 'Congratulations! I think we're in danger of winning!'

There was a lull of several weeks until 3pm on 11 December when everyone was called back to the IBA's offices for the verdict. As they went in the back door which they were using to avoid the press Robert Devereux bumped into Christopher Bland, the chairman of LWT, who was the other key figure in the rival Carlton bid. The pair shook hands in a gentlemanly fashion and exchanged platitudes like, 'May the best man lose' before they were ushered into their separate rooms. An IBA officer then walked into the BSB room and asked them all to come into the chairman's office, where Lord Thomson stuck out his hand. 'I'm delighted to tell you you've won,' he said with a smile.

Downstairs Derek Lewis of Granada chaired a brief press conference before they all went off to celebrate. It was just before the Christmas break after which the business of raising the necessary serious money would start. But there was already another reason for breaking open the champagne. Within minutes of their victory being announced the first tranche of outside funding had already arrived as a cheerful voice came winging its way over the phone lines from Down Under. 'Hello, it's Alan Bond here,' said the Australian entrepreneur who had become a national hero by winning the America's Cup for his country, and been in one of the losing consortium bids. 'It's five o'clock Aussie time and I'd like to invest in your company. How much do you want?'

The answer, by anybody's standards, was a lot. Nobody at that stage had any inkling of what a massive amount it would eventually become, but even at the beginning, BSB, in the language of the 80s, was only for major players. Even without the auspicious start of Bond's request to come on board the New Year timing for raising more money could not have been better. In October 1986, just as the first satellite hopefuls were presenting to the IBA, the City had undergone the 'Big Bang', switching to computerised dealing and sweeping away the old Stock Exchange floor overnight. London, at the centre of the new world market with its twin advantages of speaking English and being strategically time-located between America and Japan, had been caught up in the worldwide stock market boom. The government had added its own fuel to the fire by its spate of privatisations as Mrs Thatcher strove to turn Britain from a nation of small shopkeepers into a nation of small shareholders.

As the Yuppies talked up the market, global communications had become all the rage with the media sector flavour of the month. Television companies like TV-am, Thames and Yorkshire had already been floated to excited stagging activity from punters out for an instant profit, the advertising sector was soaring, and the whole media field was seen by analysts as alight for investors. The television sector peaked in April 1987 just as the money-raising was at its height, and in July the result of this propitious timing was the signing of the first round of financing which had raised £222.5 million. Of the original consortium members Virgin was now in for £25 million, Pearson for £30 million and Granada for £35 million. Anglia had put in £11.5 million.

Alan Bond, true to his telephone call, had taken the largest slice of all with £50 million, and a number of additional investors had been roped on to the bandwagon. Chris Irwin had taken a trip across the Channel to the French company of Chargeurs SA, a conglomerate with interests in textiles and communications which included films and transport. Chargeurs was in France's Top 40 companies, with very actively traded shares, and had been looking for new media interests. It had been impressed by the success of its native Canal Plus station, broadcasting a subscription film service on the French version of D-MAC, which after a shaky start was doing well and had 3 million viewers. There was a fashion in French utilities and heavyweights for investment in British television companies and Chargeurs had involved itself on a 'me too' basis. Chris Irwin thought the £24 million stake the easiest money he had ever raised.

Then there was Reed International, the plodding and diverse publishing company known in the City as the 'Ministry of Magazines'. This had previously been involved in communications with the general masses through ownership of the *Daily Mirror* but sold it three years earlier to Robert Maxwell. Reed came in for £20 million. George Davies' high-flying Next clothing chain added another £10 million; London Merchant Securities, owned by Lord Rayne and predominantly a property company, also came in for £10 million. Smallest investors of all were Invest International Holdings, with £5 million, and Trinity International Holdings, traditionally a conservative company which was based in Cheshire and best known as publishers of the *Liverpool Post* and *Echo*, with £2 million.

But one significant previous investor was already beginning to get cold feet. After being so quick to come into the original equation, Alan Sugar of Amstrad did not feel easy with the way BSB conducted its business in general. It seemed to him its priorities lay in the size of the office suites they were all going to have and he was not comfortable with the extravagance of what he had seen them planning. Most significantly of all, with the IBA proviso that the advanced – and costly – D-MAC system be used, a sizeable question mark now hung over the promise that a receiver kit could be available for £250. Never one to be profligate with what he called 'the old dosherooney', Sugar did not join the stampede to invest.

The central investment to be made with this initial capital was to be the £170 million required to buy the two satellites which would relay back from the D-MAC signal, with originally hopes of boosting British industry by giving the contract to British Aerospace. But the Hughes Aircraft company, a subsidiary of General Motors in America, had been keen to corner a new market. It offered a deal under which it would pick up a substantial proportion of the costs if the project foundered, which was a risk British Aerospace was not prepared to take. The offer had been accepted and Hughes had already started work.

The first tranche of capital raised, it was time to start recruiting staff. BSB brought in headhunters and for the company figurehead they in turn zoomed in on Sir Trevor Holdsworth, the president of the CBI, who was retiring as chairman of GKN. He was recruited as BSB's chairman, ironically by the same headhunters he was using to find his own successor at GKN. Richard Branson of Virgin, who saw him to discuss the post, remarked: 'It must be a long time since anybody interviewed you for a job,' and Sir Trevor agreed it certainly was.

BSB had already recruited its first employee in March, headhunting again in the pursuit of excellence. Graham Grist already had a reputation as a high-flier through being a former IBM Salesman of the Year, an accolade he had won when helping the National Westminster Bank to implement its Access system at Southend, which had been followed by a controversial cold-mailing of credit cards to 3 million people. Grist had joined IBM in 1968 and done seven years on systems engineering and sales before he went to BICC to become finance director of Balfour Beatty, part of the group and involved in large-scale construction projects from a dam in Sri Lanka to the Channel Tunnel.

After putting out feelers to headhunters, Grist had been approached about BSB. He was very impressed by the shareholders, and Virgin and Pearson seemed just the right blend of establishment and entrepreneur. He also liked the Channel Tunnel aspect of BSB's being a large start-up project. All in all it looked like a winner to him.

Grist was an enthusiastic executive, and many of the BSB staff were later to take as gospel the received wisdom that he had put himself through Harvard Business School. In reality it had been the London Business School, but he was still keen and self-motivated and although he knew little about television did not in any case see his job as a media one. He was so far from that side of it he actually found it slightly off-putting, but reasoned Granada's expertise would see to that end of things. The Board, now turning its attention to choosing the chief executive who was to be the one person above him, was thinking along similar lines.

CHAPTER TWO

Mr Marketing

The appointment of Anthony Simonds-Gooding as chief executive, to be known universally throughout the saga of BSB as ASG, came only after lengthy debate within the fledgling organisation. Not that this indicated any misgivings about ASG on a personal level. He was in fact one of the most popular and well-liked businessmen in Britain. Even after all the horrors BSB was subsequently to endure, nearly everyone involved was to remember him fondly at the end. It was impossible, if you worked with him or knew him socially, not to be captivated by his warmth, charm and natural gregariousness which combined to give him an extraordinary ability to motivate people. Quite simply, ASG was a born leader and people found him charismatic and inspirational.

As the shareholders got to know each other better there had been long discussions about the key position of chief executive, the pivot around which the whole company would revolve. As BSB was a different sort of television company to the terrestrials should he be a broadcaster or the alternative of a marketing man? (The job was never considered suitable for a woman.)

The shareholders had become virtually united in their view by 1 July, 1987, when with immaculate timing BSB officially became a company. Having raised its money when the TV sector of the market was peaking, 16 days after the company had been formed the London share price index reached an all-time high.

The odd man out in the chief executive debate was David Plowright from Granada Television, who was convinced BSB had to be a programme-led service. Plowright did not think there was much of a market for second-hand American material, which was awful. It was the BSB programmes which would matter. So he advocated in interminable discussions that the BSB principal should be a man who understood broadcasting, but had also learnt a degree of numeracy and cost control so he could run it as a business.

The other shareholders were largely uninterested. They did not think the programme-led philosophy was appropriate to a bull market. Derek Lewis, also from Granada but with a different background and perception, agreed with Virgin and the others. They all wanted an aggressive company driven by the twin considerations of the market and finance. The old-fashioned idea of good programming might be all right for the duopoly terrestial situation of yesterday when there was just ITV and the BBC, but Plowright then had to listen to various observations about how 'quality' television was a thing of the past. What BSB needed, the others were quite clear, was a marketing exercise, both to sell the service and make the subscriber base grow.

Hearing this endlessly repeated in meetings, Plowright reluctantly recognised how the focus in television had changed. Before the 80s companies had all had MDs with a background of programme-making, such as Paul Fox who had gone from the BBC to Yorkshire, Brian Cowgill at Thames, Brian Tesler at London Weekend, and Jeremy Isaacs who had started Channel 4 in 1982. But as the 80s had progressed a new culture had been brought in and the finance people – the men in suits – had started coming through to assume control. Nowhere was this more true than at the BBC, where Alasdair Milne, with 30 years' service in the Corporation and a background solely in programme-making, had earlier that year been sacked as Director General in favour of Michael Checkland. The appointment as DG of this accountant, predictably dubbed Michael Chequebook, had marked the end of an era. Plowright recognised that the same philosophy was driving BSB. Now the money men were in charge, programming was still held to be important but was no longer the main consideration. Reluctantly he realised the other Board members would have their way, and turned his attention instead to concentrating on steering the shareholders' programming committee.

But, before the final agonising decision was made, there was much indecisiveness and confusion. First BSB went to the headhunting agency Norman Broadbent asking them to find a chief executive who was a marketing person. Then, changing its mind, it decided it did want a broadcaster after all, and switched to the head-hunting agency GKR, which had broadcasting experience. Then it changed its mind yet again. But instead of going back to Broadbent to find a marketing man it let GKR keep the revised brief. The result at the end of the day was the recruitment of ASG, which was ironic. If BSB had gone back to Norman Broadbent ASG would not have been considered, as Broadbent had placed him in his current job and under headhunting rules repoaching was forbidden.

The man GKR now zeroed in on had risen to dizzying heights, and a dizzying salary, on the back of the marketing boom which had built up during the 60s and 70s and reached new peaks in the 80s with the marketing of the Prime Minister herself. And it was to the company which had helped promote her rise to power that BSB turned, as GKR put the heat on the man carrying the grandiose job-title of Chairman and Chief Executive of Saatchi and Saatchi Communications Worldwide.

Anthony Simonds-Gooding came from a services background and was just 50. He was born in Dublin in 1937 of an English father and an Irish mother, the daughter of 'Tiger' Riley, a famous horseman, polo-player and big-game hunter. Anthony was then whisked out to India at an early age to follow his father, Major Hamilton Simonds-Gooding as he pursued his career as a cavalry officer in the Indian Army. His was a fondly-remembered childhood, with hazy recollections of endless journeys in trains and carts as the family moved around the sub-continent and to and from the hill stations according to the season. Indian independence in 1947 had brought them back to Ireland, where they settled back at the family seat in the wilds of south-west Kerry before Anthony was sent to the equally wild countryside of North Yorkshire, to be educated at the staunchly Roman Catholic public school Ampleforth, where he was taught French and rugby by Cardinal Hume. He enjoyed the outdoor life and the school enabled him to follow his interest in games, which he continued until his mid-40s by playing rugby as a prop forward for London Irish and Surrey.

At the age of 16 after O levels, Simonds-Gooding had followed the dictates of his family background by leaving school to join the Royal Naval College at Dartmouth, graduating to a spell with the Far Eastern fleet on the frigates *Opossum* and *Mounts Bay*, based in Singapore. Then, as a sub-lieutenant, he had transferred to Faslane in Scotland on the frigate *Exmouth*, joining the 3rd Submarine Squadron which used the ship as the 'enemy' in training exercises.

Despite some rosy memories and having learned to cope with things like boredom and living with other people, Simonds-Gooding had decided there was no future in the Navy. In 1959, when he was 22 and had served in the Navy for six years, he had decided to go back into the mainstream just as if he were graduating from university. A great deal of money had been invested in his training and having made a commitment to Queen and country he knew he would have to leave the Navy in a proper manner by convincing their Lordships of the Admiralty he was going to a proper job. Seeing an advert he applied to join Unilever's management training course, a choice which their Lordships concurred with when he was accepted. He was allowed to buy himself out at the cost of £200.

Simonds-Gooding didn't know business from a pig's foot, and when the Unilever people asked him what he wanted to do, with his open background he simply didn't know. He never took himself or his career too seriously, so he asked them to outline what was involved in each of the different jobs, ending up in marketing and thereby getting in on the ground floor of an emerging industry. He then followed a textbook career by joining what was then the small division of Bird's Eye, whose staff were known as 'the barrow boys of Unilever'. As part of his training they put him on the road as a rep and sent him to Chippenham, where he was enormously impressed by the Welsh salesman deputed to show him the ropes. He was even more impressed by the device the salesman had rigged up on the back shelf of his company Morris Minor, where he had strung two parallel pieces of string on which he placed his Homburg hat upside down. It bounced along gently and could be retrieved for the next call without any creases or any dirt on it.

ASG liked that sort of thing; it was why he began to like marketing and he chuntered along as he put it, through his Bird's Eye career, helping foist things like fish fingers and frozen beefburgers on to the unsuspecting public. What intrigued him more than anything was people in every sense – the people he worked for, the people he worked with, the people who worked for him, and the general public, who were always full of surprises. There was, he always maintained, 'nowt so queer as folk', and marketing was all about understanding the market and what people did. Sales was just the direct process which followed. One of his favourite tales was of a disaster with a new Bird's Eye product of frozen apple fritters. They had researched brilliantly in test groups where ordinary people were paid to give their reaction, but then flopped in the market. The reason, he was fond of telling people with great relish, was that it was belatedly discovered people did not like getting up in the middle of their meal to fry the pud!

There were a couple of breaks as he moved from being managing director of this to managing director of that. He did two years in Brussels and Paris setting up a frozen food business for Bird's Eye and another eighteen months at Lintas, the advertising agency which Unilever owned, where he worked on Lever Brother products like soap powders, learning significant nuances which he had found wonderful such as the critical differences between the two words 'bright' and 'white'. He loved advertising and the people working in it, while advertising people in general found him enormously stimulating to work for because of his genuinely open mind.

Then came a seachange as, after 12 years, Simonds-Gooding moved to the family-owned brewers Whitbread as their first-ever marketing director. In 1974, two years after he had begun, Whitbread started the advertising campaign which made his name. At the beginning of the 70s the company, with a pedigree stretching back to the eighteenth century, was very much the fusty old brewery run by Colonel Bill Whitbread. Modern concepts such as employing a finance director and marketing director had not yet impinged on this gentleman's consciousness, and when they were explained to him he said he did the former and they already had two girls in the library to do the latter. But he had finally bowed to the insistence of Whitbread's bankers and first a finance director and then Simonds-Gooding as marketing director had been installed.

At that point, as the brewers locked in battle with the Campaign for Real Ale over the traditional British brew, the market for lager was just opening up. Whitbread had two brands, Stella Artois and Heineken, and a copywriter in the advertising agency of Collett, Dickinson, Pearce came up with an idea for an advertising campaign based on the strapline 'Heineken refreshes the parts other beers cannot reach'. The slogan researched very badly in groups, which ASG understood. He had a natural flair for advertising and knew it was supposed to come up with something new. If you did lager as an intellectual drill it came up as 1. refreshment 2. taste 3. strength. So saying it was refreshing was commodity advertising and meant you were advertising lager as such, rather than any particular brand.

But he still liked the slogan and it was one of those situations where you had to be brave and self-confident, ignoring the research, to trust in your belief that not only was it brilliant, but long-term and able to be used in a thousand ways. Even though it might not be unique in what it said, it was unique in the way it was saying it. It was expression rather than content which captured people's imagination. Simonds-Gooding backed the slogan, and it went on to become one of the all-time greats. As Heineken's share of the market soared, ASG's reputation soared with it and he was made.

At Whitbread, where he stayed for 13 years, a large marketing department to supersede the two girls in the library had just been set up before he arrived. There were a lot of people making noise, rather than music, and as he started reorganising it he self-deprecatingly described himself as 'a one-eyed man in the land of the blind'. He found that Whitbread, with the long family tradition it still maintained, already had a heritage of being excellent marketeers with brands like Mackeson, Whitbread Pale Ale and Whitbread Gold Cup, which were just that bit different. His job was to apply the modern systematic approach to marketing which was needed now everything was much bigger.

He was immersing himself in the patrician, powerful world of
the big brewers as the toyboy on the board when one of the other
directors called him in to offer a word of advice. 'We must win by
stealth,' the older man told him, drawing on his pipe, ' Remember
EHM – envy, hatred and malice.' When Simonds-Gooding looked
puzzled the director explained there was competition out in the
marketplace like Big Brother Bass. There was a famous brewing
saying that the brewers would get more out of a Britain sober than
a Britain drunk. 'Don't take the arse out of it,' he advised, 'Take
what you want, but don't be too greedy'. It was a conversation
which Simonds-Gooding was never to forget.

With the natural charm inherited from his Irish mother, ASG
moved easily within the company. Women especially described
him as a big cuddly bear of a man and found him enormously
endearing, particularly for his pinstriped suits which, although
he spent a fortune on them, somehow never seemed to fit him
properly. But he was a flamboyant character, big on emotion
and enthusiasm for life, with a ready smile and cheerful, brisk
manner. He had a warm, rich voice too, and a classless accent
that took away any suggestion of pompousness or privileged
upbringing.

Employees liked him for taking responsibility without qualms,
appearing to have adopted the old Army adage that an officer's
job was to make decisions and worry about whether they were
right or not later. If things went wrong he was prepared to
carry the can, not try to transfer the blame, and was willing
to admit that even though he always tried to do his best he
could make mistakes like everybody else. And he was generous
in his attitude, spending a lot of time walking the floor, taking a
genuine interest. In all his actions he maintained the egalitarian
spirit and knack of getting on with people he had learned in the
services to make people feel personally involved and motivate
them to do their best in their work.

As he saw it much of his role was in driving out arrogance, in
line with his central belief in never taking himself or the job too
seriously. There were two sorts of people he had to deal with –
the older brewers, who wanted all these new things to go away
and thought lager would never catch on, and the young graduates
joining the company who were equally arrogant in thinking the

older ones idiots. Simonds-Gooding came to realize he was part of a culture dating back to 1742 which was based on years and years of sound experience. Whitbread was a nice company, even if it was a bit smug, and naturally it made the odd cock-up like everybody else. But it had a very good sense of values and everybody liked it. Moving an army like that off in a new direction meant going at a speed it could take, which was in line with the 'not taking the arse out of it' advice for the market. One of the most fascinating aspects of the job was so many people doing so many different things who had to be considered.

After 13 years at Whitbread Simonds-Gooding had reached the top as group managing director, the first from outside the family, when suddenly he switched to a very different scene. Maurice Saatchi of Saatchi and Saatchi, whom he knew, asked him to join the rapidly expanding advertising company. 'Come and help me and my bruvver,' he said, 'We couldn't run a bath'.

The prospect was alluring enough to make Simonds-Gooding jump ship from Whitbread and he arrived in his new office to find it absolutely covered in roses. There was a small note on the desk reading: 'Over to you, Anthony. Best of luck. Charles and Maurice.' What sort of hand-over was this? he wondered. At least at Whitbread he had been started off with a copy of Arthur Bryant's *History of the Green Jackets* and *The History of Brewing*. This is going to be character-forming, he decided – an impression immediately confirmed when the head of the office in Melbourne, Australia rang. The sales director had run amok and he wanted to know if he had the authority to fire him, as he had only been there one day. Simonds-Gooding told him he had only been there two days himself. But he was there to make the decisions, so a decision he would make. 'Proceed as you think fit!' he advised with the old Naval signal.

Saatchi's had hired Simonds-Gooding as part of their plan to establish a global advertising agency, and a spate of acquisitions in his first four months meant the number of people reporting to him as chief executive of the communications side of the business rapidly spiralled from 4,000 to 14,000. His job, now far from marketing, was to rationalise the chaos as none of the new companies fitted together and all sorts of accounts were in conflict. He was plunged into 18 months of applying rhetoric to what was basically anarchy, seeing his primary task as averting disaster and getting everybody hunkered down in a proper manner. He finally achieved this to his satisfaction through reorganising and merging 19 different companies into seven, later dismissing as 'casual malice' the suggestion he had just done 'an Elastoplast job'. His round of applause from the Baghdad Brothers, as they were known, was the immortal econium: 'We gave you a toilet and you cleaned it. Thanks.'

In May 1987 ASG was living in David Frost's apartment in New York, on the nineteenth floor overlooking Central Park, when he was 'phoned by a GKR headhunter about the BSB job. Frantically busy with Saatchi business he brushed them off. It was not until August that he completed his mammoth task and returned exhausted to Britain having done what he had set out to do and seen the Saatchi share price climb from 350p to 750p.

All this time GKR had kept up the pressure. Different people kept ringing. 'Now, are you sure?' they would ask. 'Just stop by when you're in London and let us explain.' He fobbed them off but still they kept coming as he settled back in his home in Fulham, with excursions to his country house near Dorking, recovering from his debilitating Saatchi ordeal. In many ways he had had enough and when the headhunters rang yet again he finally bowed to the pressure. 'OK,' he replied, 'Take me to your leader!'

ASG ended up in the Virgin office in Ladbroke Grove, which he found a funny little place. Then, in bits and pieces over the next ten days, he went round meeting the other key shareholders' representatives – David Plowright, Derek Lewis, the chairman, Sir Trevor Holdsworth . . . At first he felt leery. There was no need for him to get involved in a venture like this which was obviously high-risk. But as he listened to the BSB people he got more and more interested. This was a club of enthusiasts, and the picture they were painting was compelling – more choice on TV, deregulation, developing new technology. Then there was the challenge of getting it all together – the satellites, the production technology, the marketing, the financing, the film encryption and, of course, the programming. On top of all this was the idea of rejuvenating the European electrical industry so 'all the currents were flowing in the same direction' as he put it in an unconscious pun. ASG was fully aware of how the Europeans had lost out in this field to the extent that eight out of the top ten electrical companies in the world were Japanese. All in all it sounded like a chance to make history.

Besides which these people – Pearson, Granada, Reed – were big, established companies. He had always believed in people who put their money where their mouth was and on that score he was looking at £220 million worth of credibility.

The chief executive's post would fit in with his personal circumstances as well. He was looking for a change and wanted to be in the UK so he could see more of his family. And he liked the fact that BSB was television. Personally he was only a light viewer, with catholic tastes, but television was a business that reached out to people directly. It fitted with his own interest in people and curiosity about what they did. It was glamorous as well, and there was the final attractive element that BSB was starting from scratch. Previously he had only belonged to long-established or family institutions. The only difficulty, of course, was whether it would all work.

Finally he decided to give it a go and started making appropriate noises. Everybody at the BSB end had agreed to the appointment when Saatchi's, frantic at the prospect of losing this top man, began to wheedle and he started to wobble. He rang BSB to say Saatchis had made him feel guilty and he couldn't leave. The brothers had a new megaplan of making a takeover bid for the Midland Bank, which he was involved in.

Until this point, apart from the first meeting, Richard Branson of Virgin had largely stayed out of the BSB business, but Robert Devereux, realising there was more than one way to catch a monkey, now got in touch with his boss and brother-in-law. Then he rang Simonds-Gooding back. Would he come down at the week-end to meet Branson at his country house? It was the kind of invitation ASG couldn't refuse and he went down a Saatchi man to return a BSB man.

Branson made the day a family affair, which was the way ASG liked to do things, and also enabled him to take along his greatest fan, his wife Marjorie. It was the kind of gracious occasion and world they both knew and loved, and although Branson simply reiterated what the other shareholders had already told him, in such idyllic surroundings ASG found him a compelling salesman. The two chatted amiably about Virgin Airways, with ASG getting the impression that he knew a lot more about it than its owner thanks to having flown the airline a great deal on his transatlantic commuting nightmare for Saatchi's. The previous year he had clocked no less than 60 crossings.

The day passed in a pleasant haze of lunch, swimming in the pool, playing tennis and walking round the lovely grounds, where they saw an extraordinary snake skimming across the pond. But underneath the delightfully civilised veneer was a harder cash incentive. In his virtually unassailable position ASG was able to negotiate an extraordinarily remunerative offer, even by marketing standards. If he took the job he would get a flat salary of £248,000, an additional £310,000 lump sum as a 'golden hello' compensating him for the loss of share options at Saatchi's and a dizzying selection of perks. There were BSB share options which could one day make him a virtual millionaire when it was floated on the Stock Exchange, expenses, company cars, health care, credit cards, petrol cards . . .

Virgin remained uncomfortable about the package ever afterwards, but reminded themself that ASG had been head and shoulders above anyone else. Other candidates had been considered and vague approaches made to Jeremy Bullmore, head of the advertising agency WPP, but ASG outshone them all. The specification was for a person with operational experience of a large company with a lot of employees, accustomed to working in difficult circumstances, and used to dealing with a strong board (he had become used to dealing with opinionated individuals at Saatchi's). Virgin, eventually justified the appointment in their own minds as an investment. ASG was very impressive, very charismatic, and had impeccable leadership and marketing credentials. The others were simply delighted. Chris Irwin thought him very much the dream candidate and was terribly flattered when he came on board. David McCall of Anglia thought him a man of great stature with a very strong personality, which was needed. It was going to be a big marketing job persuading consumers to buy dishes.

Even David Plowright, despite his misgivings about putting a marketing man at the head of the company, was impressed. When he met ASG he found he had real presence – a sense of humour and a missionary zeal. Probably, he thought, it was because being at the helm of BSB was as interesting as standing on the bridge of a frigate back in his old Navy days. Plowright also formed the opinion ASG was tough. Like David McCall of Anglia he had a clearer grasp than some of the other shareholders of what lay ahead. ASG, he felt sure, would be able to take it.

And as far as everyone was concerned apart from his being an outstanding character, one of the bonuses of being from outside the media was his not being linked to any established television company. That meant he was not part of either entrenched establishment or suffering from predetermined patterns of thought.

For ASG it all fitted his career pattern. Instead of BSB, he could have moved to a job with any blue chip company, but like the switch to Saatchi's this was not the first career move he had made which had surprised both colleagues and observers of the industry. He himself was describing it as 'one last run' and saying it would be 'really, really interesting to have one last big thing to do'. And big, with costs now put at £625 million, it was certainly going to be.

The lucrative deal signed, ASG, with the fitting payroll number of 007, stepped into his £4,769 (basic) a week job as chief executive on 19 October, 1987. The stock market promptly went through the floor, with share prices crashing as the long bull market ended spectacularly in what was dubbed Black Monday. For some time, as unemployment had mounted, parallels had been drawn in the Big Papers with the great depression of the 20s. Now the crash was likened to the financial disaster on Wall Street in 1929, with Rupert Murdoch's Sun strapping its headline of CRASH! with: 'It's throw yourself out of the window time, folks!' Mrs Thatcher had cashed in at the right moment with the election in June, four months earlier, which had given the Tories another five secure years.

When the bubble burst much of the froth evaporated instantly as share prices in Britain, America and across the world were cut by 25% across the board. The share price of ASG's former employers, which he had been so proud of helping double from 350p to 750p during the previous year, had already dropped

100p in the preceding three months – 50p of this when it was announced he was leaving. Now it went into a nose-dive that was to turn into a terminal spin, incidentally decimating the value of the share options he had just been compensated for. Although ASG did not yet know it, the market crash was the first indication the tide had just turned against his new command of the Good Ship BSB. All the shareholders' companies had naturally suffered as millions of £s were wiped off their market capitalisation, but for Pearson there had been a different shock in the previous month when Rupert Murdoch had taken 20% of the company's shares in a dawn raid. Although Murdoch had said he was not seeking control the unexpected move had been a major alarm.

But little of this concerned him as he started working away in a nondescript edifice in the heart of advertising land in Old Park Lane, known locally as the Pan Am building and providing unserviced and very cramped quarters. BSB's first key man, Graham Grist, was already on board and had been working for six months on various aspects of the company, including the crucial job of getting the untried D-MAC technology required by the IBA licence up and running. Grist's progress reports seemed satisfactory, so ASG let him get on with that side of the business whilst he started building his own team.

His first call was to Peter Bell, an old chum from Unilever whom he had appointed brands director at Whitbread. Bell was currently working as marketing director for the Whitbread subsidiary of Pizza Hut UK, the reorganisation of whose parent company in America ASG counted as one of his own principal Whitbread achievements. The pair had met up again in New York, where ASG had even been discussing an appointment for Bell with Saatchi's. Like ASG he was a classic marketing high-flier whose skills had been honed not in the word of creative television, but in mass-market foods, known in the trade as Fast Moving Consumer Goods or FMCGs.

Bell was astonishingly young to be considered for such a key post at BSB. Born in Catterick, North Yorkshire in 1954, he was little over 30 years old. After being educated at nearby Richmond School he had gone to Leicester University to read for a BA in Social Sciences and then, like ASG, taken the guaranteed fast track to marketing eminence by joining Unilever under the graduate training scheme. After serving his 18-month apprenticeship in selling, market research, promotions and finance, Bell had gone up the familiar ladder – assistant brand manager on pie fillings and family soups; brand manager, Cup-A-Soup; product group manager (beverages) with responsibility for Instant Soups.

In 1979 Bell had been headhunted to Whitbread, where he had worked for five years under ASG. As marketing director ASG had reorganised Whitbread's marketing on a regional basis and Bell set up a new marketing department for the East Pennines. Physically, beer suited him well as he was a large man who looked as though he enjoyed a pint and had a hearty, generous manner.

In September 1982 he had been appointed UK Beer Brands Director, where he had formulated a business plan for national ales, lager and packaged beers and developed Whitbread Best Bitter, the group's biggest hit since Heineken. At the same time he had fought to maintain the latter's market share in the face of fierce competition from 40 new lager brands which had been introduced in three years. His enormous enthusiasm for his task and dedication to marketing was not always shared by the reps to whom the latest product would be revealed, with ambitious scenarios about how it would be placed. 'Another marketing first . . . ' they would remark cynically to each other when Bell and his cohorts came on to present their spiel.

In 1986 following ASG, who was by then with Saatchis, he had moved to New York as vice president of Whitbread North America. Then he had come back to England to go to Pizza Hut, where he was just getting involved in developing a new business plan and changing the company's advertising agency when he received the call.

ASG took his old friend to breakfast at the Cavendish Hotel. When offered the job of head of marketing at BSB, Bell was postively ecstatic. It sounded like the most exciting marketing job in Britain! Furthermore, it was a chance for him to find a niche in broadcasting, which was usually impossible for marketing people. There was no challenge in things like airtime on ITV, where you could sell all you could produce, but BSB was different. It was competing with the entirely established marketplace of the BBC and ITV. They not only had a 20- to 30-year start, but absolutely no distribution problems. The entire population simply had to press a button to receive them, yet to receive BSB people would have to go through the physical act of purchasing new equipment. You could not, therefore, just treat them as viewers in the way that terrestrial TV did. You had to treat them as customers to be sold a product – and that was where his marketing skills would come in.

Bell accepted the job at once, leaving Pizza Hut the next day. As the business plan which had won the franchise was already in place, he saw his present role as a strategic one. He would be marketing the programmes once BSB was on air, but if satellite TV were to be sold as a product there was a long way to go before that. Bell began recruiting his team and organising more of the vital research on which all successful marketing depended.

ASG meanwhile had his hands full with myriad tasks. There was all the business of setting up flow charts, instructing headhunters to recruit more key staff, and generally getting things organised – which included his primary task as a marketing man of beating the drum and getting the 'good news' message of BSB going in the outside world. He had already said in press interviews that he 'would bet a pound to a gooseberry' people would not have four buttons on their set for ever and explained he had joined the venture because it had been 'like going to the tailor and finding the suit fits very well'. Friends and associates in adland watching Tony as he took the first steps of his adventures in medialand found this remark particularly amusing as they recalled his often somewhat rumpled appearance.

He had also slightly blotted his copybook by disingenuously remarking he thought BSB was a 'good wheeze' and 'enormous fun', but at the beginning of November he was back in full flow on the speaking platform where he excelled as he addressed a conference in London entitled 'Images of the Future'.

The launch of BSB, he enthused, was 'the most important broadcasting event since the launch of television 50 years ago'. By 1995 the company would be 'the largest acquirer of programmes in Europe – and only halfway along the road.' ASG put so much gusto into his task, and spoke at such length, that the tea break had to be cancelled and the next presentation, on the interesting aspect of who would pay for the various new services being excitably proposed, withdrawn. The only glitch came when he was asked about confusion over transmission and encryption standards. He could not really help on that one, he admitted. He had only been in his job for days. But, he assured them all, he was shortly to have an introductory briefing. The next speaker was applauded as he opened by commenting: 'Satellite has broader bandwidth in more ways than one!'

On the logic that BSB was to have three channels, channel heads had already been appointed and ASG was content to let them get on with their jobs unimpeded so long as they reported directly to him. Andy Birchall was running the subscription Movie Channel which was the key to the business plan after being recruited from Premiere, a cable TV film channel he had founded in 1984. Birchall, a vegetarian who did not drink or smoke, prided himself on being extremely fit and had an unusual background for a media person in having once taught woodwork in a school. He lived with his wife, who was a committed green journalist, and three children in a beautiful working mill house in East Sussex which he had converted himself, and on his own admission was not a team man but liked working alone. He had been offered the job by Robert Devereux, who had been impressed by his mixture of business acumen and programming experience when he was running Premiere, and had accepted as he saw BSB as the biggest media adventure ever. Before that he had been the development manager for the BSB shareholder, Pearson.

The second channel head was Bob Hunter, a former editor of News at Ten who had helped to set up TV-am. Hunter, who was Irish and in his mid-40s, did not suffer fools gladly and was already known for his lack of patience, but at the same time had a great sense of fun and was to become a byword in the company for his sharp dress sense. The other two channels were not so precisely defined as the Movie Channel and presently veering through various permutations of the whole gamut of sport, programmes for women, programmes for children, news and current affairs, the arts, music (both highbrow and pop), and general light entertainment. All sorts of trendy names like Zig Zag, Galaxy, Life Style and NOW were being bandied about and nobody was quite sure how each would pan out, but there was enormous enthusiasm and it was definitely agreed each would establish a different identity.

This all fitted with Peter Bell's marketing plans, which he now explained at an early 'awayday' – a feature of BSB management style through which various execs and heads of departments met together outside the office for a brainstorming session. In these early days, ASG well realised, they were a gang of coves who didn't really know each other and Bell also wanted to bring in the different agencies like design, marketing, advertising and research which were now being involved.

BSB was going to be a huge success, he enthused in a bullish presentation. It was going to introduce satellite TV to the UK, which was crying out for it. The shareholders would be getting returns within three years. And how it would all work would be through a marketing drive. The brand of BSB would be positioned first by being sold in through effective ads, promotions and PR. Then the programmes would become part of the offer. Bell fleshed out his plan by paralleling it with the business of his and ASG's previous employers. The BSB brand was like the Whitbread brand, he explained, and the channels – Galaxy, NOW, or whatever they were going to be called – sub-brands. They were like different Whitbread beers, say a white label beer and a lager beer. As such they would be promoted separately later after the holding BSB brand had been established.

Later there was to be a brief from Andy Birchall and Bob Hunter which everyone expected to reflect the same positioning. Instead Hunter got up and said that was not the way he was going to operate. He was MD of his channel and he was going to do things his way, not the way Bell had outlined. Everyone was rather surprised at his vehemence and the afternoon was abandoned, with Birchall never even getting up. It was the first public manifestation of the split which had already developed in the company between the marketing people and the programmers. They all went away wondering what was going to happen.

One of the conditions of the original franchise had been BSB's providing an effective news service, and to this end negotiations had been opened with ITN. It had all seemed quite promising as ITN already supplied a service to Channel 4, but when they moved from generalities to what he called 'talking turkey', ASG found it did not taste very nice. ITN, from its Olympian heights as the doyen of news, seemed to regard BSB as a trivial affair. The deal it offered not only meant it would preserve editorial control, but stipulated BSB would only get certain pieces of film after a 24-hour gap. That seemed a funny idea of news to ASG, and it was also clear it would cost an arm and a leg.

The IBA then stepped in to try its hand at marriage broking, helping ITN to agree that BSB would have editorial control, the team would be moved to the BSB building, and the bill reduced. But then ASG found the ITN people moaning that it was all too onerous, and the talks broke down. In line with his policy of always being honest with the regulators, he went back to the IBA and openly explained that it wasn't going to work. Sympathetically, the IBA accepted the situation, and allowed BSB to look elsewhere to fulfil the franchise news requirement.

There was much headshaking within the TV industry, where BSB was being sized up as a potential competitor, at this apparent setback. But within the company it was not seen like that. News cost a fortune, and the money men saw few signs that satellite buyers would be that interested in it. It was a side of the business of more interest to the programmers. Anyhow the loss was soon recouped from a marketing point of view. Shortly afterwards BSB really hit the front pages for the first time when the 92 chairmen of the Football League clubs voted 91–1, with Liverpool the dissenting voice, to allow the committee to negotiate with BSB for TV coverage of matches. ASG knew they were just being used to bid up the terrestrial channels, and never expected it to happen. But it was still a huge boost, making the company feel grown up as well as helping with the prime marketing objective of putting the whole satellite concept on the map.

Physically, too, it was time for a change. Larger and more suitable offices were needed as BSB was growing fast and more employees arriving to be fired by ASG's and Bell's huge enthusiasm for the task ahead of them. Conveniently space was found to rent on the Third Floor of the IBA building, symbolically reuniting mother with her growing baby. And not only was the company now cosily esconced with its protector, but for those distraught at losing the amenities of Mayfair's adland there was a major consolation. The Good Ship BSB, now docked at 70 Brompton Road, was conveniently located opposite Harrods.

CHAPTER THREE

The Empire Strikes Back

On 8 June, 1988 the rumpled figure of Rupert Murdoch rose up at the British Academy of Film and Television Arts amid swirls of dry ice reminiscent of a pop video. Behind him on a multi-screen video flashed dramatic images of a launching rocket, whilst all around thundered Carl Orff's choral work, *Carmina Burana,* a composition based on original lewd writings by sexually-obsessed monks. When the dry ice smoke – supposedly simulating burning rocket fuel – had cleared from the air Murdoch made the announcement that hundreds of media correspondents, specialists and analysts had gathered at the press conference to hear. His worldwide Empire, News Corporation, was joining BSB in the satellite business. Its station would be run under the British branch of the Empire, News International; it would be be called Sky; have four channels initially, which would be free and supported by advertising; and would begin broadcasting in February the following year. 'We are seeing the dawn of a new age of freedom for the viewer,' Murdoch concluded.

The Skyship Enterprise was to be launched, and the cosy world of the Good Ship BSB evaporated overnight.

The plans Murdoch laid out to the excited media hacks were simple and straightforward. News International was renting four channels from SES – Société Européenne des Satellites – a Luxembourg-based consortium launching a medium-power Astra telecommunications satellite that November. One channel would be devoted to films, one to sport, one to general entertainment, and one to news. Between them they would double the number available in this country.

A couple of hours later Murdoch's announcement was endorsed by Mrs Thatcher, who that day was the guest at the annual Press Association luncheon. 'Some people say it will drive televison downmarket,' the Prime Minister told the backbone of Britain's news-gathering operation, 'I have always believed there is a market for the best. I think the opportunity of more channels can enable us to have some very upmarket television.'

Whatever Mrs Thatcher meant by 'upmarket', for once she was parting company with her usually close ally Murdoch. The phrase, with its counterpoint of downmarket, was one he had repeatedly said he did not understand and was a manifestation of the British class system he so abhorred. But in those British class terms what Murdoch was planning with Sky was inescapably and horribly downmarket, both in terms of output and potential audience. Another way of putting it, which the Big Papers were quick to stress, was that he was bringing American television to Britain – cost-led, low-grade, and aimed directly at the undiscriminating audience at the lower end of the socio-economic spectrum which had telly-watching as its prime occupation. Murdoch had already given a taste of the depths he could plumb in this field when he bought into the Sky Europe cable channel, which had been piped to blocks of flats and hotels all over the continent since 1982. Bored reps and expats had watched it in a desultory fashion, mainly due to its sole virtue of being the only thing available in English, while the British TV industry either ignored it or just saw it as a bit of a joke, sneering at its 'Eurocrap' output of turgid pop videos, third-rate sitcoms and tired old soaps. Commercially it had been no more of a success, attracting some advertising but still incurring losses put at around £40 million to date.

The Empire's move into the new electronic media had been heralded in 1981 by the establishment of a New Media Group thinktank, designed to plan News Corporation's inexorable shift away from print towards electronic media. There had been initial puzzlement as to why Murdoch had originally come into Sky Europe to rescue it from bankruptcy. Now it could be seen as a means of gaining experience for this new dawn and that, behind the scenes, the Empire had been repositioning itself. With the groundwork laid, as Murdoch was now announcing, it was going into the television business with a vengeance.

So too was the grizzled person sitting beside Murdoch, to whom attention at the press conference gradually shifted. Alan Sugar of Amstrad now emerged as the engineer who would beam down the signals from the Skyship Enterprise. Amstrad's departure from the BSB consortium had released the company back into the market as a potential manufacturer.

In the climate of confusion and uncertainty between the partners Murdoch had seen his chance and he and Sugar, whom he now lauded from the platform as 'probably Britain's greatest entrepreneur', had struck their own deal. Amstrad would be supplying 100,000 receiving dishes a month and although not an exclusive supplier, with its head start and Sugar's genius at cost-cutting would obviously gain the lion's share of the dish business. Furthermore, Murdoch announced, all the electrical gubbins needed to receive Sky would be marketed at the magic £199 figure BSB had been striving for, with installation costs adding about another £40. Before he left BSB, Sugar had written saying he was convinced the equipment could not be sold for less than £400.

Sugar, with the supreme confidence of a man who had success-fully tapped the bottom of the market many times, now took over from Murdoch to tell the gathering that electrical goods retailers needed a new boom. Satellite TV was it. 'People will go for it hook, line and sinker – no question about it,' he declared, committing himself to delivering one million receivers into High Street stores and saying he hoped to have sold five million by 1995. Marcus Bicknell, the commercial director of SES, delighted at the new high profile given to Astra by Murdoch, chipped in by saying about BSB: 'They're dead.'

Murdoch had dipped his toe in the waters of British televison before with a brief period of involvement with London Weekend Television at the beginning of the 1970s. But at the time that had been only a sideshow to his main operation of turning the failed Sun into Britain's most successful newspaper. And it had been with the Sun that he had finetuned the art of hooking in the type of British punters he was now envisaging for Sky, at the same time getting his revenge on the British class system which had so irredeemably stuck him with the hated label of 'downmarket'.

When he had taken over the *Sun* in 1969 for peanuts it had been the failed remnant of the old *Daily Herald*, the Socialist newspaper tied to the Trades Union Congress. In the 30s this worthy organ had been the country's best-selling daily but had gradually died on its feet. The traditional working class had grown more and more bored with screeds of the outpourings of dull trade union leaders, and a revamp in the mid-60s to turn into the new, trendy *Sun* had failed to halt its remorseless decline. But Murdoch transformed it. Suddenly it became a cheerful, inky riot, aimed straight at the new generation he reckoned was bursting to throw off the class shackles it had been bound in by the only real alternative of the pious, Labour-supporting *Daily Mirror*.

Churned out as it was on the clapped-out *News of the World* presses which were all Murdoch had, the paper was crude and rough technically. But he didn't think that mattered. The battered hot metal look was all part of being a tabloid and distinguished it from the posh, and infinitely duller, broadsheets which were the Big Papers. Murdoch was certain the punters were more interested in the editorial style, which was a mixture of fun and an 'up yours' attitude to authority, coupled with a relentless commercial edge. Sales soon proved him right. The punters didn't want the sermonising and old-fashioned class-ridden attitude of the *Mirror*, and within seven years the *Sun*'s circulation had risen from virtually nothing to overtake it. Once ahead, it had never lost its lead, and now its circulation was over four million copies a day, making it the best-selling daily in the British language. It was ahead of the *Mirror* by more than a million readers.

Murdoch's aim with Sky was to emulate the *Sun*'s success. This time he would give the same sort of punters what they had so far been denied by the unique British TV duopoly. All the constant cant about quality, good progamming and keeping up standards was in general the spiel of the middle and upper classes, who did not actually watch much television themselves. Some of them even clung to the old-fashioned belief that the commercial channels were vulgar, and avoided watching them as much as possible. BBC programmes, they maintained, were 'better'. But what many of the actual viewers further down the wretched British class system actually wanted, Murdoch believed, was what they had so far been denied – television American-style, with lots of channels to watch, and on all the time. Sky would only have four to start with, but there was already the promise of two more.

Then there was the bonus of the Astra satellite having 16 channels in all. This had already caused the corpulent figure of Robert Maxwell, Murdoch's deadly newspaper rival, to announce plans to rent some of these and go into satellite as well, in conjunction with W.H. Smith. Maxwell's announcements were being discounted as a classic spoiler, but whether he came in or not there would at least be foreign programmes which Sky punters could watch if they had a mind to. These would probably, of course, be incomprehensible to them, but they would still be important in the new world of the TV zapper, which had arrived in the 80s with the advent of remote controls to transform the pattern of television-watching.

Until then the primary strategy of the old terrestrial companies had been to hook the audience in early in the evening under a strategy known in the trade as the 'inheritance principle'. This presumed, usually correctly, that the bulk of viewers would stay slumped in their sofas and armchairs when programmes changed simply because they couldn't be bothered to get up and walk across the room to press the button and thereby choose a different channel. So once you'd got them, the theory ran, you had them all evening, until it was either time for them to retire or you gave them the white dot which faded away to mark the end of broadcasting for the day. You then reminded them to switch off their sets and got the TV to make a loud noise in case your programming had slightly failed in its objective and, instead of gripping them, merely sent them to sleep.

On the back of the inheritance principle came the strategy within a strategy of 'hammocking'. When you asked people what they wanted to watch more of they invariably replied animal programmes or documentaries, but in reality there was great fear that the more stringent programme medicine of current affairs and documentaries was the one thing which might cause them to stir from their torpor and make the mighty effort to rise and press the button. That in turn would be a disaster, as under the inheritance principle the opposition had then got

41

them for the rest of the evening. The heavier slots were therefore carried, or 'hammocked', by softer, lighter-weight programmes like comedies or game shows so viewers, knowing they would not have to wait long before something less demanding came on, would dutifully remain seated.

The key time to 'inherit', and thereby get the possession which was nine points of the television law, was after the regional evening news, when viewers had come back from work and were settling down after their tea or, in the case of the more upmarket, their supper. The critical programmes designed to capture an evening's audience were series like Z Cars and soaps such as Emergency Ward 10, Crossroads and Coronation Street, with Dixon of Dock Green hooking them in on Saturdays. The BBC's answers in later years were Wogan and, more controversially and with much muttering that it was descending to the depths of ITV, the gritty drama of EastEnders. It was these programmes which battled it out at the top of the weekly ratings charts as the programme controllers agonised over the early evening schedules.

But the wide scale advent of remote controls and video in the early 80s had destroyed most of that thinking. Now terrestrial TV was struggling to cope with the new audience of the zappers, remote controls in hand, attention span limited, boredom threshold high, impatient of anything demanding and liable to zoom off to another channel at the touch of a finger. Zapping had even become a completely new way of watching television, with viewers deliberately hunting for anything which suited them at one particular moment, with no intention of staying with it for more than a few minutes – a problem exacerbated for the commercial companies by advertising breaks, which were now no longer seen as an opportunity to make a cup of tea or have a pee, but to zap off.

The new phenomenon had resulted in an increasing tendency for programmes desperately to clamour for attention. Previously they had been content to proceed at a more leisurely pace, confident the inherited audience was in their clutches, and therefore able to load in the more worthy, or even educational, material which had helped build the reputation of British television as the best in the world. But now the zappers were beginning to rule the new terror was that if nothing exciting was happening on a minute-by-minute basis, the audience would get bored and flick the remote to zap off in search of something more stimulating. TV programmes were therefore becoming more and more like pop newspapers, bristling with hooks and gizmos to grab attention. One way was the traditional one of capturing viewers for a limited period by unmissable events like the daily edition of Neighbours, but the newer onus was to jazz up the output. Moving captions had started running along the bottom of the screen, whilst voice-overs and background music jostled for attention and multiple images flashed and switched in a confusing jumble, providing a passable imitation of the effects produced by zapping whilst staying on one channel.

But whatever the terrestrial companies did to cater for their newly fickle audience, they could provide no substitute for a large number of channels to zap, and anyone with a Sky dish would be receiving 16 channels altogether from the Astra satellite. At the Sky press conference the hacks were excitedly talking of a breakthrough which would lead to tens, if not hundreds, of channels, each offering an excitingly different mix of light entertainment, movies, sport and news.

It was not just freedom which was being offered by Murdoch, they told each other, but the other key buzzword of satellite which was used as a massive headline in a full-page article in the next issue of Murdoch's *Sunday Times* – CHOICE. He had made this point personally at the press conference when he expanded on his vision of the future by explaining he was flying back that night to New York, where his apartment was equipped with a cable television connection which offered a choice of 30 different TV stations. Some of the programming of these was 'pretty awful', he admitted, but not all – much of it was 'enormously satisfying'. 'In Britain,' he added, 'I come in every night and find very little to satisfy'.

BSB had of course known that the Astra satellite was to be launched and it had been referred to in the original information memorandum drawn up for fund-raising by the merchant bankers Lazards, owned by Pearson, one of the consortium members. The memorandum had warned: 'BSB believes its principal satellite-based competition could be medium-powered multi-channel satellites, particularly Astra', but had then gone on to dismiss the threat by saying: 'BSB believes it will be able to compete effectively with Astra for a number of reasons ... the Astra project appears to be technology rather than programme-led'.

Peter Bell was on holiday in America, a country for which he shared the same enthusiasm as Murdoch, when the office phoned with the news. He rushed out and bought every paper he could lay his hands on, flipping through them and absorbing the details with mixed feelings.

Bell could see instantly that at one stroke Murdoch had thrown off all the constraints BSB was under. Not only was he using the Astra satellite, but the other major surprise of his announcement had been that he was ignoring the innovative D-MAC technology BSB was tied to and using tried and tested old PAL.

There was nothing to stop Sky using D-MAC in its broadcasts from the Astra satellite, but, as Murdoch had explained it, he had to use PAL as the chips to receive D-MAC were not yet available. 'This piece of so-called wizardry has not been proved to be any better,' he said scornfully. 'It is not even proved capable of manufacture. I would say the whole thing is somewhat of a conspiracy among big manufacturers in Europe to make everybody go out and buy another television set.' But even if the chips had been available, Murdoch's thinking was the same as when he had started the Sun nearly twenty years earlier. If television was to be like pop newspapers, or pop music, it should be treated as such, and therefore be cheap, cheerful, and something to get on with now – rather than trying to elevate it into some sort of art form, or expensive and complicated technological development.

Alan Sugar of Amstrad (the company name was derived from AMS, Sugar's initials, and 'trading') was just as derisive. He had always thrived on selling cheap simple products, like low-cost hi-fi tower systems more remarkable for their number of flashing lights than sound quality, and relying on proven technology. He dismissed D-MAC as 'a lot of nonsense which requires a lot of redundant components'.

Bell might not have agreed with that, but the underlying argument was obvious to him. It was such a shame BSB had to go through all the stuff it was going through with the technology when Murdoch could be up and running so quickly. BSB management could be just as quick off the mark, if only it could be liberated from all the constraints. By comparison, without restraints, Sky would be able to operate a form of celestial piracy. The warning that Harold Wilson had given had at last come true.

ASG was more bullish about the technology point when he replied to Murdoch in the *Sunday Times'* CHOICE article, peddling the line that once the superior D-MAC was on stream, old PAL would simply disappear. 'Maybe we're missing something, but we're in high good humour,' he declared breezily. 'I think Murdoch's plan is just a load of junk to tell you the truth. If I've got it right, he's going to come out with a receiver kit that is already obselete the day it hits the market. We'll make a lot of hay out of that.'

But behind the scenes there had been a moment of near-panic within BSB. Reactions to the announcement had varied between individuals, but the chairman, Sir Trevor Holdsworth, had been dismayed as he had thought BSB had a monopoly and Astra was just European. And this was the crucial element feared by all: now BSB was not just up against more Eurocrap of the diluted Sky Europe variety, but all the undoubted resources of Rupert Murdoch beamed direct at this country and tailored for the home audience.

The shareholders called ASG in for an emergency get-together, but when they had calmed down they realized the position was not so bad. Apart from its unquestionably superior technology BSB was also official and genuinely British, as its name so proudly reflected. Not only would its programmes be better, but Murdoch had a primary problem with his film channel, which he had announced would be 'clear' and not scrambled like theirs. That meant it would either have to be free of charge or supported by advertising, as it was impossible to scramble, or 'encrypt' absolutely securely in technological jargon, on the PAL system.

BSB, on the other hand, had always seen encryption and getting regular subscription payments from viewers as the key to making satellite a financial success. It was central to the business plan and had been one of the main points that had come up at the original interview for the franchise. And if BSB couldn't make satellite pay without subscription, how could Murdoch survive on advertising alone? The terrestrial television companies were already worried about how satellite would spread the advertising butter more thinly and knew the new competiton would lead to a price-cutting war. As for the gap between the two competitors, Sky would not really have much of a head start. If Murdoch was correct it would be on air in February 1989, but BSB would arrive with its superior system only a few months afterwards in September, well before the crucial Christmas season. Anyhow, the Ariane rocket had not even gone up yet. It was not due to launch the Astra satellite until November and it could fail or be late. Anything could happen.

They were carrying on, they told ASG, who once they had made the decision went back to his office clear in his mind. His job now was to provide the vital leadership for his boys and girls in the battle that lay ahead.

But the shareholders also had another point, which they raised through their direct line to government, Edward Bickham, the newly appointed head of external affairs. Bickham was a bright Oxford PPE graduate now in his mid-30s, though with his boyish appearance he looked much younger. In 1980, after leaving Macmillan's, the publishers, he had joined the Conservative Party's Research Department and graduated to being a special adviser first to James Prior then Douglas Hurd when each was at the Northern Ireland Office. He had then gone with Hurd to the Home Office and become closely involved in the various discussions about the future of television in Britain which were leading up to the Broadcasting Bill.

But Bickham had tired of being a virtual civil servant and wanted to break out into the more commercial world. At the prompting of a headhunter he had gone to see ASG at his large country house near Dorking. Bickham arrived there in the pouring rain and halfway up the garden path met ASG's wife Marjorie, who was surrounded by several large dogs. She seemed warm and friendly and he stood outside chatting to her in the rain before going indoors and getting down to business with the man himself. The result had been his accepting the proferred post, which in the convoluted job terminology of BSB was labelled Executive Director, External Affairs.

Bickham had started work in April, two months before the Sky announcement, and been given an immediate and urgent brief. A suggestion had been floated by the Home Office that the government would launch a fifth terrestrial channel, which might even come onstream quite shortly, giving BSB wholly unexpected new competition. ASG had thought when the franchise was awarded that BSB would be allowed to be born and out of nappies before there was any competition like this. The shareholders had been given the same impression and when he discussed it with them they were so horrified he saw their eyes sticking out like chapel hat pegs. Virgin in particular was insistent the government must agree to hold back on such a scheme until 1995. Bickham had immediately set up a meeting between Sir Trevor Holdsworth and Lord Young, the Secretary of State at the Department of Trade and Industry, after which Sir Trevor had been able to soothe the shareholders by assuring them Lord Young had said he 'would not undermine' BSB.

With the fifth channel out of the way, Bickham was now shoved into the path of the new and even more ghastly spectre raised by Murdoch. The first stop was the IBA. But here he was told there was nothing the regulators could do, even if they wanted to. In granting the BSB franchise they had been just as aware of Astra as BSB itself, and they had been just as taken by surprise by Murdoch's announcement. They explained to Bickham they now accepted the whole situation had changed, but pointed out they had allocated BSB the monopoly of a purpose-built satellite. This was specifically designed for beaming down high-powered DBS (direct broadcasting by satellite) signals, to be picked up by a small receiving dish. Astra was not a high-powered satellite, but medium-powered. Much more to the point, it was not a television but a telecommunications satellite, and as such the IBA had no control over it.

Abandoning the IBA, Bickham went off to put a different case to the government. Murdoch might have got round the question of a technological monopoly, but he had not broken the regulations about cross-ownership of television companies and newspapers. These were definitely in the government's camp and they were quite clear. They stipulated, as had been strongly emphasized at the original franchise application, that newspaper owners were limited to a 20% holding in TV stations. Everybody had been warned that no publisher was allowed to have more than a 20% stake in any of the applications. Yet Murdoch owned *The Times*, the *Sunday Times*, the *News of the World*, the *Sun* and *Today*, which added up to 35% of the British press – and here he was starting a satellite station under the same overall company umbrella of News International. And nobody, apparently, was doing anything to stop him,

Bickham hammered home the BSB argument to his old colleagues at the Broadcasting Department of the Home Office. Sky was British, based in Britain, designed for Britain, and beamed to Britain. Just because its signal was to be uplinked to a Luxembourg-owned piece of metal from London and then bounced back to the UK, that did not make it European. It therefore came under the cross-ownership regulations. The reaction was to tell Bickham he was right in principle, but the officials then pleaded that the matter was entirely beyond their jurisdiction. The Astra satellite itself wasn't British, but European-owned and broadcasting on European frequencies, which they did not regulate. Therefore, like the IBA, there was nothing they could do. Bickham countered that what Murdoch was doing was at least in defiance of the spirit of the law. If a service was specifically designed for Britain, cross-ownership provisions should apply even if the satellite was non-domestic. Murdoch had found a loophole through a series of unthought-out decisions, he argued, as the Whitehall officials listened sympathetically but in the end just held up their hands. And in the more influential circle of Downing Street, sympathy was rather more limited.

There was a very good reason for this, the Big Papers and members of the chattering classes who were deeply opposed to Murdoch now started muttering. These were people who held strong opinions not just about television, but the way the Dirty Digger had brought Britain rubbish and filth in the *Sun* and coarsened the whole newspaper scene. More importantly, he had switched the paper from backing Labour to urging its twelve million readers to vote for Mrs Thatcher in 1979. With hindsight it had now been realized that switch had been a crucial element in her victory. For it had been typical *Sun* readers from the socio-economic group C2, who had formerly been staunch Labour supporters from the *Daily Mirror*-style old working class, who had followed their paper's advice. Their votes, particularly coming from the younger end, had tipped the balance her way and since then they had been leading the raucous end of the new phenomenon known as 'Thatcherism'.

When Murdoch made his bid for *The Times* in 1981, Mrs Thatcher's Government had put on a three line whip in the Commons to stop the take-over being referred to the Monopolies Commission. The Murdoch papers had since then continued to promote the Thatcher vision, particularly the *Sun* under its foul-mouthed editor Kelvin MacKenzie, with his GOTCHA and STICK IT UP YOUR JUNTA! headlines on the Falklands. Again in 1987, the government appeared to be turning a blind eye to Sky. The chattering classes muttered darkly that it might have been a very different matter if it was not Rupert Murdoch who was going on the Astra satellite, but Robert Maxwell who espoused the Labour cause and now owned the *Mirror*.

But the hawks in Downing Street saw it differently. Rupert was of course very matey with Maggie, and indeed popped in to see her frequently. But the Prime Minister's office had also been monitoring BSB as an example of great British private enterprise like the Channel Tunnel and on those grounds wanted it to succeed. The trouble was that so far they had not found BSB particularly impressive. For instance, it was silly of it to assume that just because it had a monopoly of this new DBS business on Britain's official frequencies, nobody else would do it on other ones. It didn't make the slightest difference whether it was Rupert Murdoch or anyone else. The airwaves were bigger than that and we were all in the process of deregulation, not just in television, but every aspect of commerce. BSB must have known broadcasts on Astra were a possibility. Thames Television certainly had. It had even bought an interest in the Astra satellite as a wise insurance policy. BSB seemed to have this backward thinking attitude that it had some sort of God-given monopoly, and was living in the past if it thought it was just an extension of the old duopoly of the BBC and the ITV companies. That old world was breaking up. The airwaves were free and the future would belong to those who understood that these days television was being driven by advances in technology, not by making rules.

Apart from this theory, Downing Street had also met the personalities involved with BSB, and the officials who were keeping a close eye on the company hadn't seen people there who really knew about television. In September 1987, after the election, Mrs Thatcher had hosted a key seminar on the future of broadcasting and said she was determined that her government should do something about television, which she referred to as 'the last bastion of restrictive practices'. Key industry players were invited to a brainstorming session, and as it was a month before ASG started, the BSB representative at Downing Street was Graham Grist. (Sir Trevor Holdsworth had been unavailable.) Grist, shoved into the breach, had made a poor impression against silver-tongued TV hands like Jeremy Isaacs, the head of Channel Four, Michael Green of Carlton who had been BSB's rival in the franchise stakes, and Ian Trethowan of Thames. Admittedly that was stiff competition, but both Grist and John Whitney, the Director General of the IBA, seemed totally outclassed as they mumbled through their presentations.

On another occasion Grist had come along to Number 10 with ASG and Sir Trevor Holdsworth and they had given quite good performances, but somehow they were still not convincing. They didn't seem to possess the same aura as others like Bruce Gyngell, the hyperactive head of TV-am, who in Downing Street's view managed the station brilliantly, or Michael Grade, the charismatic Controller of BBC1 who inherited the mantle of Channel 4 from Jeremy Isaacs. These were all shrewd types who inspired confidence. But even though ASG had a great aura of self-assurance, somehow there was always a question mark about the project. When government officials had talked round the industry the feedback had given them an uneasy feeling. The general vibes about BSB had not been good.

When a Whitehall committee had examined the future of television Sir Jeffrey Sterling, the property and shipping magnate Mrs Thatcher had appointed to look into broadcasting, had hosted a series of breakfasts for people with an interest in TV. Key players such as Murdoch, Maxwell, the tough-minded BBC

Chairman Marmaduke Hussey, and the Director-General, Michael Checkland, had all been along, giving plenty of others for the government types to compare BSB people to. And Downing Street had found some of these people very, very commercial – Murdoch especially. But many of the wide range of people they talked to agreed those in charge of BSB were very naive and somehow not as commercial as others in TV.

Then there was the last element of the IBA. Now Murdoch was going so fast with the old PAL technology the officials saw it like this: from a purely commercial point of view BSB could be looking at a potential disaster because of the untried D-MAC technology. The IBA of course wouldn't see it like that, but it was smugly ensconced in its cosy headquarters in Brompton Road and didn't have hundreds of millions of pounds riding on the outcome. And in any case, as far as some of Mrs Thatcher's advisers were concerned, the IBA was one of the most backward-looking organisations in television and one of them even went so far as to call them "a bunch of jerks". There were so many vested interests there, BSB had become victim of them.

If your money was on the line, who cared what a bunch of timeservers thought? Why be subservient to them and accept what they had laid down? BSB should have been more abrasive and bloody-minded. But as yet there was no sign of its doing something like going back to the IBA and getting tough, threatening: 'We're switching to simple old PAL as well, and if you don't like it take away our licence and see if anyone else is willing to do it.' Instead it was just carrying on bearing the cross the IBA had handed it.

All in all, Downing Street was rapidly concluding, that it had little confidence in BSB and those running it.

These matters, meanwhile, were largely passing clean over the heads of the people now joining BSB, usually after being expensively headhunted. As they were still feeling their way into this new and somewhat baffling satellite business, Murdoch's announcement had not had much impact on them. They were much more interested in getting the feel of their new employers.

ASG had decided that a major part of his job as CE was knitting together the emerging company, and decided it had grown enough for its 70 or so employees – planned to grow to 600 – to be brought together in a suitable setting and the kind of style to which he was accustomed. He had therefore got the marketing department to organise, and pay for, a summer party at his house near Dorking where, in line with his attitude that the company should be one big happy family, employees would also meet his wife Marjorie. Although she had no official position with the company, she had already taken it upon herself to help him as much as possible in his new and already somewhat stressful job.

New employees, accompanied by wives, girlfriends or entire families, wound their way through the picturesque Surrey lanes and up the long drive to the improvised parking lot in a nearby field where they blinked at the exotic selection of Yuppie machinery – GTIs, various lethal-looking turbo-charged devices, and a plethora of BMWs, which was the most popular choice of company car.

A huge marquee housing a cold buffet had been set up for the occasion next to the tennis court, while an outside barbecue dispensed hamburgers, chicken pieces and sausages. No expense appeared to have been spared and the new employees marvelled to each other that this was clearly going to be the sort of company that did things in style. There was entertainment by a female impersonator, magician, and troupe of musicians, while a special children's entertainer had been brought in to cater for the young ones, who were supervised by a couple of nannies in a smaller tent nearer the house. After watching the entertainer they were brought out for rides round the tennis court on a small elephant which had been hired for the day.

Everybody was dressed up to the nines in their most stylish summer clothes and the party was in the best English country house style, down to the essential English element that it was raining. ASG bounded about jollying everyone along as they stepped delicately through the soggy grass and mud, joking heartily that this always happened when he held occasions here. They were all chatting and getting to know one another in a friendly fashion when the atmosphere suddenly changed with the start of the organised games. A hint of these had been given on arrival when everybody had been divided into four teams identified by different colours and given coloured bands with strict instructions to wear them round their bodies at all times. Now it became clear that the games had been designated the highlight of the afternoon.

The four teams were ordered to gather together and ranged up for a series of contests which started with 'Quads', in which they had to ride small four-wheeled machines round an obstacle course which had been laid out in a field away from the house. Nervous new employees, finding the machines running away from them and plunging into the adjacent field, wondered if their loss of control would be seen as a black mark indicating they lacked direction. Next came an even greater trauma for some as they were shepherded on to a makeshift firing range for a shooting competition using .22 rifles. An instructor was on hand to help the more feeble and those tackling the problem by closing their eyes, and to everyone's chagrin ASG's young son turned out to be about the best. Tennis followed, with an automatic machine spewing out balls the teams then had to hit back over the net, before the contest moved to its climax with the tug of war.

By now rising competitive spirit and macho behaviour had intensified to the point where everybody was playing in deadly earnest. Suddenly it was no longer party games but all out war. Team leaders were appointed and strategies worked out as winning became the most important part of the afternoon. The contests became virtual life or death affairs as the teams strained and slipped in the deepening mud to a deafening background of heckling and cheering and ASG leapt around in a tracksuit, periodically blowing his whistle as he adjudicated over the titanic struggles.

The event ended with a prize-giving of magnums of champagne to the exhausted victors, while everybody chattered in agreement that it had been a lovely party and a terrifically fun day. ASG and Marjorie had been perfect hosts and as an exercise in staff relations the event was judged to have been hugely successful. As they clambered back into their various machines any lingering thoughts of Rupert Murdoch, who would definitely not have fitted in at a do like this, were long forgotten. The unreal little world which had been created for the afternoon had imbued the newcomers with an overwhelming feeling of optimism.

CHAPTER FOUR

We're so Square

Despite ASG's seemingly unruffled air at the party, which everyone back at Brompton Road kept telling everyone else had been lovely, BSB was facing the ugly fact that it was no longer the leader in what had become the satellite race. Sky was setting the agenda, and from now on few conversations took place without some reference to the opposition. Before Murdoch's announcement the company had been producing five-year and ten-year plans as if they were going out of fashion, but with the arrival of competition long-term strategy went out of the window. From the beginning BSB had known that getting satellite TV off the ground would require a massive investment in selling the whole concept to the GBP – the Great British Public – and in April, before Murdoch had made his Sky announcement, one of the Granada representatives had summarized the position by telling the *Sunday Times*: 'We propose to throw £500 million at the marketplace. Anything less and the whole thing will just fizzle out.'

But now Murdoch had arrived the new element of time was suddenly in the equation. The need to be on the air as soon as possible was paramount, and the result was for BSB to speed up its strategy with what was known in marketing-speak as 'fastbuild'. This modern buzzphrase confused many people in the company, who later referred to it variously as 'the fast burn', 'fastburn' and 'fast burn'. Privately some used the coarser, but more traditional phrase, 'shit or bust'. But whatever you called it, the marketing department-led philosophy amounted to the same thing: BSB was now on the accelerator and it had to start spending money fast. Any faint-hearted thoughts about caution or holding back for the future were to be canned.

More urgently and immediately the company was desperate to do something to counter the way Murdoch had stolen the show. The first step, already in the process of being organised when the Murdoch bombshell dropped, was to show the superior D-MAC technical system at work. Chris 'Motormouth' McLaughlin, who had been hired from the PR company of Charles Barker to take charge of public relations, had been given the task of putting together a demonstration, and the company had booked the IBA's presentation theatre at the beginning of August for a week-long display of live satellite pictures from the D-MAC system operating in Norway. The demonstration was to be in lavish style, masterminded by Rapier, the top of the range design consultancy.

That had been fine until Sky had been announced. Now it would no longer be a headline-stealer. BSB's USP – its unique selling proposition – in the market had lain in being Britain's only home-grown satellite company. Now that had disappeared the marketing-led strategy required that it had something to distinguish it from its new rival – something unique round which the BSB brandname could be built.

Then, with seeming serendipity, the opportunity to acquire something really different popped up from nowhere. A phone call came into the office from a man called John Collins, who explained he was developing a new type of aerial in conjunction with a laboratory in Leatherhead. He thought BSB might be interested in it. The task of meeting this intriguing caller was given to David Eglise, who had become involved with BSB through his previous employers, Mars Electronics, a division of the world's largest privately owned company. Eglise had been there for 11 years with the job of looking for new ventures, and when Mars got interested in manufacturing satellite receivers had done a presentation to BSB. Following that he had been headhunted and had joined as director of technical services shortly after ASG.

But when he arrived and looked at BSB's business plan, Eglise had a major surprise. It wasn't the sort of thing he was used to at all. He thought it was more like a glossy magazine – this is how we're going to do it, this is our licence to make money, this is the amount of money we have. And by the way, David, here's a blank sheet of paper – now how the hell are we going to do it? The plan, he rapidly concluded, had zero substance. He also came to the conclusion that nobody in the company realized the enormity of the project because they were rapidly getting out of their depth. Timing was another major worry. The aerial was just part of that. At this crucial point he had just a blank sheet of paper and no aerial deal. It had simply been planned to show a 12″ round dish at the IBA demonstration.

Eglise went to see Collins by a stroke of irony at the Ariel Hotel near Heathrow airport which by a further stroke of irony, considering what was to come, was a round building which had been considered 'mould-breaking' when it was built. He turned out to be a stocky, smiling man in his mid-40s whom Eglise judged to be not so much an inventor as an entrepreneur. He was immediately interested by what Collins had to say. Like everybody else in the company, Eglise knew all about the enormous pressure to get BSB an identity. Here, he thought, was something which might well take it further on that front.

Collins explained he had been working on VSAT (very small aperture terminal) technology, a form of communication used for business and military data transmission in the USA, and when he read about satellite TV he started thinking about its development for this emerging field. Collins did not pretend there was anything new about these flat aerial receivers, as they were called. They had been used by the military for 30 years and the Japanese company of Matsushita had even demonstrated one for its domestic satellite market the previous year. But it had been much bigger than the one Collins now put forward.

As Collins explained, a normal parabolic aerial worked by reflecting waves off the rounded dish and collecting them in a raised node antenna sticking up in the middle. But a flat aerial which was square was quite different, collecting the signal in a combination of many small aerials spread over its surface, which were then networked to an output. The aerial he was working on had 144 of them, each in its own little cavity. What Collins had done, in what he later modestly described as 'a replumbing job', was change the way the network of wires was incorporated through what he called a 'suspended stripline' which made for lower impedance and therefore higher efficiency – the key to making it suitable for BSB, both in terms of working better and being cheaper than the previous military models. In addition, modern developments now enabled the aerial shell to be manufactured with sufficient precision in injection-moulded plastic, rather than the more expensive aluminium of the previous military models. This, he told Eglise, made it as cheap as the shell of a telephone if it was manufactured in quantities of over 100,000. Eglise, however, found out from Collins that so far the inventor had only patented details of the construction through his tiny company, Fortel, based in Fife in Scotland.

Eglise returned to Brompton Road to report the conversation and found the flat plate receiver rapturously received by ASG and the marketing department. Here was the new USP BSB was so desperately searching for! This was the peg it could hang its hat on! The new technology and better picture to be demonstrated by D-MAC was one thing – but a square aerial, that would really grab people's attention! The major credibility problem of having nothing to show had been solved!

Trying to rein them back, Eglise explained in no uncertain terms to the non-technological trio of ASG, Bell and Grist that there was still a long way to go with the potential product. The device had not been developed. So far it was just a model and there was no question of even a working prototype at this stage. But as he talked he could see that by now all rationality had gone out of the window. Bell's gut feeling was that it was the wrong idea to talk about the technology and it could turn out to be a terrible mistake but, like the others, he felt a terrible need to say something. As far as Eglise was concerned they were simply salivating for it, saying: 'We want it! We want it!' and ASG said that they would go with it. Providing leadership was his duty to the shareholders, and he said he would take responsibility.

Grist was sent off to conduct a frenzied series of negotiations for an exclusive deal with Collins' company, which after an all-night session was finally signed at 5.30am on the morning the D-MAC demonstration was due to start at the IBA theatre.

Around 8am the press office was given the go-ahead to make an announcement, McLaughlin put together a press release, and two hours later the first square aerial was presented to the world at the opening of the D-MAC demonstration. A copy of the device, smaller than a record album cover at 25cm, and square, but designed to be mounted on a wall so that it looked diamond-shaped, was brandished by a smiling Grist, prototypes promised by Christmas, and the cost of the receiver package held at £250. The required photo-opportunity was arranged by having a delicious-looking girl from the marketing department pose decorously on the IBA roof.

Amongst those present it was not just members of the press who were surprised by the square aerial announcement. By now three electronics companies had been chosen to manufacture the receiving boxes. Again this had unfortunately negated the dream of reviving the British electronics industry as BSB's choice had been the old white hope of Ferguson, which was now owned by Thomson of France; Salora, owned by Nokia of Finland; and Tatung, from Taiwan, the heartland of the real Far Eastern enemy. Ferguson and Tatung had partly retrieved the situation by announcing they would be manufacturing in Britain specifically at Telford. Representatives of the three companies had come to the IBA to show off their own prototypes, only for their jaws to drop when the square aerial was waved about. None had known anything about it, never mind having tried to use one to interface with their part of the complicated electronic package.

But BSB was not interested in their wonderment. The value of the exercise was apparent the next day, when press cuttings were assembled and scrutinised, column inches measured, the number of pictures added up, and the PR exercise adjudged an oustanding success. The original D-MAC demonstration it had been piggy-backed onto had been efficiently presented by Nick Ross and the Rapier people. All had gone smoothly, thanks to the racks of equipment and converters and the power lorry backed up behind the IBA building, and amidst much discussion the picture had been dutifully adjudged better than PAL. But it was the square aerial demonstration which had really done the business. As the marketing department had hoped, it had provided a fantastic lead into the story which the press had really latched on to. BSB had succeeded in its marketing-led objective. Now it was seen as not just saying it would be different, but producing something to prove it.

And the presentation had been such a triumph it had even surmounted the most major problem of all. Apart from the fact the Fortel contract had been signed at the last minute, there had been a very good reason why the receiver box manufacturers had not yet had an opportunity to interface with the new device, which all the enthusing media had completely failed to notice. The 'squarial', as it was dubbed after a brain-storming session in the pub, which Grist had been holding up was nothing like a prototype, or even anything close to it, but simply a piece of wood cut to the appropriate size and shape.

The small size of the squarial, as with the original ordinary 12" round dish which it had now superseded, was in some ways as important to BSB as its shape. Both BSB's and Sky's aerials had to be accurately positioned to within a degree or two to collect the signal, and set on the side of buildings, rather than the roof, because of current planning regulations forbidding their erection above roof height. The difficulty for Sky was that Astra was not just a medium-powered satellite, but also had a footprint with a signal strength concentrated on the prosperous middle regions of Europe. Britain was only on its edge, so customers would need huge dishes to pick up its signal. Prior to the Sky announcement a handful of people in Britain had bought massive dishes at a cost of £2,000, which they installed in their back gardens to receive a ragbag of foreign broadcasting like Russian TV. A Granada representative had claimed earlier in the year that reception of Astra with an 85cm dish would be 'totally unacceptable', and the clash between the two technologies had set off a noisy advertising war which trumpeted round the papers as both sides bought space (or in Murdoch's case used its own products) to proclaim the relative merits of their own systems and rubbish the opposition.

Alan Sugar had weighed in shortly after the Sky announcement when he sat in his armchair in his Brentwood office, pointed at the television set and declared to a reporter: 'I'll offer £1 million in cash to anyone who can make a better picture than that. Everyone keeps talking about better picture quality. It's rubbish. D-MAC television sets haven't even been developed yet.' Sugar's point was that although existing sets could receive D-MAC pictures, if they did not have the equipment inside them they would simply relay them like old PAL, in a similar way to playing a stereo record on a mono player. Taking up this challenge BSB claimed any set 'with a Euroconnector' would show the better D-MAC pictures and fired back with monster ads reading: 'Dear Alan, Looks like your PAL just cost you a million', and calling on Sugar to send the money to the charity of his choice.

Sugar's reply was that he would only send the £1 million if anyone improved the picture on the actual set in his office. 'The picture on my set and more importantly on 95% of the televisions used in the UK cannot be improved,' he claimed, sparking off more complicated technical disputes which the trade papers delved into before announcing the reality was probably that half the sets people had bought could get the full benefit of D-MAC, whilst older ones owned by the other half could not.

The Sugar activity, and the barrage of claims, counter-claims, obscure literature and muddled demonstrations only served to confuse potential customers with the complex technical issues and also brought in to the mix the advertising agency which BSB had chosen – Bartle, Bogle and Hegarty, or BBH, as it was universally known.

The key to any successful marketing strategy, once the market has been identified, is the advertising, as ASG well knew. Here he was on home ground as much of his acclaimed success had been built on his natural flair in that field. He had picked BBH to execute BSB's mammoth planned spend, in preference to the larger and more established agencies, as one that both he and Bell knew well. BBH was still young, having been started in 1982 by the three partners of John Bartle, Nigel Bogle and John Hegarty, who had all left jobs in bigger agencies, announcing they were jaundiced with most of the clients they had to deal with. In future, they said, they would only work with people they liked, two of whom had been ASG and Peter Bell at Whitbread, one of the three accounts with which they had started up in business.

The agency had since risen rapidly in adland status, prin- cipally through its best-known campaign of 'Vorsprung durch

Technik' for Audi cars, and a small budget campaign for Levi 501 jeans which received the ultimate ad accolade of being so successful it had to be pulled because the shops had run out of stock. In 1986 the success had been made official when it had been voted Agency of the Year by the trade magazine, *Campaign*. When ASG hired it for BSB, BBH had no media accounts, although it was later to get the *Independent*, but was in fact recovering from a brief and bruising experience in the field which had put it at the sharp end of a steep learning curve. Earlier that year, as the advertising agency, it had been caught up in the disastrous launch of the *News on Sunday*, an attempt by members of the trendy Left who normally read the Big Papers to establish a decent tabloid-sized 'paper for the people'.

News on Sunday had been started by the kind of single-issue campaigners who had clustered round Tony Benn and zeroed in on Ken Livingstone's GLC, and was fuelled by the outrage of these 'Right-Ons' at the way the hated Murdoch, and his loathsome *Sun* in particular, had supposedly debased the high standards of British journalism. BBH, hired to dream up a campaign enabling the Right-Ons to communicate the new paper to the masses, had focused on its stated intention to be non-sexist by not having things like Page Three girls, whilst at the same time being gutsy and campaigning. The result had been the attention-grabbing slogan NO TITS BUT A LOT OF BALLS, which BBH proposed running in huge white letters on a background of screaming pink. The slogan had been thought to be brilliant by the research groups of 'ordinary people' it was tried out on, but had then led to a riot on the paper itself, where the Right-Ons running it had been outraged by its sexism and forced it to be withdrawn.

Not just the advertising campaign, but virtually every other aspect of the paper had then fallen apart as it gobbled up its £6.5 million of funding, mostly provided by trade unions and councils pilloried in the *Sun* as 'Loony Left'. It then immediately descended to the bottom line by going bust on issue three. To make matters worse it had gone down just as the June 1987 general election was announced, causing potential massive embarrassment to Labour. The situation was temporarily relieved by the paper's being rescued by the flamboyant party supporter and Lancashire millionaire Owen Oyston, better known for his ownership of Blackpool Football Club. But even Oyston's vigorous management style failed to save it and the paper had expired just as ASG was joining BSB.

BBH had described the *News on Sunday* débâcle as the worst experience any of the three partners had ever had with a client, but placed the blame for their series of horrific experiences fairly and squarely on the *NOS* management. They knew this would not be the case with ASG and Peter Bell. When these two had both been at Whitbread, Collett Dickinson Pearce had been the lead agency. BBH's founding account was on smaller brands and local advertising of products like Chester's Best and Poacher Bitter – which had involved them with Bell's Pennine activity – Gold Label Barley Wine, Murphy's stout, and Kaltenberg lager. As far as they were concerned both ASG and Peter Bell were very good news – ASG in particular. He was the kind of client whom BBH saw as sophisticated in his use of advertising agencies. Other agencies obviously agreed, as ASG had once been voted best client in one of the rather spurious awards the adworld liked running. BBH found some clients viewed their agencies as partners and equals, whilst others regarded them as hired servants whose job was to produce packaged goods with an appropriately grovelling 'yes sir, no sir' attitude. ASG fell very much into the first camp – so much so that his personal penchant for loud socks and even louder and more flamboyant ties made some people think he was actually a full-time adman himself. (Best tie of all, it was universally agreed, was a colourful number sporting Gauguin's Tahitian nudes.)

ASG had taken BBH on board the Good Ship BSB soon after his appointment when the agency did a successful presentation at its 80s designer black and white headquarters in Great Pultney Street, Soho. The account was being handled by Nigel Bogle, who had not expected really to start on the campaign until nearer the launch. But now the advertising offensive would have to start earlier and Bogle was called in to handle the problems arising out of Murdoch's extensive British press ownership. His placing huge ads for Sky in his own papers was something BSB could do nothing about, but it was a different matter with editorial copy. At BSB outrage had started from Day One at the puffing articles appearing in what had once proudly advertised itself as

'The Top People's Paper' of *The Times*, down through *Today*, to the most influential newspaper in terms of delivering the raucous socio-economic C2s, the *Sun*. The Comic, as its readers called it, had led off the day after the Sky announcement with a front page panel headed 'A Dish come true – satellite telly for only £199', backed by an ecstatic double page spread inside lauding the service to its twelve million readers. *Today*'s front page headline had been £199 FOR FOUR TV CHANNELS and *The Times* had headed its report: 'The £199 Dish that will launch a television revolution'. A count revealed that the three Murdoch papers had devoted 217 column inches to their reports, whilst the other eight nationals ran to only 124 inches between them.

Nigel Bogle's job was to deal with more Sugar-type claims over the respective merits of the two systems. This had continued after the squarial demonstration when *Today* attempted to defuse BSB's PR triumph by stating: 'Sky satellite dishes, made by Amstrad, cost £199 and will be the size of a dinner plate.'

By now ASG had arrived at the point where he could feel his blood pressure rise every time he opened a Murdoch paper. He was learning rapidly about the media, which previously he had not thought about a great deal, just reading the papers like everybody else. Now he was gaining personal experience of the naked sort of way newspapers could serve the interests of their proprietors and he thought this kind of outrageous statement was taking matters too far. The BSB chequebook was taken out to buy space in which to fire back, and mystified readers opened their papers to be confronted by large ads illustrated with a place setting of dinner plate, knife and fork. Under the obscure headline of: 'Dear Rupert, If your satellite dish is a dinner plate, you must eat whopping dinners', the copy leant on the weighty authority of the British Ceramics Manufacturers' Association to state that the average dinner plate was about 10″ across. Sky dishes in the south, on the other hand, would be 60cm – 23¹/₂″ – across. If you lived north of Manchester they would be even bigger at 75cm. And for the few Scots inhabiting their country north of Aberdeen, they would be 90cm. Above that size, and in the Outer Hebrides, you did not just need a bigger dish, but planning permission.

The squarial, on the other, would be a mere 25cm, or 10″

across, like a real dinner plate, and as the BSB signal was purpose-designed for Britain and centred on Manchester, would be uniform in size the length and breadth of the country. WE'RE NOT KEEPING YOU WAITING FOR NOTHING, the ad signed off defiantly. Puzzled newspaper readers looked in wonder at the huge displays, but BSB was emphatic that this high-profile approach was the only way to respond.

The News International reporting was causing its own fallout in the newspaper world, and hacks on rival papers bemoaned the way it further demeaned their craft – with varying degrees of sincerity. But eyebrows genuinely shot up when Jonathan Miller, the media editor of the *Sunday Times*, which had kicked off its coverage with the glowing CHOICE article, was suddenly reincarnated as Sky's Director of Corporate Affairs. Miller, a large man with dark hair and a smug attitude who was occasionally confused with Dr Jonathan Miller, had been unpopular in many quarters in the *Sunday Times*, but there was still shock at this naked crossing to the PR side of the fence. Theoretically that was only occupied by the sworn enemies of good journalism.

To make its point and raise its profile, BSB zeroed in on the Autumn 1988 party political conferences with elaborate stands and enormously expensive glossy presentations. At the Conservative conference, before each debating session delegates were greeted in the main hall by BSB promotional videos blasted out at deafening volume on the giant screens later used to amplify the conference speakers. ASG himself spoke at a conference fringe meeting in Brighton attended by Tim Renton, the Minister for Broadcasting, where he questioned Murdoch's impartiality by stating in ponderous fashion: 'The unique prominence given to Sky Television in News International's newspapers and the seeming mixing of promotional references with editorial matter must give rise to doubts about whether News International's objectivity may be undermined by their wider commercial interests.'

Official bodies were pulled in to bolster the argument. A complaint was sent to the Office of Fair Trading about unfair Sky ads, which was then passed on to the Advertising Standards Authority, and the European Institute for the Media was commissioned at a cost of £15,000 to produce an independent report on coverage of satellite TV in Murdoch newspapers versus the rest.

But the advertising and editorial war raging in Britain was still nothing to what had started up in Rupert Murdoch's adopted home of America, where he had taken out citizenship in order to conform with American laws on ownership of newspapers and television stations. For late, and thinking on his feet as he was, Murdoch had known when he announced Sky that despite its headstart BSB had still left the door open to the most important aspect of satellite programming – films. And Roop, operating on familiar territory in Hollywood, was not the sort of man to pass up an opportunity like that.

CHAPTER FIVE

Film Wars

Both sides in the satellite war which had now broken out in earnest knew the battle would essentially be won or lost over films. Every ounce of market research and experience, both at home and abroad, confirmed this to be the aspect of satellite TV of most interest to the potential audience. People would have to pay through subscription, which was expected to be £10 or more a month. The bait would be no longer having to go out to the video shop and pay the money there instead. For the subscribers' money BSB planned to show them between six and eight movies a day, giving a UK premiere on television to 20 films a month. As part of his strategy the head of the Movie Channel, Andy Birchall, was planning to cut down the number of repeats compared with other specialist film channels, such as the cable Home Box Office in America. Really big films might play as many as ten times, but would be screened at different times of day for the convenience of viewers, while poorer offerings and box office disasters would only be put on once or twice, thereby maintaining the overall quality of the service.

In the spring of 1988, before the announcement of Sky, Birchall had said publicly that BSB was close to doing a deal with five of the major studios, but when Murdoch dropped his bombshell these remained uncompleted. There were a number of reasons for this, not least of which was the newness of the company and the fact it was setting up in Britain in competition with the existing terrestrial channels. To Hollywood BSB was an interesting but unknown ancillary form of revenue, and the failure of satellite attempts in America in favour of cable TV did not make it any more attractive. For all the moguls knew it might not be around for very long – if it ever got off the ground at all – whilst both the British terrestrial networks had long been steady customers. Even with the thriving video market these were still prepared to pay good prices as they continued to rely on the blockbusters for their star attractions at peak times like Christmas. For them the entry of this third player into the market had been most unwelcome, and despite hot denials Birchall heard they had been muddying the waters by telling the studios that if they sold to BSB they would no longer buy from them.

But this had been only a minor irritant as the Hollywood moguls, seeing this new boy in town, were in no rush to conclude any deals, knowing there was plenty of time and that anyhow they held the whip hand. There wasn't even any automatic fixed price and to a certain extent it was a question of what BSB was prepared to pay, although as Robert Devereux had told the IBA franchise committee, if the money was right they would certainly sell. But what had really held things up was a concerted drive by Birchall to try to 'close the video window' – the amount of time video had exclusive rights before a film was allowed on television. The normal release pattern was three to six months in the cinema, followed by 12 months on video, 12 months on pay-TV where it existed in countries like America, and finally playing on ordinary television. For the existing British terrestrial companies the timing was not so much of an issue, as they had to accept that when everybody could see a film for nothing, taping it if they wanted to, this effectively destroyed most of its value to the video rental business.

But with the subscription Movie Channel BSB was not seeing conventional TV as its main competition. Instead it was looking at the video shops, knowing their main attraction to customers was the opportunity they offered of watching films as close as possible to their cinema release. Trying to mirror this, Birchall had accepted there was little chance of simultaneous release on BSB and into the video shops, but now put forward the argument at length to the various Hollywood moguls that the existing 12 month video window should be closed down to at least six months. In excellent presentations he produced reams of BSB-commisioned in-depth research and analysis of the rental market which showed that films in the video rental shops peaked in popularity within two weeks as eager punters rushed in to get the latest offering, and obtained 80% of rental revenue within six to eight weeks. The moguls were impressed by the study, which had been exhaustively carried out by consultants, and found it intellectually convincing. They told Birchall they had always felt instinctively this was the case and it was interesting to have data which proved it. But despite many weeks of trying to convince Hollywood of the justness of the BSB argument, Birchall got nowhere.

The trouble was the studios had heard it all before. The cable pay-TV people in America had been continuously lobbying for the same deal for years, and although they were sympathetic the studios told Birchall that however correct he might be they simply could not afford to alienate their lucrative customers in the video industry. The industry in turn had naturally hotly denied the BSB research, and no matter what sort of money BSB was prepared to pay the studio figures spoke for themselves. Video rights could now bring in $1 million a film, with Warner, for example, obtaining 30% of its revenue from this source, compared to 28% from the cinema and 42% from ordinary TV.

The position was still deadlocked when Murdoch made his move.

The entry of Sky put paid to the highflown video window strategy, and instead the studios rubbed their hands as the two players came to town alongside terrestrial channels carrying on business as usual. Murdoch already had a head start through his ownership of 20th Century Fox, which gave him a library of 100 films, including Aliens and Wall Street, as well as a profile in Hollywood, where in the incestuous, jealous atmosphere he had friends as well as enemies.

Initially though he was at a severe disadvantage. The studios guarded their products carefully and were not impressed by his idea of running Sky's Movie Channel supported by advertising and without subscription. That would mean films being interrupted by advertising breaks, which they disapproved of. As Sky ran under no regulations these could not be limited as they were on British terrestrial channels, and whatever assurances were given there was the horrific prospect of films being mercilessly chopped up as they were on American TV. Just as importantly, if they were transmitted unscrambled they would be able to be picked up by anybody who had a dish without any extra payment, which was not pay-TV and brought problems in dealing with the terrestrial companies who were next in line, as well as grumbles from the video trade which preceded them.

But by autumn that had changed as Murdoch announced he had found a way to encrypt the PAL signal from the Astra satellite. The system which he was evolving was similar to the one used by the French film channel, Canal Plus, and utilised a 'smart card' inserted into a decoder. Its secret, in contrast to the incredibly sophisticated chip being developed by BSB to go inside the receiving box, was that almost all the intelligence on the Sky system was in the card itself, using a technology known as Video-Crypt.

The smart card itself was an impressive piece of technology, which dealt with the scrambling process which had chopped up the picture's 625 lines and then rotated the bits to render it unwatchable in a way which varied every few seconds. This system was not as secure as the one being planned by BSB, and Sky therefore announced that to get round this problem and outsmart hackers that new cards would be issued every three months.

Initially, because of Sky's encryption problem Hollywood had told Murdoch it would only deal with him over old films which had already been on TV enough times for nobody to become excited about seeing them again. But now it was accepted Sky's movies would be encrypted after an initial bedding-down period whilst the technology was got together. The channel would not now be carrying any advertising and so the two satellite suitors were on equal terms.

Back in London, for the shareholders' representatives, ASG, and everyone in the company the Hollywood melodrama which followed was a baffling, confusing and highly expensive process which effectively blew out of the water all the carefully-laid business plans of the Good Ship BSB as it began paying the price for not having closed its deals earlier. It was not just the sums of money involved, which soared ever upwards to unheard of heights, but the way its supply was coming under pressure. Previously BSB had been banking on buying most of its stock on the basis of pay as you play, meaning money would not have to be forked out until individual films were actually screened in the long-distant future. But Murdoch, with more money behind him, then played his trump card by introducing the idea of upfront payments and forward guarantees. Suddenly BSB needed a lot more money fast.

As Birchall shuttled backwards and forwards to Hollywood negotiating with the various studios, alarm escalated in Brompton Road and the number of meetings increased as the various shareholders' representatives struggled to agree on how much more they were prepared to throw into the kitty.

They knew that it was 'either live or die by the deals' for both sides, but the situation was complicated by there being seven major studios to deal with, all of whom were watching each other closely and in no hurry to make the first move. Meanwhile both satellite opponents were in a hurry to tie up their business as quickly as possible. Birchall likened it to grilling, frying and baking all at the same time as he dashed from one studio to another, meanwhile continuously phoning London or flying back to bring the latest figures to the attention of an increasingly distraught Board.

ASG himself had been across to this extraordinary American world in Los Angeles, where he was chauffeured about in a stretch limo as he attempted to bring one of the deals to a successful conclusion. He had sat waiting for the money men to come out with their price, having told the others if it was unacceptable they would simply get up and walk out. It had been and they had. But the brave gesture had turned out to be futile as the deals still had to be done, now seemingly at any price. And as ASG had also discovered, Murdoch was really serious competition. It wasn't just a question of money. Everywhere he went Murdoch seemed to have been there before him in person, either ringing and going over everyone's heads to talk to chairmen, or just as often calling round in person to discuss possible deals face to face.

The nightmare had finally climaxed in one of the last deals –

the crucial one with Paramount/Universal. Birchall described it as 'the real ball-breaker' as Paramount was the most senior of the studios and by that stage BSB had realised it would have to get it. Birchall also respected both companies for listening very carefully to what was said, knowing a lot about the opposition, and being very good technicians in broadcasting, always thinking about how their product was going to be used.

At the beginning of December Birchall went to his first meeting to start negotiating the deal at a building known as the Black Tower on the Universal Studios lot. Although it was ultra-modern it was stuffed with antiques and the higher you went inside the more senior the people became and the more exotic and expensive the antiques. Birchall's destination was the long boardroom on the top floor, with a stunning view over the San Fernando valley. He walked in alone to be confronted by a team of 12 people from the other side. They seemed surprised there was just him and asked if the rest of his team was coming. When he said no they just replied 'Oh', and Birchall realised this was something special. Then they suddenly offered him an enormous deal which quite dumbfounded him. It was not just for all their films, but every piece of TV material they had lying round the place. It was so comprehensive that Birchall thought it probably included the security tapes.

Although the deal was mega, all this additional material was a problem which had also been cropping up with the other studios. They all wanted to unload their TV offerings for extra money as part of the film deal and one horror had already involved having to take dozens of hours of aerobics. They were being parked as possible cheap fillers for one of the other channels. Playing for time, Birchall said he was interested and shot back home for advice.

Whilst he was in London there was a strategy meeting at which a sharp division of opinion arose between those arguing that the technology of BSB was so powerful it did not need to win simply on movies, whilst the other side maintained that if you could control movies you could control everything. None the wiser, Birchall returned to LA with a small team to get the deal together. He informed Paramount BSB did not want the comprehensive package which was on offer, but was prepared to talk about a film deal, perhaps with a bit of TV attached. BSB had better make its mind up quickly then, he was told, as the studio was negotiating with another party.

Birchall made an appointment for 10am the next morning and went in to start haggling, keeping in constant touch with London by phone. By 9pm there was a deal in principle, despite desperate attempts by Murdoch to interfere by phoning and sending his own team round, which was refused entry. The madness was given an extra spin when the head of Universal drove out of the studio gates just as a lunatic born again Christian trying to get to the actor Michael Brandon, who was filming on the set, was also refused entry by the security guards and promptly shot two of them, killing one on the spot and fatally wounding the other.

Birchall, who had missed all this drama, now told the Paramount people the BSB team would go out for a meal break whilst the agreement was being drawn up in legalese before being signed. Instead they hotfooted it across town to meet the man from Warner at Hamburger Hamlet in Century City. BSB had already done one deal with Warner for back numbers like the Mad Max series and Clint Eastwood, which had been regarded as a notable event as Warner had traditionally resisted selling to pay-TV. Now, in the restaurant, Birchall tied up a second deal for all their current films and the ones they would be making over the next five years. The payment was agreed at $40 million, with the additional advantage that Warner settled for a commitment but no money upfront.

All this time Birchall had been keeping in contact with ASG, who in turn had been securing the continuing agreement of the various shareholders to the escalating sums on the Paramount deal. At one stage Sir Trevor Holdsworth had even been called out of the opera to play his part. Finally, at 4 am, Birchall concluded the Paramount deal and phoned ASG with both that news and the agreement in principle with Warner. It was a huge advance, he said. If they did get Warner it would crash Sky's Movie Channel. But ASG's reply was that they simply couldn't afford it. The shareholders had only given authorisation up to a certain sum, and it wasn't enough to get Warner as well. They had already been pressured into committing huge sums of money and there had been ten meetings. If he had been the owner of the company with real power, like Murdoch, and not just the chief executive, it might have been a different matter, but the shareholders had had enough for the moment and there was nothing he could do. It was a major turning point and later Birchall blamed himself for not pushing enough – a blame he thought was shared by the people back in London for not understanding the crucial importance of the moment. But the decision was made and he flew back to London. Murdoch, in a final sprint, then made sure there was no chance for BSB to change its mind and go back by moving in over the weekend to tie up the Warner deal for Sky. At the last minute he had saved his bacon as without it his Movie Channel would have been irreparably thin.

When the dust had settled the damage was heavy. Both sides claimed to be winners, and although generally the pundits gave BSB a 60/40 advantage, it was clear neither had succeeded in knocking the other out of the satellite race.

BSB's massive £200 million deal with Paramount and Universal had brought in 800 films and television programmes including Fatal Attraction, Crocodile Dundee II and Out of Africa. An £86 million deal with Columbia and Tri-Star Pictures had netted The Last Emperor, Roxanne, Blind Date, Ghostbusters and The Karate Kid I and II, with other features like The Adventures of Baron Munchausen, Ghostbusters II and Steel Magnolias still to come, as well as 'classics' including Bridge Over the River Kwai, The Way We Were, Absence of Malice, Tootsie and The China Syndrome. After a harrowing blind auction at which each party put its bid in a sealed envelope, a deal with MGM/United Artists worth £50 million had been concluded in conjunction with the BBC, netting 198 films including A Fish Called Wanda, Rain Man, Cher's Moonstruck and Rocky IV. Sky, as well as getting the future Warner output, had gone into a £100 million joint venture with Disney and Touchstone Films, makers of Who Framed Roger Rabbit? and got Platoon, Robocop and 165 others from Orion to add to its existing Fox output. Altogether, Birchall reckoned up afterwards, the two sides had committed $1.2 billion (£670 million) in payments and guarantees for the next five years, with $700 million of that coming from BSB. A furious Murdoch, accused BSB of paying silly prices, but the pundits agreed that although Sky had been unwilling to pay top dollar to start with, its deals at the end had been just as punitively expensive as BSB's. It was the Hollywood moguls who had been the real winners and although with hindsight it was agreed both sides had paid too much, that did not mean they would not have done the same thing given the circumstances all over again. There was no other choice.

But for the BSB shareholders' representatives the practical result had been embarrassing trips back to their parent boards to sanction a huge injection of another £131 million of funding, bringing the new total up to £353.5 million.

Just as bad whilst the whole saga had been going on had been the loss of one of the major shareholders as Virgin, which had been a prime mover in driving the BSB equation from the start, pulled out. The primary reason given was Richard Branson's decision to take his company off the Stock Market and back into private hands, with the explanation that the banks funding the move had taken a dim view of a £25 million high risk investment which would not generate any cash flow for years to come. But the bankers' reluctance was also extremely convenient, as Virgin's view of the whole project had changed with Murdoch's entry. It had partly been the new competition, but also the way that like Alan Sugar, Robert Devereux had become more and more unhappy with the style in which the project was being run. Virgin's original intention for BSB had been a £250–350 million total investment, with a lean and mean emphasis on programming. Instead it had watched the company ballooning up in a way which made Virgin feel completely and utterly uncomfortable. According to Virgin thinking, if you were in a new venture with a high risk you cut corners. Yet here were salary levels they found absolutely unbelievable and chauffeur-driven cars like the one ASG was swanning about in, when they thought an MD in his sort of start-up situation should count himself lucky just to have a car of any sort.

Just as importantly Devereux had seen the role of the Board gradually change. At the beginning it had been running every-thing, but particularly after Chris Dickens and Peter Bell had arrived to join the management team the position had begun to reverse itself. The management team was now running the business and the shareholders' only job these days was to deal with major policy and financial decisions, while the executives simply made presentations to them. Even David Plowright's programming committee had ended its life not long after the franchise had been won and responsibility for implementing its decisions handed over to the channel heads.

The Board also met monthly and was huge. It was composed of twenty disparate people who knew each other well and had a fairly common view, which Devereux realised made it inevitable it would be difficult to make decisions. Everybody sitting round the table also held a full time position of high responsibility in their own company, which meant they did not really have much time to give to BSB. He knew he himself often forgot about it once he had left a meeting. Yet nobody had seen fit to plug the gap by appointing some non-executive directors who would have more time. Then ASG's way of going about business was just different to theirs. Somebody had mentioned to him ASG didn't like dirtying his hands negotiating, which after some thought he had decided was true. Virgin was not like that. Everybody there had dirty hands all the time.

Devereux had tried raising points like this at the cumbersome Board meetings, but found himself not just alienated from the way the company was going about its business, but from the rest of the Board itself. The heavyweights of Pearson, Reed and Granada seemed quite comfortable about the direction BSB was taking and would reply to his objections by saying things like: 'OK we take your philosophy, Robert, we might save £10m a year on that – but what's £10 million in a £1 billion venture?' Devereux, thinking this nonsense, despaired. BSB was now so radically different from what Virgin had first envisaged he had the feeling of a great big ball running down a hill. But with the rest of the Board apparently quite happy, and the odds so against him, he saw there was little point in trying to rock the boat. It was even possible they might be right.

He therefore went to see the chairman, Sir Trevor Holdsworth, and ASG to explain Virgin had to leave and then rang the heavyweights to give them the news, taking the opportunity to sound them out and see if any would be interested in taking Virgin's 11% share. When it was pretty clear they weren't, Richard

Branson offered it to Alan Bond, who took it immediately. Virgin neatly sold it on to him at a profit of £1 million, increasing Bond's stake from his original £50 to £75 million, giving him a share of 36%, although a complex system of voting rights prevented him having more than a 30% share in corporate decisions. Relieved, Virgin had effectively been out of the kitchen by the end of the year, although it took it another four months to get the money out, at which point they went out to dinner and broke open a bottle of champagne.

At the same time BSB, which had been keeping its fingers crossed that Murdoch's gamble would still not succeed, had its hopes dashed when it became clear Sky was going to happen with the successful launch of Europe's first Ariane 4 rocket on 10 December. This had always been the most nerve-racking aspect of the operation, and not just for Murdoch, as the rocket was also carrying a Skynet 4 satellite owned by the Ministry of Defence which had cost the British taxpayer well over £50 million. If the rocket had failed Sky would have lost its key advantage of time, as a replacement could not have been launched until 1991, which would have reversed the positions of the two rivals and put BSB, with its planned September 1989 launch, well into the lead.

The launch to place into orbit the Astra satellite, built by RCA in America, was from the European Space Agency's complex at Kourou in French Guiana and a nail-biting affair. First it was delayed for 24 hours after cloud came within 10km of the site, bringing a risk of lightning strike, and then there was a minor technical hitch before the Ariane rocket successfully lifted off. SES, whose profile had increased enormously as a result of Sky and had by now sold ten of its sixteen channels, was deeply cheered although there was still widespread dis-belief that Sky could have the rest of its operation in place in time.

Meanwhile, back in England, Rupert Murdoch had been furiously pursuing the key to the launch of Sky – the date he had announced of 5 February, 1989. Just as when he had launched the *Sun* on a gobsmacked British public nearly 20 years earlier, Murdoch's primary decision had been that speed was of the essence. The first satellite station to get on the air would grab the initiative. Whether it was the best was purely a secondary consideration.

What the station needed first was staff, and a mass headhunt started for mainstream television people. Although Sky's closest role model was the American cable stations, ignoring his own American television interests Murdoch returned to his Australian roots for most of the senior management. In a whirlwind recruiting campaign he rapidly persuaded a number of respected and reliable television executives on board. Gordon French, the head of production, came from Channel Nine; John O'Loan, the Head of the News Channel from Channel Ten; while David Hill, the dynamic head of the sports channel, Eurosport, was an old Kerry Packer man. All were hardened professionals, known to be amongst the toughest in what was regarded Down Under as a highly competitive business.

Their immediate task was to recruit more staff, both for on and off screen, while a parallel hunt went on to find a base for the operation. Wapping was not ready and the old Sky Europe channel only had a couple of West End offices. Sky was going to require much more space than that, and in any case a W1 address – even if handy for Soho's production facilities – was completely out of keeping with the spirit of the new venture. Sky was not only going to be low cost, it was to look it, as became evident when it was located on a couple of vacant lots bought on a trading estate not far from Heathrow Airport grandly entitled the Centaurs Business Park. The estate at Osterley was a dismal-looking place far from glamourland. In ironic counterpoint to BSB's headquarters opposite Harrods, it was situated opposite the famous store's furniture warehouse. In an attempt to upgrade it, the powers that be inside News International decreed it would be referred to as Isleworth, the classier name of the next-door borough. But although the new name appeared on the headed notepaper, it never caught on amongst the staff.

The location was a disaster for TV people, like those from the BBC who habitually moaned about the low grade of the restaurants and shops round Television Centre in Shepherds Bush. At Osterley there was not a restaurant or shop nearby to complain about, and no public transport, giving Sky the additional trouble and cost of laying on shuttle buses backwards and forwards for staff.

Whilst building work started, the Australians and their early recruits squeezed into the old Sky Channel premises and a West End office in Ogle Street which had housed the *News of the World* magazine before it moved to Wapping. Construction workers, carpenters, plumbers, engineers, and Sony operatives toiled for long and painful hours but, as winter came, progress seemed pitifully slow. No matter how hard everyone worked it seemed inconceivable that the place would be ready in time. Constructing a standard office block and getting it operational would have been difficult enough in under six months but a television station was a vastly more complex undertaking. Twenty-four-hour broadcasting, especially when much of it was going to be live, required sophisticated engineering, good communications systems, and the installation of highly complex equipment like transmission suites, a master control room, a variety of computer systems, studios, and editing suites.

Murdoch saw the only way to drive the project forward was to appoint a mover and shaker, and anyhow the existing managing director of the Sky Channel, Jim Styles, who was known as a Mr Nice Guy, had already decided to resign. Styles was therefore kept on as a consultant in the interim and Murdoch decided to choose a Brit to head the team of mostly Australian management already assembled to run the station. He called in Andrew Neil, the editor of the *Sunday Times*, as executive chairman. Styles eventually left to retreat back Down Under and exchange the hassles of Sky for the relative peace of the book trade in Brisbane.

To most people setting up a television station would be a fulltime job. For Neil it was not enough; he would continue to edit a major Sunday newspaper as well. Now aged 40, he came from a respectable working-class family who had lived in a tenement in Paisley, Glasgow, but had been sufficiently bright and hard-working to graduate from Glasgow University. His need to prove himself and his status outside the English establishment had appealed to Murdoch, who had taken him from being the UK editor of the *Economist* to play a crucial role in the move to Wapping. Neil was also reknowned for his wiry hair, which had given him the nickname 'Brillo Pad', and a curious line in tight-fitting suits which gave the impression of having been sprayed on. When he had arrived at the *Sunday Times* a crude joke had circulated: if you can't plug it into the mains or fuck it, the editor's not interested. This had subsequently been reported in *Private Eye*, at which Neil had been so amused he had the cutting framed and hung in his office. The aphorism had some point as he was well known for his activities about town with attractive women, which were shortly to lead him first into the headlines and then into the libel courts through his association with the notorious Pamela Bordes.

Neil had been proud of the way he had helped clear the unions out of Fleet Street, and as a devotee of anything American he was a huge Sky fan. His own tastes were defiantly downmarket and he had once told a friend his favourite television programme was Blind Date. He was also a consummate media mouth, reluctant to decline an invitation and working furiously, often giving the impression he could be everywhere and do everything. On one occasion he appeared on a live BBC discussion which ended at midnight and returned to Television Centre by 6am to review the newspapers for Breakfast Time, whilst in the space between the review slots he rushed off, without removing his makeup, to appear live on an independent radio breakfast show. Then he started a normal day like everybody else.

Neil's enemies were to accuse him of spouting Murdoch propaganda on behalf of Sky, but the reality was that as a fervent believer in deregulation and the free market to usher a version of America into Britain he had been advocating something similar for years. And with him on the scene an added vigour was given to the recruitment campaign as he started hitting the phones to everyone he could think of. The feedback from the established TV channels was not encouraging. Sky was perceived as tacky and downmarket and many TV hacks did not consider working for Murdoch a respectable occupation. But Neil had two cards to play - money and opportunity. Sky's hallmark was lean and mean and it was later to become famous for evermore draconian cost-cutting, yet in the short-term race to get on air the policy was quite different. The equation was being driven by time rather than cost, and as conventional TV wisdom dictated the project to be impossible anyway, the only way it had even a chance of success was to fling ever-increasing sums of money at it.

Neil started singling out those who might have a personal reason for wanting to make the journey to Osterley. Jeremy Paxman was rising fast inside the BBC to claim the mantle vacated by Robin Day and had tired of presenting Breakfast Time. He was keen to move to the heavier and more prestigious Newsnight, but so far had not been asked, so Neil called him from the carphone in his Jaguar to offer him £75,000 a year – more than double his existing BBC salary – to present the Sky clone. After a few exploratory meetings Paxman declined.

Neil had more luck with Frank Bough, who was experiencing lean times thanks to the activities of other News International newspaper editors. After what television regarded as a glorious career, first on Nationwide and then as one of the founding presenters of Breakfast Time, Uncle Frank had been rolled by the *News of the World*. Bough did not deny the allegations and had instantly been taken off the BBC's screens, so when Neil offered him the opportunity to rehabilitate himself with a show on Sky he happily accepted, along with the not inconsiderable sum that went with this therapy. Derek Jameson, the former tabloid newspaper editor and supposed inspiration of Sid Yobbo in *Private Eye*, was then excitedly splashed across the Murdoch papers as he signed for a nightly chat show at a reported salary of £250,000 a year.

At a less exalted level Neil led a hunt by Sky executives to scour the BBC, ITV and even occasionally Channel 4 following a strategy of wholesale talent stripping. In the television watering holes around Charlotte Street and Shepherds Bush mutterings arose about offers of fabulous salaries, whilst in the boardrooms annoyance mounted at this new interloper crashing in on traditional television arrangements. Training had always been a sensitive subject in the industry, with the BBC spending up to £20 million a year and employing 150 staff solely for this purpose. The result was that no one else really bothered very much, as after imparting its superb training in programme-making the Beeb proceeded to pay well below market rates, enabling the commercial companies to lure its graduates away with higher pay.

But now Sky entered the fray to beat them at their own game, targeting middle management figures and relying on them to persuade their chums to 'come across'. Nearly 30 staff from the BBC alone accepted with alacrity, only to exhibit mixed reactions when they stepped into the new operation. Some loved the breezy, no-nonsense atmosphere and relished the egalitarianism of its Aussie backbone, despite the enormously hard work. Others found it chaotic and shambolic and left within weeks.

As Sky began to take shape, people in the business remarked that in many ways the closest parallel to the emerging Sky News was TV-am, which had also come from outside to challenge the old cosy news duopoly. An early Sky signing had been Kay Burley, one of the cutest of the TV-am sofa team, and the satellite interloper then zeroed in on the burly young political editor, Adam Boulton. Despite impeccable establishment credentials and having worked for the BBC, Boulton was impatient within the cosy world of broadcasting and was acknowledged as gifted and hardworking, if a trifle dishevelled in appearance now and again.

One Sunday morning in late-November he came into the make-up room at TV-am as Andrew Neil was being groomed for a discussion programme on the recent election of George Bush to the American presidency. Boulton was also on the show and after the two had started chatting about Sky News, David Frost had a word with Neil. 'Promise you won't come after Adam,' he said. 'I can't make any promises,' Neil replied as he zoomed off back to his Wapping HQ. The next day he called Boulton and asked him to come to the offices in Ogle Street. In order to preserve confidentiality Boulton was interviewed by John O'Loan, who was in charge of the news operation, in what appeared to be a storecupboard. O'Loan was deeply sensitive to charges of poaching, especially from a 'mate' like the Australian head of TV-am, Bruce Gyngell, and Boulton had anyhow just signed a lengthy contract. But the cloak and dagger operation was instantly negated when on the way out he bumped into a pair of TV-am colleagues, entering the building to be interviewed in the same furtive fashion.

Back at TV-am's trendy building in Camden Town, Boulton

thought hard. He was barely 30 and quite fancied the thought of starting up his own operation and picking a team from scratch, while in terms of serious coverage he had been promised all the resources he wanted. In any case he liked John O'Loan's laid-back Australian approach. He decided he trusted his judgement about Sky being a serious operation and nothing like a celestial Sun. Picking up the phone to his lawyer he started talking about how he could get out of his TV-am contract.

Popping backwards and forwards to Ogle Street he saw the offices filling up with more and more familiar faces as the numbers went up daily and the atmosphere grew increasingly frenetic as people competed for desks and telephones. A few people came from the existing Sky Europe service, like Gary Davey who was involved in setting up the film channel, and Neil also tapped another source within the Empire by giving talented individuals from the Murdoch papers a chance to spread their wings. Although Sky had neither time nor inclination for TV training it was assumed bright hacks would rapidly absorb television technique by osmosis. The key job of News Editor on the News Channel was therefore given to a razor-sharp young hack from the Sun, Nick Ferrari, who had been marked out as one of Rupert's golden boys and was moving up fast through the Empire. There were other resources at Wapping to be tapped and as Sky represented such a huge investment Murdoch, at least temporarily, put in some of his best managers such as John Alwood, who had overseen the successful move to Wapping and now became finance director.

Wapping had been one of the crucial factors in Murdoch's decision to start Sky, as his successful ending of the print unions' monopoly had led to massive newspaper profits which would finance the operation. But as far as the TV unions were concerned the way had already been cleared in dealing with the 'last bastion of restrictive practices', as Mrs Thatcher had described the industry. Just as in newspapers, tales of the excesses of television technicians like camera crews and picture editors were legendary, while manning levels clashed horribly with the technical reality of shooting on video rather than film and using the new ENG (electronic news gathering) cameras which could virtually be operated single-handed. There were fabulous overtime agreements leading to massive earnings when 10- and 12-hour breaks between shifts were broken and triggered double and treble hourly rates, as well as bringing in a whole complicated substructure of days off in lieu. The problem had become especially acute on coverage of disasters or long-running news stories, with the climax rumoured to have been reached during the Zeebrugge ferry disaster in March 1987, when a TV-am video editor had earned £93,000 through these so-called 'golden hours' payments.

But by the time he announced Sky, Murdoch already knew there was no need for him to do a Wapping in television. In February 1988 TV-am had dismissed around 250 ACTT technicians and started running the station without the unions. When Sky was made public in June disconsolate and angry pickets were still standing outside its headquarters of Eggcup Towers, lamenting the end of the good times as they leaned on their parked BMWs and Granadas. But there was little sympathy, never mind any of the bitter pitched battles with the police which had characterised Wapping.

Inside the station the flamboyant and hyperactive Australian chief executive, Bruce Gyngell, along with Ian Irvine, the granite-faced accountant who was company chairman, held their ground while eager young kids, previously unable to obtain the prized ACTT union ticket which was the only way to a job, learnt quickly – if not always smoothly – how to output television programmes. The ACTT shook its fist and the Labour Party boycotted the station, but the course of history would not be swayed. The new buzzword was 'multi-skilling', ending the old situation where a registered scene-shifter had to be called in if the smallest piece of backdrop needed moving, or a plug could only be changed by an electrician of a suitable grade. Throughout the TV industry other managers looked on with glee as they contemplated reaping the rewards of the taming of the unions without even having to dirty their hands.

There was therefore never any question of the unions gaining a foothold in Sky, even though when it was announced there were 30 ACTT technicians working for the old European Sky Channel. The ACTT agreement was simply terminated from 1 September, with those wanting to stay being offered an immediate 5% pay rise, with a further 5% at launch in February. Those unwilling to accept were asked to leave immediately, with two months' salary as a pay-off, making Sky the first entirely de-unionised broadcaster in Britain. Ironically many of the ACTT technicians who had been locked out of TV-am now came to work there, reopening old wounds as they bumped into members of the so-called 'scab labour' who had also been given jobs. Even toughened Australians looked on in some surprise as tempers boiled over and occasional fist fights erupted between the Pommies in the corridors. Tim White, the shop steward who had led the strike, showed his face for the odd freelance shift, and even the most famous beneficiary of the old regime eventually made his way to the station. 'Do you realise you've employed the £93,000 man?' a former TV-am employee asked John O'Loan one day. The head of the News Channel looked puzzled until the riddle was explained, at which he gave a smile. 'That's the last overtime he'll be getting,' he replied with some satisfaction.

The destruction of union power had eradicated the previously punitive overtime agreements, but Sky still caused a minor stir, even in the new realistic climate, when it announced it would not be paying any overtime at all. Things became even more radical when the station then stated it would not pay for employees' lunches when they were out of the office. The decision was rationalised on the grounds they would be having lunch anyway wherever they were. This might have sounded reasonable to the general public, but in televisionland and the old Fleet Street world of Lunchtime O'Booze lavish expenses-paid lunches had always been a traditional perk. Technicians like camera and soundmen were a byword for reading the menu from right to left so as to order in a way which would extract maximum value from their employers and the thought of paying these bills themselves made them feel positively ill. Even those hired on high salaries began to get an uneasy feeling this might not end up as the gravy train it had superficially appeared to be.

Even more sickening for some were the pay differentials. With the unions out of the way pay was negotiated on a personal level and some were better at it than others. It did not take long for new arrivals to realise the person next to them, doing an identical job, might well be being paid a wholly different wage. Most galling were the national differentials. Many of the Australian bosses had encouraged mates lower down the pecking order, like cameramen, secretaries, technicians and producers, to come to England from television companies Down Under. After they had arrived with surprisingly few work permit problems it was only slowly that the Brits discovered most of them were being paid at significantly higher rates than the home grown talent.

By the end of the year progress of a sort had been made at Osterley but the place was still little more than a building site. Andrew Neil had been down to kick arse and send heads rolling – a process known to the Australians as 'giving the flick' but work was still hopelessly behind schedule. On December 29, with just five weeks to go, Murdoch, impatient with the slow progress, decided to pile on the pressure by ordering the last staff out of their cramped, but at least warm, West End offices. The new arrivals cursed as they fell over cables and swelled the queues at the hot dog stands which were the Centaur Business Estate's staple catering facilities, while the rest of the time was spent huddling round the few available fan heaters. But as jokers on the staff pointed out, if hot dogs did not get them, ulcers from the pressure would as Murdoch continued to demand the start-up date of February 5.

CHAPTER SIX

To Boldly Go . . .

On the same day the remaining Sky staff were being herded down to Osterley, a Cathay Pacific jet landed at Gatwick to disgorge the small Antipodean figure of Ben Hawke, wrapped in an enormous black greatcoat. As he emerged blinking into the weak sunlight, still befuddled by jetlag, he shivered and pulled the coat round himself. It had been handmade for him in Hong Kong out of the finest wool, with 'Specially Made for Mr Ben Hawke' embroidered on the lining, for just such occasions as this, and now Hawke congratulated himself on his own foresight. He had forgotten how bleak the London winter could be, and for a moment wondered if leaving Sydney had been such a good idea. He had been given a cheap ticket to start with and later, as he huddled in a taxi trying to find some place way out in the sticks called the Centaurs Business Park, his doubts began turning to deep gloom. He began to wish he had never heard the words 'Sky Television'.

Just three months earlier it had all been very different. Hawke had been holding down an enviable job as a senior producer on Australia's top-rating current affairs show, Sixty Minutes. This in turn was one of the jewels in the crown of Channel Nine, the pinnacle of Australian commercial television, which BSB shareholder Alan Bond had bought from Kerry Packer for Australian $1,000 million in 1987. As well as being good at his work, Hawke liked it. He had come up through the ranks, starting as a cub reporter for Rupert Murdoch's broadsheet newspaper the *Australian*, before moving into television by joining the respectable public television channel, ABC. Finding TV suited him, he had then crossed the commercial bridge to Channel Nine and worked his way up to Sixty Minutes, for which he had travelled all over the world making current affairs documentaries. It was not just a plum job but a lucrative one. At Channel Nine they did things in style and from the boss, a free-spending television mogul called Sam Chisholm, downwards the channel oozed money.

In late September Hawke, as part of his Sixty Minutes lifestyle, had sat down to a programme lunch at the swish Sydney restaurant The Peacock Gardens – one of those easy affairs so good it turned into dinner. As the wine flowed and the stories of heroic television endeavour grew ever more extravagant, a colleague casually mentioned she had been called from London by John O'Loan, offering her the job of heading the features department of Murdoch's new Sky News. On balance, she confided, she had decided she wasn't inclined to uproot herself for such a risky venture. Hawke, however, was interested. Despite the prestige of his job and the undoubted financial rewards, he was restless. He was still only in his early 30s and had anyhow always relished new challenges. Through a haze of Chardonnay, he told her if O'Loan called back she could mention he might be interested.

He had been snapped up and within days, although O'Loan had never met him, officially offered the post of Head of Features, Sky News. Hawke had tried to check it all out with friends in London, who had faxed out some newspaper cuttings, but the station was so new he hadn't been left much the wiser. Deciding what the hell, he'd negotiated his terms and accepted. Now, just as the year was turning, here he was in Pommieland going to take up the appointment which had seemed so exciting at the time.

But as the taxi finally ground to a halt at the Centaurs Business Park he looked out in horror and disbelief at a dismal, muddy building site. What had he had let himself in for? All he could see were a series of what looked like unfinished railway goods sheds, with disconsolate workmen shoving wheelbarrows and humping piles of TV equipment across acres of freezing mud. Paying off the cabbie, he picked his way towards one of the sheds to take a closer look. It just got worse. There were mounds and snakes of cables everywhere, with only perilous walkways above the ducts, and more teams of workmen hurrying about and banging away. The landline phones could not have been installed, he realised, as what he presumed were the members of the Sky News staff were walking round shouting into portables. Periodically they cursed as the networking went down and the machines cut out. Hawke couldn't see any furniture or anywhere to sit, but he supposed that made little difference when parts of the building were still unfinished and wide open to the elements. It was obviously too cold to sit still for long anyway.

He turned up the collar of his coat and drew harder on his cigarette as he went in search of his new bosses. That didn't help much either. The details he had been sent in Australia were now confirmed. According to the press release heralding his appointment he would provide '. . . at the bottom of every hour, a comprehensive mix of exciting, informative and entertaining programming, which runs the gamut from hard-hitting discussion shows and business reports to the world of showbusiness'. This Sky Television outfit, he realised in amazement, was planning to be on air in precisely five weeks and his part in the operation was starting six new shows from scratch. In the world of normal television that would take months, yet he was supposed to do it in less than forty days – whilst at the same time operating out of this rathole.

The weeks soon turned into a blur as he was plunged into 16- and 18-hour days spent in a frantic mixture of trying to find ideas, persuade on-screen talent, hire staff, commission graphics, approve studios, and co-ordinate the thousand and one other details involved in putting any programme together. Because Osterley was miles away from mainstream televisionland of Soho, he soon found he had to spend much of his time in the back of minicabs shuttling him between various facility houses. But rather than dreading these long car journeys, he soon grew positively to welcome them. He had a mobile phone, so he could keep working as he sat in the gummed-up traffic, and the cabs were better equipped than his so-called office in being at least warm and having something to sit on.

Every midnight, and sometimes later, Hawke would return exhausted to the bedsit he had rented in Richmond and crash out. There was no time to find a house, or any point in doing so, and he was just relieved that he had left his wife and two small children back in Australia. It was a shame in some ways as they'd always dreamed of spending a couple of years in Europe whilst the children were still young, but at least now he would not have to uproot them. Once this madness was over and the whole scheme had flopped he could go back home to rejoin them. He just hoped Sixty Minutes would still have a place for him.

During the day Hawke's mind was preoccupied with a myriad other matters. What he had been catapaulted into, he gradually became aware, was a totally new way of making television. On normal stations programmes had to argue their way on to the schedules as there was always too much material. Producers would wring their hands in anguish as their precious material was ruthlessly chopped back, or even canned altogether, and great agonising would go on about how new programmes could be slotted in round crucial 'junctions', like 9pm across BBC1 and 2, or 10 pm across ITV and C4, when the news came on and viewers were likely to reach for their remote controls to switch channels.

There was no agonising at Sky, just huge gaping holes which needed to be filled somehow. Instead of buying in material and then working out how to compress it, Hawke found his new and unique job was to try and stretch it. After getting a good deal on buying in a one-hour special on Iran he examined it carefully and saw that with a little ingenuity he could spin it out to make three separate half hours. Getting on the mobile phone, he hired the veteran ITV reporter Llew Gardener and a producer to drum up some suitable wallpaper material, stretched it to the three half hours, and made provision for several repeats. A few more holes had been filled in.

Creating entirely new material, as his brief demanded, was harder. He saw the obvious possibility of a nightly entertainment show, and immediately created a programme called Wild West End to interview stars and preview their new shows. The programme could be based on the acres of free promotional material ladled out by the showbiz PR companies. There was bound to be an endless stream of celebs desperate to get their faces on any television channel which would plug their current effort. The problem was where the programme would be made.

The Osterley plans optimistically showed three studios, but in reality there was only a fighting chance one would actually exist by launch date and even if it did, it would be used fulltime for the rolling news show. Hawke cut through the morass by booking a nightly studio in Soho. Then he threw some of the advertising people out of their nearby office, rearranged their desks to install his production people, and Wild West End was ready to go. More holes had been filled.

Casting round for more traditional and well-worn subjects, his next scheme was a show about the press. A colleague dreamed up the title 'The Editors', which got them so far, but Hawke sat shivering in his greatcoat wondering who would actually present it. One of the keen young staff he had just hired from the BBC asked him if he knew of somebody called Anthony Howard. Hawke had never heard of him. 'He's just left his job as Deputy Editor of the *Observer* and he enjoys doing television,' the ex-BBC producer explained excitedly, looking up Howard's home number in his contacts book.

They rang and asked if they could come round. It was a filthy night and pouring with rain, as they knew full well without even bothering to look outside. The roof had still not been sorted out and to add to Hawke's miseries he had by now caught a stinking cold. As he huddled in the welcome warmth of the minicab he mused that even if Howard turned out to be no good, it would be worth the trip just to spend a few hours in the more civilised environment of the journalist's Holland Park home. Hawke was beginning to forget how other people lived.

When they arrived Howard ushered them into the kitchen and offered them coffee, and as he seemed keen Hawke got straight down to business. The format, content, and Howard's contract had all been discussed almost before the coffee got cold and they then sat around chewing the fat until Hawke could delay things no longer and they clambered into the womb-like minicab to head back to the Osterley wilderness. 'In the BBC that would have taken us at least three months of meetings,' the amazed ex-Corporation man commented as they ground their way through the traffic. Hawke just grunted, already preoccupied by how to fill the next hole.

Periodically, along with a couple of colleagues, he would beard

O'Loan or any other senior exec who would listen to protest that the whole thing was madness. 'Look, mate, why can't we give ourselves just a few more weeks?' he would demand, 'This is ridiculous! It just can't happen. Who cares if we start on 5 March instead? BSB isn't around and the outside world barely knows we exist. Why such an insane rush when we could do things properly if we had just a little more time?'

O'Loan, so busy he was permanently on the run, generally held meetings standing up or as he was striding about. On average they lasted two minutes. The reply to the moans was always the same: the instructions from Empire HQ were non-negotiable. Sky must stick to its schedule. Murdoch had said the station would start broadcasting on 5 February and, come hell or high water, that was what was going to happen.

One of Hawke's major problems in trying to recruit top line talent was that although he would try to see people away from the 'office', sooner or later they would arrive to view Osterley and he was always convinced that once they saw the chaotic building site they would be bound to try and pull out. Above all he was casting around for a good presenter for the evening current affairs show. He thought he might persuade John Stapleton, the likeable and highly experienced BBC man from Oldham in Lancashire, who had done a long stint on the now defunct Nationwide and was currently fronting the BBC's Breakfast Time. They had one meeting before, unavoidably, Stapleton showed up at the building site to fight his way past the diggers, cement mixers, and men in hard hats into the cavernous space Hawke was supposed to work in. He looked shell-shocked.

On the wall Hawke had stuck together several photographs to make up a glorious panoramic display of golden sunlight and warm-looking water. He waved his hand laconically. 'That,' he explained wistfully, 'is the view from my house in Sydney.' Stapleton looked in amazement at the very different scene surrounding them. It was raining again, drips were still coming through the roof, and the place was so bare Hawke appeared to have the only desk and chair. With some effort a second chair was found for Stapleton and the two men sat down in their overcoats to discuss terms, with Stapleton voicing the familiar BBC doubts about working for Murdoch.

'You know, John,' Hawke replied with a grin, 'I've worked for Packer and I've worked for Bond. They're all evil men, John – but they are very rich.' Stapleton laughed at the joke. He already liked Hawke's direct Aussie approach.

Stapleton, along with his wife, the presenter Lynn Faulds Wood, had been involved in the famous beginning of TV-am so he thought he knew something about television start-ups. But Osterley was something else, as he told Lynn after he had gingerly picked his way through the mud of the building site and returned home. 'The place is TV-am with knobs on,' he explained in wonderment. 'It hasn't a hope of even falling on the air, never mind getting on it – it's a complete and utter shambles.'

Back at Osterley Hawke had been immediately diverted by fresh problems as shows he thought he had safely bought and tied up started falling apart. Searching for suitable ideas to lift he had combed the schedules of the American CNN (Cable News Network) and emerged with a likely runner in Crossfire, which he also conveniently knew happened to be one of Murdoch's favourite current affairs shows. The programme's format was a double act featuring a pair of presenters from opposite ends of the political spectrum, one left-wing and one right-wing, who then interviewed a guest.

After some judicious lunching and several more minicab journeys to civilisation Hawke had persuaded Norman Tebbit to play one half of the required Laurel and Hardy roles. Tebbit had by now retired as Conservative Party Chairman and therefore had the time, while his nickname of the Chingford Skinhead bore testimony to his aggressive attitude which Hawke knew would make for good television. As Tebbit's opposite he had roped in Austin Mitchell, Labour's shadow Trade and Industry spokesman and a veteran of Yorkshire Television's local current affairs magazine, Calendar. Studios had been requisitioned, the contracts all signed, and Hawke had been happy that at least something looked as if it was going to work well.

But days before the 5 February launch date a letter arrived from CNN informing Sky that the American network wished to complain about its ideas being ripped off, plunging Hawke's show into a complex series of negotiations. He was just about to despair when he was finally told the programme could go ahead –

but only if it was given a new name. The message came through on Friday, with thousands of pounds already committed to shooting the final title sequence over the week-end. The graphics were already designed and there was no question of postponing the shoot – not just because the studio time was paid for. There simply wouldn't be another chance in the few remaining days before they went on air. As the agreed design for the opening graphics featured gun sights, Hawke now had hours to find a substitute title to blend in with this central visual feature. He already knew the Centaurs Business Park gave little creative inspiration and in any case, like all Murdoch business establishments, was dry. So he drummed up a couple of mates and took them to the nearest pub, where he bought them each a drink and told them nobody could leave until they came up with a new name acceptable to CNN.

The first suggestion was the limp effort of Sky Crossfire, which was predictably rejected when proffered to the Americans. The trio returned to the pub, staggering out two hours later with the next suggestion of Target which no one was really satisfied with. But alcohol had failed to produce anything more inspired and when CNN gave agreement it was decided it would obviously have to do. The graphic designer was phoned and given his new instructions.

Avoiding an injunction from CNN by the pedestrian title of Target saved the Tebbit-Mitchell roadshow which immediately, even before Sky had gone on air, proceeded to give the station the first real blast of the publicity it craved. Until then there had been little apart from the breathless columns of prose served up to Murdoch readers alongside increasingly desperate full-page ads puffing the station's tiny handful of celebs. The buzznames of Derek Jameson, Frank Bough and Tony Blackburn had been endlessly paraded, but when they were joined by Selina Scott, the blonde ex-News at Ten newsreader, Sky immediately ran into trouble. Scott's pert face was featured in a full-page ad in the *Sunday Times* claiming: 'Sky signs top presenters for 24-hour news', but 40 lines into the smaller print came the crucial admission: Sky had not exactly signed up Ms Scott, but just bought in a programme called West 57th from CBS in America, on which she happened to be one of four guest presenters. Ms Scott had not signed up with Sky, her agent trilled, and was seeking legal advice. The ad was not repeated.

Otherwise workmen might toil night and day at Osterley whilst shouting Australians rushed around getting the programmes together, but despite reams of press releases as far as the majority of the GBP was concerned Sky was still virtually invisible. Non-Murdoch Big Papers which ran anything about the station mostly sneered, predicting varying degrees of downmarket activity which they made clear was not expected to appeal to their readerships. Then on 1 February, four days before launch, the Labour leader Neil Kinnock stepped into the breach by announcing that Austin Mitchell's role as a twice-weekly Sky presenter of Target meant he would be unable to carry out his front bench duties. He was therefore being relieved of them.

The next day was a slow news day and this last-minute publicity godsend made the front pages everywhere. The *Daily Express*, emphasising how the Labour leader had shot himself in the foot, ran an editorial saying: 'Sky should think of sending Mr Kinnock a little something in return for the free publicity he has directed its way'. Taking his cue, the oleaginous Corporate Affairs Director Jonathan Miller ordered a case of champagne and instructed it be sent to Kinnock's office with a thank you note.

The reaction in some quarters at Osterley was not however approval but incandescent rage. Hawke was furious at this unasked for interference in a delicate situation, while ex-BBC and ITN types experienced a nasty sinking feeling that they might have made a ghastly mistake. Despite all the assurances they had been given, it seemed as if Sky was going to be the tacky, tabloid telly they had all feared. And treating the Leader of Her Majesty's Opposition with such contempt was not just tacky but, like the Sun, right-wing tacky. The political editor, Adam Boulton, was especially furious given all the efforts he had put into the sensitive matter of establishing satisfactory relations with the Labour Party.

One of the new arrivals even rang Andrew Neil to complain. 'It was just a joke,' Neil answered lightheartedly. 'We do things like that all the time in Fleet Street,' he added. 'This is not Fleet Street and television does not work like that,' replied the angry journalist. But, as always at Sky, recriminations were soon overtaken by events. Despite the Kinnock-led publicity bonus the venture still looked as impossible as ever and the atmosphere at the Centaurs Business Park was rising to a pitch of subdued hysteria. All through the night of Saturday the fourth teams of workmen struggled to cover the mud of the car park with a veneer of asphalt, whilst mounds of potted plants were heaped up in the entrance and yards of turf unrolled at the approach to make it look halfway decent. Round the back and in the corridors, which the distinguished guests would be kept well away from, there was just a sea of wires.

Unperturbed, Rupert Murdoch inched his way around a big hole in the floor. Luxuries like floorboards were still to come. He grinned at Boulton and said 'Good Luck'. As 6 pm approached executives and a host of celebrities from on and off screen, including even the top brass of the BBC, gathered with Murdoch at Osterley, whilst across town more junior staff had been invited to watch the launch in the comfortable environment of the Selfridge Hotel behind Selfridge's where a party had been laid on. As 6 pm came round there was a hush as people stopped eating, put down their drinks, and joined in the countdown to a voice loaded with TV gravitas which boomed out: 'This is the television revolution! A revolution in quality! A revolution in quality and choice!' On the multiple screens Eurosport, Sky News and Sky Movies burst simultaneously on to the air to broadcast the same promotion. The only slight glitch was Sky, a revamp of the original Sky Europe, being six seconds late. After announcing in unison the glories of the new celestial future the four channels then split away from each other to screen their own separate programmes.

Sky Movies, still unscrambled and free, kicked off with Project X, a mediocre science fiction film about a US air force pilot who becomes involved with the secret military training of a chimpanzee. Later in the evening things were to improve with two of the channel's blockbuster offerings – Paul Newman in The Colour of Money and Bette Midler in Ruthless People, both of which were already earmarked for multiple repeats due to the problem of some Hollywood studios being reluctant to provide recent movies until scrambling and subscription were in place. As a result Sky had already had to announce its early films would primarily be 'classics' – television-speak for ancient B-movies which had long since run their natural course.

The Eurosport channel began the evening with tennis, followed by skiing and cricketing action featuring Australia versus the West Indies. Eurosport was a joint venture between News International and the members of the European Broadcasting Union, which included the BBC, and was planned to show a mixture of European and international sporting events 18 hours a day. Established filming rights given to other companies made many jewels of the sporting calendar unavailable and, with all that time to fill and the restricted budget, it was obvious there would have to be considerable emphasis given to obscure events or minority sports. Under the leadership of David Hill, one of the more exuberant of the Australian imports, Eurosport had been determined to procure its own exclusives in due course, but a major problem had loomed with the European Commission challenging alleged anti-competitive practices in the tie-up with the European Broadcasting Union. But at this point, like most legal actions, it was proceeding only at a snail's pace and no one was going to let it spoil the party. There was also an optimistic attitude at Sky that dedicated sports fans could be hooked into anything, with hopeful pointers in the way 'sports' like darts, bowls and American football had been made popular by the British terrestrial channels. The Wrestlemania series of American wrestling might well inherit the popularity British wrestling had once had on ITV, and who knows, they told each other looking at their future schedules, surfing in Hawaii could well develop mass appeal.

As the members of staff at the Selfridge Hotel munched on their breaded chicken legs they turned to the third channel, Sky News, which had opened with its regular format of a half-hour news bulletin, starting every hour on the hour. The 'back half hour', as it was called, was filled with a mixture of Ben Hawke's offerings. Visually Sky News looked very neat, with slick and classy presentation and John O'Loan's original vocation as an architect showing in the studio set. Sky had gone for the same format as the 9 O'Clock News on the BBC which had recently been redesigned to give an impression of activity and immediacy by placing the newsreader against a backdrop of the working newsroom. Sky News, it was universally agreed as staff nodded in vigorous approval, had succeeded rather better at the same thing.

There were two 'exclusive' opening stories, one about ten Britons taking up an offer from a German to sell their kidneys for £20,000 each, while the second reported the favourite tabloid hate figure of Myra Hindley as being about to return to hospital for further cancer checks. Both were duly rubbished in the papers the next day as hoary old chestnuts, but that was accepted as time-honoured Fleet Street tradition. Meanwhile, the critics were mildly taken aback. Contrary to some of the horror scenarios bandied about by the chattering classes there seemed to be little to grumble about. News, after all, the critics had to concede, was news, and Sky News seemed to be making a perfectly workmanlike stab at it. And as its slogan of 'We're there when you need us,' emphasised, it was always on.

The fourth channel, simply called Sky, was the only one of the four with a chance of being seen on launch night much beyond a few West End hotels. In a carefully worded press statement News International had claimed 600,000 homes in Britain and the Irish Republic would be able to see the station, but in reality most of these were on old cable systems and restricted to this one channel which had been the old Sky Europe. An eleventh hour deal with the Cable Television Association had slightly boosted the potential audience by including another 53,000 homes linked up to more modern cable systems. Sky, later to be renamed Sky One, was puffed as 'an up-graded version of the existing family entertainment service' which, according to the information pack, 'had strong audience loyalties across Europe'. In a demonstration of the fare that had built up this following the channel opened with an old Dolly Parton show, preceding a formula of tired Australian and American soaps with titles like General Hospital and As the World Turns. Nostalgic trips back to the black and white days of the 50s were promised by Lucille Ball's comedy show I Love Lucy, in line with the entertainment policy of the airline TWA, which showed it on all its cross-Atlantic flights.

The only sign of anything that could be regarded as home-grown, if not original, was the prospect of Tony Blackburn hosting a women's chat show called Sky By Day; a remake of the veteran

ITV show Sale of the Century; and starting in March a nightly chat show with Derek Jameson, no longer the Fleet Street editor with a left-wing background but now rethemed as the archetypal Cockney cheerful chappie. Jameson's opening show straddled his two different worlds with the newspaper in-joke of putting a ferret up someone's trouserleg – the expression used by *Sun* editor Kelvin Mackenzie to galvanise his staff.

At the Selfridge Hotel, once the initial excitement had worn off, the staff soon turned their backs on the screens to concentrate on the more important business of piling into the free bar, while at Osterley the executives were cock-a-hoop. What did it matter if the output looked pretty unexceptional on the screen? It was the extraordinary achievement of getting it there in so short a time that they had reason to be so proud of. At a height of 23,300 miles above Zaire the Astra satellite had taken its allotted place in the Clarke Belt, named after the science fiction writer Arthur C. Clarke who had first suggested the feasibility of a 'geo-stationary' satellite in the late 1940s. Clarke had worked out that if a satellite was at this particular height the speed of rotation necessary to keep it in orbit would match the angular rotation of the earth and therefore, seen by an observer on the ground, it would appear to be stationary in the sky. By the time of the Sky launch, satellites had been used for interchanging TV pictures from one continent to another for several years but now the Skyship Enterprise had boldly gone where no other TV station had gone before by beaming the signal from Osterley to be bounced straight back to earth. The *Observer's* TV critic John Naughton told readers that Blue Peter had computed the return journey from Osterley to a house in London as 71,546 kilometres which, he commented acidly, 'would make Murdochvision the longest garbage-run in history'.

But at Sky that night there was nothing but jubilation. On the ground the whole thing had been a triumph of organisation and technology, with hardly a hitch except for a few minor sound problems.

Earlier in the day at a press conference Rupert Murdoch had been in more restrained mood as he revealed he had so far spent £25 million to add to the £40 million he had already lost on Sky Europe. 'Now the money will start to go out seriously,' he said, but denied there was any chance Sky would plunge its parent company of News International into the red. Saying it would 'raise and modernise the standards of the BBC and ITV', Murdoch parried a question about the percentage of American content by replying: 'Downhill skiing from the US might involve British skiers, British cameramen . . . how do you define it?'

After Murdoch had hailed the arrival of 'television's new age', the guests were invited to the nearby stately home of Syon House, the microwaves and robot dispensing machines of the Sky canteen having been judged unfit for the task of feeding such a distinguished multitude. The canteen, to which the only alternative was the Centaur Business Park's hotdog stands, had been built as a brave new world of cookchill cabinets and microwaves avoiding the need for any catering personnel. Former BBC types, accustomed to moaning about their old canteen had hardly been able to believe all they were now getting was a wall of machines. But although much loathed the canteen had already come in very useful with pilot news bulletins, as Sky's arrival had coincided with the height of the listeria and salmonella scare. When pictures had been needed of the sort of food that could be dangerous and of harmful methods of cooking, a crew had simply been sent upstairs to film there. 'Meals like these can make you ill,' the commentary line had run. At the infinitely more civilised Syon House about 500 execs and guests dined by candlelight, although in Sky's typically chaotic style numbers had been miscalculated and there was not enough room for everyone to sit down. Norman Tebbit and his wife sat at the top table with Murdoch, full of praise for the successful enterprise, while mavericks muttered that the grandiose scene reminded them of The Draughtsman's Contract, the trendy Channel 4 film made by the director Peter Greenaway.

A nearby pub, The London Apprentice, had boasted that it sported 'one of the first dishes in Britain', and here there was a more informal gathering of staff who had been working on the transmission and unable to get in to town to the Selfridge Hotel Party. Even though it was more than a mile from the Centaurs' wilderness, with its unofficial status as Sky's local the pub had got an extension of hours and later that night, in typically egalitarian mode, Murdoch made sure that he left the formal dinner to rub shoulders with the troops.

Ben Hawke joined him there before, tired but elated like all his fellow employees, eventually struggling back in the early hours to his bedsitter. As his head hit the pillow he was hardly able to believe it had all gone so well, but the next morning he suddenly did not feel so good. It had been one thing celebrating the launch, he realised, but now the baby was born it had instantly become a monster which demanded constant feeding to satisfy its voracious 24-hour-a-day appetite. The initial adrenalin gone, he dragged himself back to the building site, stepped over the already wilting grass, and sat down to start blocking up holes once again.

Who he and the other 200 members of staff were blocking up the holes for was open to debate. Although the station was broadcasting, Murdoch had still paid the penalty for moving at such speed. There were optimistically claimed to be 100,000 punters on the waiting list, but virtually no receiving equipment in the shops. Murdoch went to great lengths to emphasise this had not been the fault of Alan Sugar, who was immensely experienced at fast-tracking electrical goods to flood the market. Instead there had been a hold-up over specifications which had put production back by four or five weeks. Andrew Neil put a brave face on it by telling the *Daily Express*: 'When the BBC started it had less than 400 viewers. There will be 400 able to watch Sky when it launches,' and telling those disappointed at not being able to buy on day one: 'It's not a matter for apology'.

The result was a curious irony for a service supposedly ushering in the new world of narrowcasting, where in theory audiences would divide and the sports fan, movie fan or cartoon addict would sit alone in different rooms indulging their separate tastes. The initial dearth of dishes produced the opposite effect. Viewing of Sky became a communal enterprise as entrepreneurs all over the country installed early dishes in pubs such as The London Apprentice and halls which they hired for big one-off occasions like boxing matches. In its infant days Sky-watching was to be the most sociable television activity since the nation had gathered together to view the first televised Coronation in 1953.

PART TWO

CHAPTER SEVEN

BSBBC

The morning after the Sky launch a familiar broadcasting figure sat in the IBA building, lolling back with his feet on the desk as he watched the television. John Gau had not been invited to Osterley the previous night and now, as he flicked the remote and idly zapped between the four channels, he was seeing Sky for the first time. In the run-up to the launch Gau had keenly studied the station's published schedules and as he watched the reality on the screen it all looked much as he had anticipated – pretty dreary. Switching off the set, he settled back to work.

Although only 48, Gau was already an accomplished elder statesman of the television industry, universally known as 'the best Controller of BBC1 that the BBC never had'. His eventual recruitment to BSB as Director of Programmes was seen as a major coup for the station. Gau had always been in television, going straight to the BBC after leaving Cambridge in 1963 to start his career as a humble assistant film editor. He had risen through the ranks to be editor of the daily magazine and current affairs show Nationwide, from where he had been promoted to become an able and popular Head of Current Affairs. Then came Carrickmore, the notorious incident in 1979 named after the village in mid-Ulster where a Panorama team was alleged to have co-operated with the Provisional IRA in filming a roadblock. If it had not been for this, it was universally agreed, Gau would now be leading the BBC's reaction to the new satellite competition. Even more importantly he would be to trying to retain the corporation's standards in the face of the government's virulent espousal of private enterprise, which had already led to rumpuses about the licence fee.

Gau had not known about the Carrickmore incident when it happened and only found out about it later at a party. But when recriminations began after wildly distorted press interpretation, with Mrs Thatcher calling for the BBC 'to put its house in order', he took full responsibility. The extraordinary esteem in which he was held by his subordinates was enhanced by the outspoken memo defending his team which he sent to the BBC hierarchy and duly resulted in his being reprimanded. Then, when it was time to pick a successor to Bill Cotton as Controller of BBC1, Gau got his comeuppance. Although he was the obvious choice and the management wanted him, the increasingly interventionist and politicised BBC Governors, now under the Chairmanship of the Conservatives' choice of George Howard, instead gave the job to Alan Hart, Head of Sport.

Seeing his way was blocked, Gau soon left and with typical shrewdness and foresight turned his considerable talents to the newly formed independent production sector. It was just before the start of Channel 4, which had been planned not as a producer of programmes but as a station which would commission and buy in programmes from independents. Realising this new model of publisher rather than producer was the way television was going, Gau set up his own company which in his blunt style he simply entitled John Gau Productions. He recruited a number of old colleagues and was soon busy making programmes for the new channel, eventually being appointed to the Channel 4 Board.

Next it was the BBC itself which gradually came to terms with the new world of the independents, and JGP programmes, like the series Reaching for the Skies, were duly commissioned and sold back to his old employer. Athough Gau had lost his comfy cushion there he thrived as an entrepreneur and rapidly succeeded in the hard commercial reality of programme-making as a successful business, while at the same time not compromising standards. As a result the majority of the JGP output was at the serious factual end of the spectrum, leading one of the trade magazine profiles to remark that 'John Gau Productions would not make the kind of programmes that BSB is likely to buy for its first two years on air'.

In the previous month's New Year's Honours list Gau had received a CBE that combined with a term as head of the Independent Producers Association and Chairmanship of the Royal Television Society to duly confirm his status as a grand old man of the independent sector. He underlined this by his balding, tubby appearance and his preference for safe and dull attire so very different to the average Armani-suited independent earnestly networking round the Groucho Club.

Before Gau was approached by BSB the original idea approved by ASG, of each channel head controlling his own empire and organising separate scheduling and presentation, had run into trouble. Each head was supposed to report directly to him, but ASG soon discovered it wasn't working out like that. Instead he found himself, as he put it, like Solomon, acting as peacemaker between the constantly warring channels. There was endless confusion about what was to appear where. The Lifestyle women's programmes began by being classified as information and were therefore put on the NOW channel along with news. Then NOW was rebranded a male channel to feature sport and news, so Lifestyle was reclassified as entertainment and switched to the Galaxy channel along with the Zig Zag children's programming. Then Gunnar Rugheimer, the Galaxy channel head, was instructed to report via Bob Hunter, the head of NOW, to ASG. Most problematic of all after the breakdown with ITN was the endless talk of 'different' news coverage, with ideas veering wildly between a rolling 24-hour show and one broken into two-hour segments.

Much of the muddle was caused by the fact that at that stage BSB only had three channels. The IBA had five official ones to dispense and had originally said there would be a three-year period of grace for BSB before the other two were released. But after Sky had announced four and potentially six channels, BSB had urged the IBA to offer the empty two for immediate tender. It would compete for them alongside others, and assuming it won – and there was every reason to think it would – it would then have a five-channel package to take on Sky. That would be good for the station but, as ASG realised, it would not be good for him. Trying to cope with three warring channel heads was bad enough.

The prospect of five, each blowing their own trumpet, was unthinkable.

ASG realised he needed someone to pull all the programming together, and if necessary bang heads. Opinion amongst the shareholders was divided. Virgin, always pushing for a lean operation, was dubious about recruiting another highly paid executive, especially someone straight out of the BBC culture. (They were later loudly to eat their words about the choice of Gau.) But David Plowright from Granada Television was still adamant that BSB required more programming expertise. The IBA was also getting anxious and kept on asking when a programming supremo was going to be appointed. One or two half-hearted approaches were made to ITV programmers without success before ASG bumped into Bill Cotton, who had retired from being managing director of BBC Television to become chairman of the independent production company, Noel Gay Television. Cotton suggested trying John Gau, of whom ASG had never heard, and even obligingly popped down to John Gau Productions in Putney to ask if he would be interested.

When Cotton turned up at his office the concept of BSB had barely touched Gau's consciousness, but as he listened to what Cotton had to say he became quite intrigued. What appealed to him most of all was the newness of the project. Gau had been only a junior minion at the start of BBC2, and although around at the beginning of Channel 4, had not been at the heart of the operation. Now he was being offered every broadcaster's dream of the chance to take the leading programming role in a completely new venture. Gau knew most broadcasting start-ups, like BBC2 and then Channel 4, were fiascos to start with, but they came right in the end. And even if the first six months were a nightmare, what was six months in a franchise which was to last 15 years? He was certainly interested enough to agree to Cotton's suggestion he had breakfast with ASG at the Hyde Park Hotel.

The two men got on immediately and ASG, instantly impressed, was keen to bring Gau aboard. Gau in turn was becoming more and more attracted by BSB but, as he now explained to ASG, he had a problem with the success of his own company. He was not prepared, he said, to ditch something he had so carefully built up to sail uncharted waters in the Good Ship BSB. And while he could leave Susie, his wife, to run the company there was no guarantee she would be able to bring in new business as effectively as he had done in the past. The two men talked through various ways of arranging compensation, such as BSB buying the company, before ASG came up with the answer. BSB was effectively going to be like Channel 4 and follow a commissioning model rather than make its own programmes. So, paying little heed to the conventions and moralities of the television industry, which he was anyhow unfamiliar with, ASG suggested solving the problem by commissioning Gau's company to make programmes for BSB. That would assure it had work, and the amount involved for BSB – out of a total programming budget of £220 million – would be tiny. In any case the deal could be independently scrutinised to protect against any allegations of conflict of interest.

Gau replied that with compensation like that he would be happy to join BSB for three years. He worked out that his company would probably lose £3 million a year in turnover if he was away from it, so the equivalent amount of business would be needed from BSB. The total profit, or production fee as it is called in the independent sector, would be some £1 million. That was in addition to a salary of well over £100,000. The two men shook on the deal.

Unfortunately, in a routine which was becoming all too common at BSB, the presentation of the issue was not well handled. The rumour first went around that they were getting a senior programmer and then, just after it was official and Gau had joined as Director of Programmes, news of the JGP deal broke separately. Gau had been very upfront about it beforehand and informed the press office it could tell anyone it liked. But there had never been any announcement, so when details of the arrangement appeared in the newspapers it gave the impression of an embarrassing leak.

Journalists rang to ask if it was true Gau was making £1 million out of BSB for his company and the press office primly replied that it was true JGP was producing programmes for BSB as part of a normal contract, the value of which it was not prepared to discuss. The media had a field day playing this up as fat cattery. Ray Snoddy, the doyen of the media correspondents who wrote for The *Financial Times*, the most weighty of the Big Papers, even questioned whether this was really on and the shareholders would be happy about it. Phillip Whitehead, the former Labour MP who was now one of the most established of the independent producers, pronounced he would never be able to look at himself in the mirror if he had signed such a deal and there was outrage throughout the industry.

Both Gau and ASG provided acres of justification but privately Gau had to admit he had made a mistake. The level of fuss which the arrangement had created was quite extraordinary, and he thought afterwards that if he had had his chance again he would have found a better way of arranging his compensation. Dealing with one's own company at arm's length was a tricky business, even though it was his wife who was officially acting for JGP in sorting out the deal.

But contrary to Snoddy's conjectures the shareholders did approve the arrangement, and as for ASG – he couldn't give a hang about the flak. He was just delighted to have on board such a wonderful person, for whom he had enormous admiration. Not only could Gau do anything in broadcasting, he had also acquired the shrewdness that came from being an independent producer. He was exactly what BSB needed. The same feeling spread amongst the staff when he duly arrived, and he inspired a deep sense of awe as he stalked the corridors there. Gau, they knew, had the precious TV commodity of 'bottom', otherwise known as gravitas, which gave a feeling of weight to the whole programming side.

The channel heads Bob Hunter and Andy Birchall, who had previously reported directly to ASG, were naturally less than happy. In the hierarchical-conscious atmosphere of BSB they did not like the idea of someone coming in above them and assuming overall control of the programming side. More practical was the point that if Gau was such a good idea, why had no one thought of putting someone in his position earlier? It was something Gau soon wondered himself. He had not long been at his desk before he had the sensation of groping for the stable door after the horse had bolted. It was all very well appointing him programming supremo, but a lot of the point was lost if, as had happened, many of the programmes had already been commissioned and millions of pounds committed to them before he arrived.

In the good old days, when television was first the monopoly of the BBC and then the duopoly of BBC and ITV, it generally made its own programmes in-house. Anything else, such as films or American soaps and serials, was labelled 'acquired programming'. But from the mid 1980s, television companies were busy trying NOT to make programmes, and although BSB may have seemed like a television company to the outside world, it was actually a clearing house and publisher of programmes that were either specially commissioned or bought in in the old 'acquired' way. Sky had begun by going down a similar route, gathering large amounts of acquired programming, the joy of which was that it could be very cheap indeed. In some cases, like the daily series on business or health it cost nothing at all. Specially made programmes, even when Sky commissioned them and set the rate, could never quite do that.

The average cost of making television programmes varies hugely. At one extreme, high-profile original drama can cost £450,000 an hour, with £100,000 an hour for good documentaries involving filming abroad. At the other end of the equation the genre known as talking head shows can cost little more than a studio and a presenter's fee. On average the BBC's costs for network television were over £82,000 an hour, with ITV spending more, yet Sky was was claiming that it could come in at £6,000 an hour. Commissioning original material from outside was only a temporary measure whilst it got its act together. It planned to continue to buy in the bulk of its programmes and in the long term not commission anything, but revert to the old days by making its own programmes in-house. That would cost even less and give even greater control over output and costings, as well as being more flexible.

But BSB was not Sky and enticing invitations to tender for programming had started appearing in the spring of 1988. The process had taken off from there, and now Gau was gobsmacked to find how much had been decided months beforehand and how his hands were tied. When he sat down to start planning his schedules he found there was an awful lot which needed unravelling, yet many of the crucial deals which would shape the station's output had already been signed.

After the breakdown of negotiations with ITN, the BSB commitment to being 'different', a word which consistently came up on all subjects, had ended up on the news front with awarding the contract to Crown Communications in a consortium with the London Radio station LBC and IRN (Independent Radio News) which won against ten other competitors, including names like Eddy Shah. Crown's previous TV experience, however, extended primarily to making corporate videos, and it had merely said 'different news' would consist of things like 'the reporter getting more involved with the story'.

Gau thought otherwise. As a former boss of BBC Current Affairs he was deeply sceptical of the 'different' concept especially on news. In any case news was already well and expensively covered by both the BBC and ITN. The addition of Sky News provided sufficient coverage for even the most addicted junkie. BSB was supposed to be about adding choice and in this field Gau thought there was nothing to add. He told ASG at once that a news channel was out of the question, while the IBA wrung their hands. But, as Gau pointed out, the original franchise requirement of news taking up half a channel's output had been stipulated eighteen months before Murdoch entered the field. Eventually the IBA gave way and Gau was left with the messy task of reducing Crown's annual contract from nearly £12 million to £4 million, scrapping the plan for four rolling two-hour news shows in favour of two-minute summaries. For some of the Crown people, after months of dithering and indecision by BSB, it was a relief to be have anything concrete at all.

Gau found himself facing similar problems on the other channels. The five-hour daily entertainment output on Galaxy had been contracted wholesale to the independent Noel Gay Television at a cost of £12 million a year, while he would have preferred to have spread the commissions around. He thought it mad to give this sort of power over scheduling to an outside company. Deciding when programmes should be screened was a different art to making them, and one Gau was extremely skilled at. He set about clawing back some measure of control, making it clear to the others that directors of programmes could not give away that kind of autonomy without making a nonsense of the rest of the output.

The story with the sports programming was much the same, although in this case Gau did not feel so strongly about using one company. What did bother him was the extraordinary deal which Mark McCormack, the sports promotions mogul, had managed to negotiate for his subsidiary Trans World International. Not for nothing had McCormack written a book about what was not taught at Harvard Business School. BSB had agreed to pay his company £25 million a year, including financing a specially equipped building, and given all manner of guarantees and hefty management fees, all for a five-year period.

When news of this deal leaked out there was much hilarity over at Sky that anyone could make such a crazy commitment to such long-term arrangements. Sky's deals were the other way round – short and sharp. Then, if they didn't work, they were thrown out. Of course satellite television was risky, but if a company didn't want to take the risk Sky would just find someone else who did. It seemed to the Sky negotiators that BSB took a different view which sounded like: 'Tell us what you need and of course you can have it. Copper bottom guarantees – no problem. Anything extra you'd like?'

Gau then moved on to the next headache, the Lifestyle women's programming. This had also been given out in a single block and, as far as he was concerned, to quite the wrong company. The invitation to tender had produced a shortlist of eight competing consortia packed with familiar names. Anna Ford and Gloria Hunniford had appeared on two tenders each and the proposal from a consortium led by the former Nationwide reporter Bernard Falk read like a re-run of that show with John Stapleton, Frank Bough, Sue Cook and Falk himself all featuring on the presenters' list. Other proposals had scoured the land to find suitable female executives, coming up with the former Wogan producer Frances Whitaker, who led the bid by Hawkshead, Andrea Wonfor, with a good reputation at Zenith, and Lis Howell, who was Head of News and Current Affairs at Border Television. (Howell was later to be reincarnated as the respectable non-Australian face of Sky News when she joined as managing editor). Other reputable

Lifestyle contenders included Phil Redmond's Mersey Television and Hilary Lawson's TVF.

On 10 August, 1988 the BSB executives had assembled for two days at the Berkeley Suite of the Mayfair Hotel to conduct the final interviews. But the whole process of briefing, shortlisting, research and deliberation had all essentially been a front. One proposal, from a consortium of Yorkshire Television and the *Daily Mail*, had been brought together by the producer Mike Hollingsworth, the boyfriend of Anne Diamond, and as the current doyenne of sofa television at TV-am she herself had been brought into the line-up. Before the interviews BSB, in its normal style, had commissioned research which had come up with findings such as the astrologer Russell Grant 'is extremely popular with the C2s', presenter Gloria Hunniford is seen as 'a bit old and mumsy', while 'Anne Diamond is perceived as over-exposed and not a popular presenter'. But despite this, for ASG there was still no real choice. This consortium offered the opportunity of having a national newspaper on BSB's side, and that was too good an opportunity to miss.

At the Mayfair the interviews proceeded in a brisk fashion on the first morning. At 2 pm the Yorkshire/*Mail* group, led by the *Mail*'s editor, Sir David English, entered the room exhibiting an air of supreme confidence. Hollingsworth, Anne Diamond and the rest of the team had prepared extremely carefully, hiring the Berkeley Suite the day before for a dummy run and experimenting by moving the table and chairs about to achieve the best line of sight. Afterwards they had sat up until 3 am reworking their script and that morning hired the room immediately above for yet more rehearsals. Over the lunchtime break they had then got the hotel staff to rearrange the furniture in the actual suite precisely as they wanted it.

At the interview Sir David held up a picture of Murdoch and looked at the row of BSB executives. 'You have heard nothing yet but the rattle of small guns,' he told them. 'Mark my words, he will obliterate you and that's why you need us.' ASG already needed no further persuasion. The next day he wrote to Sir David awarding him the contract, which offered a cool £8.5 million plus management fee for three hours a day of women's programming. Part of the deal was that the *Mail* would help promote the face of BSB towards the public. The other defeated independents were furious at what they felt was a stitch-up, but BSB held firm.

Inside the BSB hierarchy, however, there was not universal delight at the choice of the consortium, which was eventually called New Era Television or NETV for short. Hollingsworth, and to a lesser extent Diamond, were well-known in the business as prickly characters who frequently launched legal actions.

At BSB there was a similar pattern of acrimony, this time over Diamond's proposed salary and signing-on fee. Hollingsworth, who was supposed to be in charge of contracts, awkwardly had to leave the room whenever the subject was discussed, and when the final offer came Diamond was displeased. She had some justification as the sum was rather less than BSB would later offer to stars such as Selina Scott and Robin Day. Then Hollingsworth fell out with the *Mail* and Diamond was displeased by a feature in the paper on their wedding in Australia. Eventually they both left the consortium. With their departure things became a little smoother, but New Era was never to be a happy outfit.

Gau, examining the problem after the contract had been awarded, was not concerned with these petty personality problems. He just thought that BSB had made a substantial editorial mistake. It was all very well craving promotion in the press, but surely that kind of support could have been arranged by some other means? Not only was New Era the wrong choice, but it was the product of the same misconceived notion of giving out so much programming as a slab. Once again he was left to pick up the pieces and make the best of what he had been handed. If only less had been done before his arrival his task would have been so much easier, he thought grimly – except for the Movie Channel.

Gau could hardly believe the tales of titanic Hollywood battles with Murdoch for the various film rights. Movies were the cornerstone of the operation and it seemed to him crazy BSB had not got these deals under its belt long before Sky loomed into sight. He had heard all the justification about BSB constantly seeking better prices and further shrinking of the 'video window', but he was sure if he'd been in place by then there would have been a lot less messing around and much more decisive action. It reminded him of the saying that 'the best is the enemy of the good'. BSB always seemed to be seeking after the best instead of settling for the good. The result in this case had been getting the worst with such hugely expensive films.

It was only when he really started studying Sky that Gau's general gloom lifted. Just as he had predicted, it was offering a pretty thin diet of cheap acquired material, mostly culled from abroad. The Sky entertainment channel looked much like the original Sky Europe cable output, except the re-runs of American soaps were now just dated instead of positively ancient; Eurosport was a bland and pretty uninspired offering for a British audience; Sky News was, he had to admit, pretty impressive. But even there if you looked closely there were many hours of foreign-acquired programmes, with endless current affairs shows from Australia and the United States.

All this only confirmed Gau's instinct that the way forward for BSB was to be more British. He saw his job as crafting a schedule with a distinctive and predominantly home-grown emphasis, worthy of a station calling itself the Third Force in British Broadcasting. Already described by one former colleague as 'the incarnation of John Bull in television', he was the ideal person to promote such a strategy and his first port of call had been to Auntie herself to ask her to open her treasure chest. Within days of his arrival he started negotiations to gain access to the BBC's spectacular archives of familiar comedy and drama shows – the kind of material which had become part of the national TV heritage. A handful of these key offerings, like Dr Who, Dad's Army, Steptoe and Son, Are You Being Served? and Porridge, would be an enormous boost for BSB and the vision of the 'Best of British'.

Gau knew persuading the Corporation to part with this material would be tricky. But he had contacts right to the top of the tree, starting with his friend Paul Fox, who was Managing Director of BBC Television. The biggest potential problem was not however with the BBC itself, but the minefield of the actors' union, Equity. Hitherto this had not allowed any repeats until each actor in an old programme had given his or her individual consent, and then negotiated a suitable fee. But Gau was confident that ultimately it would see reason and find a way of negotiating collectively on behalf of its members. This would probably mean a quid pro quo of originating new British drama to provide work for union members, but BSB could live with that. It would be able to give guarantees of investment in original production which Sky never would, even though it was hankering after similar material. So far Sky had obtained a few ITV archive programmes, but these had only been in areas like natural history which by their very nature did not feature paid-up Equity members.

Gau was not being esoteric but thinking commercially as he started crafting the BBC1 image for BSB. Sky might single-mindedly hunt down the C2s as the quarry more likely to splurge on a dish, but he was pursuing a longer-term goal. Although the key satellite 'dish drivers' were films and big sporting events, there was more to it than that. Further down the line the advertisers were not just after quantity, but quality of audience, just as they were in terrestrial television. Advertisers might have a primary interest in ratings, but they were also keen to tap high-spending AB viewers even though this meant lower numbers overall. A prime example was Thames Television's City Programme, a financial magazine transmitted at 10.30 pm on a Thursday with a total audience figure less than a third of the regular rating for a prime-time soap like Coronation Street or Thames' own gritty cop show The Bill. The advertisers loved it as they knew that in the break they were talking to rooms full of Yuppies, or at least small investors with money to spare. That was an infinitely more interesting prospect than wasting money on the impoverished or unemployed.

After talking to the ad sales people Gau was even clearer than ever that he must deliver the popular BBC1 audience who are ultimately more attractive to advertisers. One of the reasons for the *Mail* winning its contract had been that its readers were just the type of people BSB was after. The ITV-type audience, traditionally more C2-ish, was much more Sky's territory. It all fitted together with Peter Bell's marketing plans, the tasteful squarial business, and the talk about 'discrete' and 'discerning' viewers

Gau had in mind an assortment of goodies to tempt them

beyond his promise of more things British. He envisaged unex-purgated opera and arts programming over the weekends. Then there was the association already set up with Britain's most prominent film maker, David Puttnam, which gave BSB exclusive rights to his work ahead of other television stations. There was even a worthy bursary at the National Film School sponsored by BSB to bring on new home-grown talent.

Most of Gau's planning was geared towards a five-channel package on the presumption that BSB would be able to expand from its present three. The closing date for applications to run the extra two official channels was in March and he had produced a reasoned case why BSB should succeed against the other six outside bidders. With five channels BSB's programming as he had structured it made much more sense. In addition to the one-subject film channel, the all-important sports programming was to move off the NOW channel to one of its own. Galaxy was to be entirely entertainment, catering for children during the day and offering drama, soaps and general entertainment in the evening. Here, alongside the products purchased from the BBC, BSB would commission its own soaps and dramas, which might one day become national institutions themselves. The fourth channel would be an 18-hour daily offering of rock and pop music, eventually to be called the Power Station. That would compete head to head with MTV, which was thrilling youngsters on Astra. Finally there was the NOW channel, which Gau was not so sure what to do with. It would have to inherit the Lifestyle women's programming now moving back from Galaxy, but he needed to get more to grips with this material and devise a schedule based on information programmes with themes like travel, gardening and medicine.

Although NOW and the New Era brief still needed sorting out, the rest, providing he pulled off the deal for the BBC archives, was slowly taking shape and a coherent philosophy was emerging. As Gau sorted through the material he was confident the IBA would see the logic of his scheme and the five channels would go ahead as planned. The announcement of who would get the two extra channels was expected in June. But while he was waiting for confirmation and putting the finishing touches to his plans, Gau slowly became aware that there had been an awful miscalculation. The microchip needed to get his programmes into peoples' homes – the navigation system of the Good Ship BSB – did not yet exist.

Gau was horrified. When he had taken the job no one had ever mentioned this to him, and he had never even thought to ask. Of course he knew there was a slight risk with the rocket launch, which couldn't be relied on 100%. But beyond that he had assumed – naively, as it now turned out – that the rest of the technology had been locking into place behind the scenes. Now it wasn't never mind the quality, or even the width. The more pertinent question was when, or even whether, anything – good, bad or merely indifferent – would actually reach his target viewers.

CHAPTER EIGHT

The Chips are Down

ASG and Graham Grist never really got on from the day the new chief executive started on Black Monday. ASG may have been a team player, but at BSB he wanted a team he'd had a hand in picking himself. As Grist was employee 001 ASG had obviously not picked him, which he could live with – providing he was dealing with a person who thought and acted like him. But Grist came from an entirely different business culture, with a different way of doing things, and his whole attitude was different from ASG's more laid-back style. Although ASG found Grist very clever and extremely hard-working, at the same time he thought that was not necessarily a good thing. He lived for BSB, seven days a week, and seemed to ASG to be obsessed with it. There were, after all, other things in life.

But Grist's real problem, as ASG saw it, was tending to always see the worst side of everybody. He was like the girl with the curl in the middle of her forehead – when he was good, he was very, very good, but when he was bad . . . Taking him aside, ASG had a long talk with him about his management style, backing up his homily by booking him to go on a high-powered leadership course run by consultants. ASG was a great believer in consultants. Grist in turn, as he watched ASG at work, had his own thoughts about the loose way he seemed to operate. The other execs had soon cottoned on that sooner or later the two men would clash.

(In typical BSB style Grist never got to the course at the time, but went on it later and was very proud of leading the team that was first in the competition to build a bridge.)

David Eglise, Grist's deputy who met John Collins at the Ariel about the squarial, was also amazed by the way his boss worked. He was a man without an off switch. Like ASG, he found Grist to be utterly single-minded in the way he lived for BSB, disregarding office hours in his passionate enthusiasm for the company and the job it had to do. At work Grist was a whirlwind of activity, seldom at his desk, always on the move, carrying three phones. Eglise found having a meeting with him incredible. The phones would be ringing all the time and he was astonished not just by how much work Grist got through, but by his unbelievable power of recall and attention to detail. One of the things that first surprised him when he joined BSB was how few people there were to do so much. He soon found out what that meant in practice when his own in tray zoomed from empty to eight foot thick.

Grist, with his frenetic energy, powered through these mountains of work. But as he watched him doing so, Eglise shared ASG's view that his management style was over-aggressive. Eglise was finding himself in a position he likened to being Grist's minder, continuously running round trying to placate people and keep them happy. Physically, however, the roles were reversed, and people in the office would smile at the spectacle of the large and bulky Grist zooming about with the much smaller Eglise trotting in his wake.

Grist's abrasive style caused the most severe ruction with the regulatory authority of the IBA. Chris Irwin, the man who had helped kick off the original application for the franchise, had always seen the IBA engineers as a low-cost consultancy resource. But Grist's attitude was that BSB was a commercial project and therefore could not possibly rely on other people like them. He told Eglise the IBA people might have expertise in some areas but business wasn't one of them, and matters then worsened when Grist and one of the IBA people seriously fell out. Before Irwin left, at Christmas 1987, he took on himself the last job of mediating between the two sides, which he saw rather than working together had got into a terrible fight. The IBA had been keen to take over and engineer the uplink to the satellite for what Irwin thought the 'peanuts money' of around £100,000. But Grist had firmly rejected the approach and in doing so, in Irwin's opinion, thrown away millions of pounds worth of expertise. Relationships had gone so sour between them that Irwin had to pour time and energy into working out some sort of mechanism by which they could continue to consult each other. As he did so he thought how absurd it was. There he was, supposedly working for the same company, but ending up playing shuttle diplomacy just like Henry Kissinger. His diplomatic work done, Irwin thankfully departed, eventually returning to safe ground on the relatively uncomplicated shores of the BBC.

After ASG had taken over the reins of the new company, Grist's multifarious activities had gradually been reduced so that by the beginning of 1989, with the Sky launch only a few weeks off, he was left with just the biggest unknown facing the new venture – the innovative and complex MAC technology. ASG didn't know anything about the technology, and as primarily an advertising and marketing man, didn't want to. Grist, although he had worked with computers in the past, was no technological expert either, and ASG realised he was leaving him with the stuff he didn't really want to handle. But, as ASG told him, Grist just had to do it because he had set up all the contracts before the CE arrived. 'I'm trying to get your round peg into a round hole,' ASG informed him.

The technological challenge facing BSB had been made even more daunting by the IBA regulators grinding their own axe. Sorting out the technology would have been easier if the company had been allowed to use D2-MAC, the lowest grade of the MAC variants which had already been developed in Europe. In France the government had even given financial help to get it off the ground. In the private enterprise world of Britain it was taken for granted there would be no state aid. But a complication arose because the IBA's engineers favoured not the French-style D2-MAC but the technically superior D-MAC, and it was this MAC variant which had been foisted on BSB as a condition of the franchise. The industry had lobbied to change the specification to D2-MAC, with much emphasis on how this fitted with 1992-type thoughts of moving towards a common European standard. But the IBA had remained aloof from the uproar and now BSB was lumbered with the task of developing this untested technology.

The key component for the IBA-ordered D-MAC system was the microchip which would decipher the signal sent from the satellite. It was this that made D-MAC different from all current television systems and why it was seen as the way forward for the future. In the PAL system the black and white picture, known technically as the luminance, and the colouring information, the chrominance, were transmitted simultaneously. This caused various forms of distortion – in particular patterning and cross-colouring on the screen when fine black and white pictures foiled the receiver into thinking colour information was present. But in the MAC system the two constituents were transmitted separately and then recombined by the chip in the receiver box. This got rid of the spurious effects and ghosting to give a much enhanced picture.

How much difference this would make to the average viewer, when many people couldn't even be bothered to adjust their aerials correctly, was not so obvious. But that part of the equation did not concern the engineers. They were just immensely excited by their visions of the technological future and already pointing to other innovatory aspects of D-MAC. It had, for example, scope for carrying several stereo sound channels, so multilingual transmissions would be possible. From the programme-makers' point of view this was interesting, but raised obvious problems with lipsync, which ruled it out. Again, that end of things was not the engineers' concern. But whichever way you looked at it, engineers and non-engineers alike agreed the chip technology was extraordinarily complex and right at what was known as 'the leading edge'. And it was not just the D-MAC chip BSB had to develop and have mass-manufactured. There was the receiver box which would go on top of people's sets to hold it, the encryption chip to unscramble the pictures for the film channel, and the aerials, whether round or square.

Grist, getting the technology side of the company on the road when he started work in March 1987, had two companies to choose from to make the chip. One was the Dutch company of Philips, which fitted the Euro-dream and already had the track record of having developed D2-MAC. The other was the

American giant of ITT, which had also worked on it. After intensive lobbying from Philips, BSB decided the Europeans were going to be slower – the French system had been eight months late – and more expensive. The exclusive contract therefore went to ITT and was signed a month before Eglise joined as Grist's deputy. When he was asked to look at it and give an opinion, his immediate thought was that it was too expensive – a development contract worth $2 million, with the further order for 4 million chips priced in sterling at £25 each.

The decision to go with ITT alone had been the result of the Grist strategy, with which ASG concurred when he took over as Chief Executive. BSB could choose between two different ways to go for its various contracts – either putting them out to competitive tender amongst dozens of companies, or the way Grist and ASG decided on of staying with only one or a few. Grist worked by enticement, and Eglise watched his boss with awe as he cleverly negotiated with manufacturers, helping on occasions by chipping in with the bullshit speech: BSB was going to spend £100 million not just on promoting itself – it would promote the whole concept of satellite TV. In the UK people had an insatiable appetite for TV . . .

The pitch was that BSB had no money to put up front. What it was offering was an opportunity. The manufacturer would have to take the risk, but in return would be made an exclusive supplier for the next three years, or at the very least be given a guaranteed manufacturing capacity. Volume sales could therefore be counted on, and the price per unit could come right down from the beginning. This would mean BSB avoided the previous problem of ordinary TV and video which had been very expensive until sales picked up. ASG knew the strategy did not really fit with free market principles, but he still thought it necessary. By technological standards BSB was in a hurry, and he found manufacturers leery when the company tried the other route and asked a number of them for competing quotes. There were endless arguments about price depending on volume, and who would make what, while the bureaucrats did not help by seeing it only as an arcane conversation as to which country would have its own interests best served.

As the squabbling continued, eventually ASG put his foot

down. The endless conversations and meetings couldn't go on for ever. If things were not simplified they would just go on and on talking. So the brutal decision was taken to go exclusively to General Instruments in America for the second most important part of the technology, the encryption system to scramble the film channel and fulfil the business plan by making viewers subscribe their £9.99 a month. The European manufacturers were furious and ASG found it all got very hairy, with lots of people shouting at them. But GI had been at that sort of thing for a long time, and most importantly ASG found it a company willing to talk turkey, whereas most of the Europeans were not.

As other people joined there were mixed feelings about the chip contract. Ellis Griffiths had been headhunted from his job as chief engineer at Channel 4 to be director of operations and had brought his team with him. As he had left, Channel 4's programme director, Liz Forgan, had told him: 'BSB is a bigger and better train set to play with', but Griffiths had arrived to be bitterly disappointed. The job was not the one he had been expecting, and he was not to be involved in the chip and encryption discussions.

Griffiths believed the contract should have gone to competitive tender between Philips and ITT, as that way the best man would have won. As it was, now ITT had been awarded the contract Philips had reduced its level of activity. Whereas if BSB had said it would have a competition, with the contract going to the first company to have a working chip at a set price, both of them would now be beavering away. Griffiths thought being with only one manufacturer was like being on a one-way street when you didn't have a map. You just had to hope you came out at the right place at the right time. Yet equally he didn't think it sensible to expect everything to come good on a large-scale project like this, which was on a very tight schedule as well as being price-sensitive.

Grist however disagreed, especially when he gave the receiver box manufacturers the choice and found they all wanted to work with ITT rather than Philips.

The ITT contract was to develop two chips. The first, the 2280, was a further development of the one already produced for D2-MAC to bring it up to the higher D-MAC standard which the IBA required. By the end of 1988 progress on that was good. The other, the 2285, dealt with scrambling the picture, was more specific to BSB, and much more complicated. ASG had been out to ITT's factory at Freiburg in Germany and got some inkling of how far BSB was at the leading edge when he saw the circuitry. It was so intense at first it looked like a block of solid colour. When he went closer and examined the wall chart he saw a plan of 300,000 circuits, all of which were to be produced on a chip the size of your thumbnail. Then it had to be refined to a prototype for mass production. ASG gained a further insight from meeting the development engineer, Manfred Junke, and discovering he was about 28 years old, 6' 6" tall with a beard, and was wearing sneakers. Seeing how far Junke was from being a man in a suit, ASG realised with some awe that making the chip was an essentially creative act involving expertise which was way beyond all of them. It wasn't the normal sort of thing, where if anything went wrong you could solve the problem by doubling the workforce. BSB was very much in Manfred's hands.

ITT's way of working, of which it was very proud, was to take the design off the computer to 'a first silicon' and then start making a series of fast modifications in cycles of six weeks which were known as 'iterations'. (ASG was to say later that it was a word which was written across his back.) The iterations were a linear process of development and meant once the chip was working to a certain level you consolidated and then moved on to the next stage. Development of the 2285 scrambler chip had seemed to be going all right until towards the end of 1988, but then progress had stopped and it had staggered through its iterations until February, eating up the allowance built into the project for slippage.

By this time alarm had developed at the executive board meetings as a finished prototype obstinately failed to appear and instead Grist and Eglise kept reporting the chip to be a certain 'percentage functional'. At a meeting at the Mayfair Hotel the execs all adjourned for lunch along with John Korda, a key consultant who was the space segment manager brought in from Telesat, the satellite launching company in Canada. Korda turned to Ellis Griffiths and asked him if he had heard about the 'functionality' thing during the war, as it very much reminded him of the meeting. He then told Griffiths the story.

'During the war Hitler called in his top scientists and told them: "I've got a problem. The country is desperately short of butter because all the fields are being dug up by war machines. But we've got lots of horses and they generate lots of horse shit. So I want you to go away and develop a method of making butter out of horse shit. Come back in three months."

'At the appointed time the scientists returned and the leading one stood up and said: "We're 50% functional." "What do you mean, 50% functional?" Hitler asked. "Well," the scientist replied, "it spreads easily".'

During lunch the joke circulated to nearly everybody except ASG, Grist and Eglise, and in the afternoon when the meeting resumed, with Eglise this time reporting the chip to be '85 percent functional', there was much ill-suppressed chortling.

But really, as everybody knew, it was no laughing matter. No matter how percentage functional the chip was, if it didn't work, it didn't work. There had already been one moment which had given the non-technical execs some inkling of the depths they were swimming in. Ellis Griffiths had sat in the executive board meetings very depressed at hearing promises he thought there was no prospect of fulfilling. But when he challenged them he was told to shut up, mind his own business, or that he didn't understand. At a meeting trying to make a judgement about when the chip was likely to appear, there was talk of two weeks late, four weeks, six months . . . Suddenly Griffiths asked: 'What happens if it never happens?' Then he told them: 'You could end up with a project that never comes to fruition.'

As the execs, many of whom had only a dim grasp of the technological side, struggled to find out more, Eglise remarked: 'Let me be clear with you, so you understand that I understand the problem. There was a chip set I was involved with at MARS which was four years late. So I do understand the problem. But this is not the case with this one.' 'Hang on a minute . . .' Peter Bell started in worried fashion, but Grist immediately interrupted. He assured them Eglise had not meant there were problems like that with their chip. He just meant he understood the kind of difficulties which could be involved.

But the disturbing lack of clear information on the chip denoted only one of the many technical problems building up behind the scenes. Eglise, seeing the fuller picture, felt the executive board should be told about them, but Grist told him not to alarm the others. Eglise was terribly torn. At the same time he was seeing Grist put over the message that everything was going reasonably well, and that was not exactly right. Grist, he knew, was holding things back. At the executive board meetings the others would be saying things like: 'Graham, we've heard from John Korda that everything is terrible and that he doesn't know what's going on. The satellite is OK but I don't think they know what's going on with the aerial. What's the problem?' Grist would reply: 'Everything's perfectly all right – nothing's wrong. It's all going smoothly.' More probing would lead to more general oil pouring: there were difficulties, but they would be overcome; it was moving in the right direction; don't worry, things are on track . . .

ASG would take note, but like everybody else did nothing to take the bull by the horns. Some of the other execs, noticing this, thought he should be less courteous and become more authoritative to force Grist and Eglise to open up. But it was obvious he was keeping the baffling technological side of the company at arm's length. He had delegated it to Grist, and he in turn had delegated much of it to Eglise. And they had to recognise that, like all of them who were non-technical, ASG was in a difficult position. When they all knew so little in the field, what could they say?

It was here that the clash of business cultures between ASG and Grist reached crisis point. ASG always emphasised that he liked to run an open ship, on which information was to be jointly shared and handed around, while Grist believed this philosophy was completely overdone. His IBM training had taught him the opposite approach that it should only be handed out on a 'need to know' basis. His further experience in banking, finance, and the toughly competitive world of international construction had reinforced his ideas on the value of information. It needed to be controlled tightly. At Balfour Beatty meetings it wasn't at all unusual for numbered copies of bids and inside figures to be handed out and then withdrawn at the end, so nobody could take them outside the room. ASG, on the other hand, was much more relaxed. He was the communicator par excellence and some people in the company even felt he had a compulsive need to do it. He had once alarmed Grist with his open attitude by remarking: 'I can't remember what I should be saying and what's secret.' Sir Trevor Holdsworth too had problems in this area, and had once inadvertently divulged some information, which Grist thought ought to be kept secret, to an interviewer from a trade magazine, which had then printed it.

And at BSB another factor had come into the mix which only confirmed Grist in his own approach. The company had a high-level leak. Time and again stories popped up in the press disclosing what had been discussed in confidential meetings. Grist had now formed the view that some people at BSB thought it more important to get a story in the papers to improve their personal kudos with the journalist concerned than to do the best deal for the company or surprise contract competitors by keeping things quiet. He had therefore taken a policy decision. The project must override everything and 'need to know' was paramount.

Ellis Griffiths, with a better grasp of the technical intricacies than the other execs, had worked out by Christmas 1988 that the chip was obviously very late. But he had no hard information to go on. Whenever he tried to discuss it he just got the brush-off, with Grist following 'need to know' by telling him there were things attached to it he didn't want to discuss, and therefore he didn't want to talk to him. Meanwhile, as Griffiths was becoming aware, the chip delays were starting to have a knock-on effect which was disrupting other developments.

Tension in the company really started to rise in February, around the time of the Sky launch, when Grist and Eglise reported more percentage figures to the executive board. This time it wasn't chip functionality but the odds on when equipment would be manufactured and in the shops. There was a 50% to 60% chance for August, 75% for October, and 99% for Christmas. The launch was scheduled for September and right at that moment, staring them in the face, was the irredeemable damage done to Sky by its failure to get stocks in.

Chris Dickens, who had joined the company as sales director to sell advertising on the station, was immediately worried. Dickens had been in New York pursuing his career as a media director for TV for the agency Young and Rubicam when the BSB approach had come through one of ASG's friends. Dickens had known ASG previously when he moved to Esher in Surrey and joined the local Esher Expendibles rugby team as a winger just as ASG was finishing his playing days. He had also known he was not the first choice for the post. There had been an embarrassing moment when the man he knew was number one walked into the Inn on the Park just as he and ASG were having a confidential chat.

But Dickens had still got very excited about BSB and the potential of what it could be by the end of the 90s. He saw it as a mega-company, with a very high profile and great opportunities for success – the biggest thing ever likely to happen in broadcasting in the UK and about to expand dramatically what Joe Public did in his leisuretime. Seduced by the prospect, Dickens had first shaken on the deal in London. Back in New York he had then driven out to the Brit Lounge at Kennedy Airport to meet Peter Bell, who had come across on the Concorde morning flight to firm things up.

Now, as he sat listening to Grist's percentage news, he insisted BSB must be 100% sure of having equipment piled high on launch day. A 75% probability was simply not enough. He thought anyhow that announcing a September launch date, which had been done immediately after Murdoch announced Sky, was a mistake. It was just making the company a hostage to fortune. But Dickens' voice was drowned out. There was no question of moving the date and instead he was told there was anyhow a slight fallback – the launch could slip back until early November before it finally became too late for the Christmas market.

Dickens was unhappy about this, but had already decided the lack of firm direction on the shareholders' main Board was being echoed on the executive board now making these reassuring noises. More and more the executive board was becoming the main power base in the company, but with 18 members was so large and unwieldy no real decisions were being made. Dickens had suggested to ASG that he reduce it to a group of five, but nothing had happened. Instead the regular

18-person meetings usually consisted of going round the table, with everybody giving a report and telling everybody else what was going on, whilst ASG made utterances. Other members of the board also recognised another creeping aspect. More and more, internal politics was becoming the main business of the day. Some individuals' primary concerns seemed to be working on constructing their own empires, which they expressed by huge attention to who sat where, and who had responsibility for what on paper, rather than what they were actually going to do about it.

Edward Bickham, who had by now been put in charge of the press office, was exhausted. He had gone on holiday to Mexico, so Chris McLaughlin, as his number two, went to attend the executive board meetings in his absence – only to be asked to leave. Obviously, McLaughlin thought, there were things going on they didn't want him to know about, and he soon worked out from furtive conversations and swapping of notes in the corridors that it was beginning to look obvious BSB was not going to make the autumn launch. A distinct sense of unease was permeating the senior execs as the D-MAC system started to be perceived differently. No longer was it necessarily the technological wondercard. Worried thoughts were turning to great previous brown goods disasters of the 70s and early 80s, such as eight-track stereo and the videodisc. They had seemed fantastic on the drawing board and been raved about by the technical people, but had been overtaken by events in the marketplace and failed miserably. Most pertinent for BSB was the showdown that had taken place between the two videotape systems, VHS and Betamax. VHS had been acknowledged to be inferior in quality, like the PAL Murdoch was using for Sky, but it had still won by being the cheapest and getting in first by persuading the cheapo video rental shops to adopt it as their standard.

John Gau had a different way of looking at it. An awful lot of energy was being poured into state of the art technology, which was perfectly proper in a monopoly but totally unnecessary if you were fighting a tough battle with an aggressive competitor. D-MAC, he thought, was becoming the real killer. It was a typically British thing imposed by the IBA, just as it had insisted on TV studios being built in Nottingham for ITV after local lobbying. The technology was beginning to haunt them. They had often been told only D-MAC could be encrypted to scramble channels, yet Murdoch had since encrypted PAL. The whole thing was becoming a shambles, with each of them playing by different rules. D-MAC was becoming BSB's Nottingham – an uncommercial cross it had to bear.

Until the worm of doubt started gnawing at the executive board things had not looked too bad. BSB had always known that with his furious philosophy Murdoch was bound to be first which was damaging but so far not considered terminal, especially now they had seen Sky's dishless start. In many ways Murdoch's seven-month lead was something BSB was happy to hand to him. Single-handedly Sky faced the daunting task of blazing a trail into the boneheaded consciousness of the C2s throughout the summer, when they had plenty of other things to do. And there was a parallel feeling that Murdoch was having problems like faulty dishes which either melted in the sunshine, or let rain into their works, and the way Sky was being slung together, somehow it was not for real. A saying had developed on the board: 'Our bullfrog's bigger than his bullfrog today', referring to how much noise each was making at the time.

In addition there was a very positive way to look at the situation. The Dirty Digger was ploughing the satellite furrow and preparing the ground. BSB would then sow the quality seed in the autumn and reap the harvest in the big push before Christmas, which was when both sides knew the real sales would be made. The figures showed 75% of all electrical purchases were made in the last three months of the year. As Peter Bell put it, Murdoch would make the market 'go faster'. And in September, the theory ran, when the GBP actually saw the superior D-MAC pictures which boosted BSB's quality edge, along with its higher quality programmes, Sky's rough PAL pictures and low-grade Americana would be blasted off their screens.

But there was another very good reason for having to think positively like this. If BSB did fail to launch in autumn 1989, Murdoch would have a Christmas to himself. The harvest would then be his.

It was precisely this fear which had persuaded BSB to sign the contract with Hughes Aircraft to start work on the satellite before the contract for the franchise had been formally signed, risking $5 million in penalty clauses. Now, as the grapevine started humming and the number of closed-door meetings increased, word started going round that it was not just the chip that was in trouble. The much-vaunted squarial, round which the company was now branded, was obviously progressing very slowly as well. The breezy promise of a prototype by Christmas had yet to be fulfilled even though it was now months later.

When Grist reported in April that the 2280 D-MAC chip was alright but there were problems with the 2285 film encryption chip, with ominous mention of contingency plans, even ASG began to feel delay was inevitable. He did not want to believe it, and with something as complex as this it took time to go from severe doubt to certainty. But events were pressing on them and BSB had to get to grips with when the hardware would come on the market. By now ASG's relationship with Grist had become very terse. Like everybody else he kept asking questions but getting nowhere. Various execs, their suspicions growing, tried to pump Grist's sidekick Eglise but he stuck loyally by his boss, giving out what he afterwards described as 'an Iraqi version of the truth' – not actually telling lies, but not actually being as honest as he should have been.

Finally, as press speculation started to increase and the muttering in the corridors grew louder, ASG decided they had to get to the bottom of the whole thing. It was difficult, because if you gave a bloke a senior job you must allow him to do it, but there came a point when the evidence against them was overwhelming and you had to intervene. As it happened, Grist was also moving to assess the whole situation through Andy Coleman, a small, affable, hard-working man who had spent 17 years on the computing side of the Midland Bank. Coleman had come to BSB as information technology director and Grist was moving him across to become project manager. ASG now asked him to 'give his opinion on what the form was'. Coleman already knew how each person had been working separately, with Grist holding the strings. His attitude was that you had so much to do you just got on with your bit and trusted your colleagues to get on with theirs. But as early as March he had still gleaned enough to suggest to Grist that the launch be delayed.

In an effort to sort things out Grist and Coleman went first to the ITT factory in Germany, where Coleman set about carving his way through the management ranks to get into the actual room where the chip development was going on and find out the true situation from the engineers on the ground. Meanwhile Grist flew on to America to assess progress at General Instruments. He had just arrived when there was a call from Coleman. He had been over everything time and time again and finally got the ITT engineers to admit it: there was no chance of the chip's being ready for a launch that year. After demanding whether he was absolutely sure, Grist then took a deep breath and rang ASG at home to give him the news. ASG took it very badly. He blew up and shouted at Grist they had nothing to put in its place. What were they going to do instead? Grist said he didn't know.

The shareholders and the boards of their individual companies were deeply shocked when they learned of the situation. The Board had firmly taken the same view as Chris Dickens that the launch could only take place with the technology in the shops. Now it was obvious that could not happen the project was at its lowest ebb. Things could no longer be hedged and the autumn launch would now definitely have to be delayed. There wasn't even an alternative date they could substitute. BSB, they began to realise, was in a totally new ball game and now nobody knew when it would make it. How many more six-week iterations would the chip have to go through? Or – perish the thought – as Ellis Griffiths had ominously warned was possible, might it never come right at all?

The day before the final decision to delay, Chris McLaughlin was told there was a likelihood the company would have to put out a statement. He asked if they wanted a note on how to handle the announcement. ASG said yes, but the others said no. In fact, they didn't want to tell anyone anything at the moment. They would prepare something and then announce it in a few days. McLaughlin was incredulous. Didn't they realise that the story would inevitably break one way or another? They had to have their excuses ready now. If nothing was in place it would be a disaster. His advice was ignored.

Ray Snoddy, the media hound who was always snapping at BSB's heels, struck immediately with a scoop revealing all on the front page of the *Financial Times*. The story was devastatingly accurate and gave full chapter and verse on the disarray. BSB, as McLaughlin had predicted, was caught on the hop. But when he rushed into the office to deal with the fall-out he found that rather than tackling the problem, everybody seemed more interested in trying to identify the source of the leak.

Grist, his 'need to know' attitude fully vindicated by the way the information had been instantly leaked, had washed his hands of the whole thing and retreated into his office. McLaughlin instead sought out ASG, who had become very overweight over the past few weeks. Now he appeared punch drunk with worry and stress – so much so that McLaughlin thought he resembled someone who had been shouted at and abused in an EST session for an entire weekend and still hadn't come out the other side of it. McLaughlin had already got some people over from the Charles Barker PR outfit to help with the expected deluge of phone calls and now he told ASG he must make a statement.

The team waited for it all morning, but by lunchtime had been told nothing. McLaughlin felt the situation was getting out of control. Then, at 2.30 pm, he was told to bring the waiting press in. ASG had agreed to talk. He immediately rushed in to advise him to stick to a prepared statement. The hacks were pissed off at missing the story, he warned. Although BSB had a long history of leaks they would still think Snoddy had been given the tip-off as a special favour, with the added conspiracy theory that it was all because the *Financial Times* was owned by the BSB shareholder, Pearson.

Three reporters had turned up for an interview – Will Stewart of the *Express*, which had missed out on a chance to scoop its deadly rival the *Daily Mail*, and the media correspondents of the Big Papers which were more supportive of BSB, Maggie Brown of the *Independent* and Georgina Henry of the *Guardian*. As they were ushered in McLaughlin saw with a sinking heart that ASG's appearance had not improved. His eyes were glazed and his suit appeared even more ill-fitting. Then, instead of reading a statement as McLaughlin had urged him to, ASG just asked the hacks what they wanted to know. They replied they wanted to know what was happening. ASG waffled on in reply, but he was obviously not inspiring much confidence.

After the hacks had left in disgruntlement McLaughlin urged his CE to put out a statement to the Press Assocation. That at least would send what BSB could salvage from the mess down the wires to all the different media, who might even use it. But ASG declined and the matter was left at that.

McLaughlin, judging the dreadful sequence of events to have been a complete PR disaster, simply switched off for three months. He had given it everything, but these people hadn't even had the courtesy to involve him as acting head of the press department. He even went so far as thinking of leaving, and had two interviews at Sky with Pat Mastandrea, who had been brought across as joint managing director from Murdoch's Fox Television in America where she had been senior vice-president in charge of sales and marketing. But in the end it had sunk in on him that he couldn't cross over. What would he then tell journalists – that he'd realised Sky was better?

At the Centaurs Business Park there was jubilation at the BSB delay and the renewed breathing space it opened up. But there was nothing else to cheer about. Despite gleeful ads saying 'Sky on Air, BSB hot air', the absence of Sky had become a standing joke, with the irrepressible star of Target, Austin Mitchell, developing his own batch of one-liners. 'What's the difference between Sky and the Loch Ness Monster?' he would chirp. 'Some people have seen the Loch Ness Monster!' In the middle of a late night Commons debate when an opposing MP accused him of rambling unduly, he replied: 'Sorry – you see, working for Sky means I'm no longer used to speaking to an audience!'

Joking aside, in the grim outside world of sky-high interest rates, the reality was frightening. Chris Liveing, the marketing manager for TV, video and satellite of Granada Rentals – whose company admittedly had an axe to grind – informed a seminar on satellite broadcasting that in February Sky sales and rentals, theoretically fuelled by pent-up demand, had totalled only 8,400. In March sales had risen slightly to 10,200, but in one week in April they had dived to just 1,748. That roughly translated into one sale per outlet per week. Liveing estimated 100,000 dishes were now sitting in the warehouses and forecast sales levelling off at 7–10,000 a month throughout the summer. Sky lamely countered with the 'good news' that its own commissioned research indicated that where dishes had been installed, satellite was taking 51% of viewing, with an average daily time of 131.8 minutes. Of this 22% was devoted to the Movie Channel, which was still free of charge and not carrying advertisements (another Murdoch problem, as unlike BSB Sky had made no special deal with the studios to carry ads). Sky-buying households were revealed as larger than the national average, with 3.5 people, and most of the audience, as expected, young male C2s with 44% in the 25–44 age group and 36% between 15 and 24.

Meanwhile, the advertising front was looking equally disastrous. One of the major points made by Murdoch in defence of the free enterprise culture had been that Sky would open up a new world to smaller advertisers. Previously these had been priced out by the astronomical rates on ITV, where peak 30-second slots like the break in News at Ten sold for sums as high as £70,000. The prices had been an endless source of complaint from the adworld, but with Sky having so few viewers not many companies were rushing to take up Murdoch's proffered window of opportunity. By launch the station had only signed up 30 advertisers, although it was reported to be trying to plug the gap by offering free slots to the 170 companies who had supported the original Sky Europe Channel.

Beecham's had been one major company mildly attracted, advertising Lucozade, Brylcreem and Badedas on the opening night, but then saying it planned 'a speedy withdrawal' to consider its long-term strategy. Other big advertisers like NatWest and Thomson Holidays were reserving their positions and there was general scepticism in the industry. Companies said those on higher incomes were reached more effectively through newspapers, and raised the 'zappers' problem afflicting all TV advertising. Viewers were now fleeing from the ad tyranny they had previously been subjected to by zapping off whenever there was a commercial break. Some were even pursuing a deliberate strategy of achieving a whole evening's viewing without seeing any ads at all. This was more complicated than it first sounded, as you easily zapped into a break if you crossed to a commercial channel, and these days even the Beeb was not safe with its endless plugs for *Radio Times*.

The advertisers' initial response to Sky was so poor that by May the station was offering slots at the ludicrously low price of £10, although the advertising trade press reported it intended to 'harden' the rate to £20, which still made it cheaper than the local newspaper. Sky's answer, whilst denying it was carrying out a relaunch, was to unveil an £18 million advertising campaign in the unlikely setting of the Natural History Museum, leading to snide observations about the doings of dinosaurs. Alan Sugar, his confident launch prediction looking as sick as the proverbial parrot, weighed in by committing Amstrad and Fidelity to another £3 million to get the dishes moving. The new Sky campaign, it was explained, would move away from the techno-battle which had so bedevilled both sides to focus on programmes.

This then touched on fresh problems. There was no sign of the sixth Sky Arts channel, which it had been announced would be launched later in the year, featuring arts and educational programming. According to the original promotion, Sky had been 'forging links' with major arts bodies and would be commissioning and purchasing a variety of programming ranging from live musical performances and drama to films on the visual arts, opera and ballet. 'Sky Arts will be a cultural asset to the country, as well as a commercial asset to the company,' Andrew Neil had manfully proclaimed. This project was still nascent, and had anyhow been written off by the Big Papers as mere window-dressing.

But Sky had experienced a truly disastrous loss with the Disney Channel, previously hailed as the station's masterstroke and dubbed 'a fairy-tale romance' by the *Financial Times*. Apart from films, Disney was seen as the crucial 'dish driver' which would rope in entire households. Some films could do that, but the second most popular channel, sport, was overwhelmingly watched by men of the breed labelled 'couch potatoes'. These gents archetypally slobbed in front of the telly, can of lager in hand, and slagged off the participants with oafish opinions culled from a mixture of their own ignorance and recycled material from 'expert' commentators. By and large women were either not interested or positively hated it. What Disney could do above all, apart from bringing pressure from children to buy, was promote Sky as something all the family could watch together – even if only on the minimalist grounds that its wide-ranging appeal and determination not to offend made it something everybody could at least put up with.

The Disney deal had been announced in a trans-Atlantic press conference the previous November, with Andrew Neil so over the moon he had happily posed for a photo-call cuddling a giant Mickey Mouse. Sky had then planned to launch the Disney Channel as the centrepiece of its subscription service, selling it along with the Movie Channel as a two-channel package. But just before the BSB launch delay announcement the deal had fallen to pieces. Murdoch had now launched a ferocious lawsuit accusing Disney of fraud and using unfair tactics, and claiming $1.5 billion in damages.

Over at BSB this was all extremely cheering, and when the shareholders examined Sky's viewing figures there was even more to cheer about. It was now claiming 1.3 million homes in Great Britain and Eire, but what News International was not stressing in its brightly-worded announcements was that most of these had not chosen the service but merely been passively connected to it through existing cable systems. In addition nearly half of them were in the Irish Republic, where they were of precious little interest to advertisers or anyone else in what was supposed to be British broadcasting. All in all, it could be concluded at BSB when you looked on the bright side – and positive thinking was positively encouraged within the company – despite their own catalogue of unfortunate mishaps there were plenty of good reasons for forging on. Apart, of course, from the horrible feeling that they were all locked into the whole thing anyway. But that was just negative thinking.

CHAPTER NINE

Mission Impossible

As Andy Coleman started delving into the technical position, ASG found out more about Graham Grist's IBM-led 'need to know' policy. First he likened Grist to a rugby player who grimly hung on to the ball rather than passing it to his colleagues. Then he decided it went further than that. Grist actually ran about the field with the ruddy thing tucked under his vest!

It wasn't just that Grist and Eglise had kept things from the executive board and the shareholders on the 'need to know' basis, but the various aspects of the technology had then been compartmentalised. There was virtually a complete lack of information between the receiver manufacturers and the chipmakers, the chipmakers and General Instruments, and on and on, right down the line. Matters had been further complicated by the extraordinary logistics of the manufacturing side. The satellite was being made in Los Angeles, ITT was iterating the chip in Germany, General Instruments making the access control module in San Diego, and the receiver base manufacturers of Ferguson, Salora and Tatung working in Telford and Taiwan. Above all this made the project one where massive co-ordination was required, but ASG began to realize no cross-conversation had been encouraged. BSB had been a postbox, with everybody at arm's length, and rather than being the team player, Grist had been very much the policeman, not letting anyone talk to anyone.

It was obvious, ASG decided, that whatever commercial justifications Grist had for keeping the different manufacturers in the dark, a leopard couldn't change its spots. The new openness he wanted just wasn't Grist's way of doing things. ASG now had enough confidence in the feedback from Coleman, and the consultants who had been called in, to act decisively. At the beginning of June, when Coleman returned from a two-week sailing holiday round the Scottish Islands, ASG called him into his office. Grist was going, he explained, although he didn't yet know it. He would be telling him in the next 30 minutes. Meanwhile, would Coleman now step into the breech to take overall responsibility for the technical aspects as project co-ordinator? Coleman was stunned. This was a position which he thought should have been created at least nine months previously, and which Grist had anyhow been moving him towards, but only under his direction. What he was now being asked to assume was a much greater and more awesome responsibility. But as well as wanting BSB to succeed, Coleman had his own personal problem. He had moved down from Sheffield to a nice terraced house in Putney, only to be trapped by soaring interest rates and the announcement of various monster road schemes which had rendered the place unsaleable. He decided to accept.

ASG then called Grist in. 'I'm afraid, Graham, that's it,' he told him, 'I want you to resign – of course, we'll look after you.' Grist told him it was disgraceful. 'I don't feel so good about it either,' ASG replied, but he didn't change his mind. Grist was out.

Eglise was astonished when Grist phoned him at home with the news. He had been expecting a shake-out, but until then had not known who was going to get the short straw. There were mixed feelings in the company over the dismissal and Coleman's new appointment. The general feeling was that Grist must have had a period when he had known there were problems. He had hoped it would all come right without his having to set off any alarm bells, but now it had gone wrong he had to take the consequences on the chin. But at the same time, although the technology was the one thing which could blow the Good Ship BSB out of the water, ASG had always let Grist handle it, never trying to understand it himself. The execs noted that even now he was not taking direct control but giving it to Coleman. Yet it was a problem which desperately needed to be handled by one person, and the only one who could really do that was the CE.

BSB then stopped dead in its tracks as the orthodoxy changed to one of project management. An army of consultants poured in, essentially to go through a reteaching process. All had to have explained to them what had been done up to now before they could assess where things had gone wrong. All in all it was to take 13 weeks to sort it all out. Coleman believed that until this point it had not been visible to the others in the company, apart from Grist and Eglise, just how pioneering, difficult, and high-risk the technical development was. ITT was developing one of the largest and most complex consumer chips ever made and the danger signs had simply not been flagged. Coleman's style was entirely different to Grist's, and much more what ASG was looking for. He saw his first job as getting people to talk to each other. They had to be made to believe the project was technically possible before the different manufacturers could all be got behind a set of revised plans.

Each manufacturer was briefed in turn about the management changes at BSB and the different approach to involving them. A week after he had been put in charge Coleman got most of the major ones round a table along with the IBA. At first he sat at the end but then, realising that wouldn't work, got up and walked around, feeling like a lion as he paced up and down soliciting contributions from the various elements and drawing together their pool of knowledge. One major problem he soon identified was that the various different companies were all perfectionists, who until now had been reluctant to let their bit go until it was 100% completed. But they all had early versions they could exchange, and once that was done it would enable everyone to progress. Gradually, as Coleman got to work in harness with Ellis Griffiths, things began moving.

It was when Eglise opened up to confess all that ASG discovered the full extent of what had been kept from him. One of the reasons General Instruments had taken the $200 million contract for the film encryption was its having been heavily involved in military encryption for B52 bombers. The company had then seen its chance to get into scrambled TV for the American cable market, where HBO (Home Box Office) had been a great success. But when work started for BSB, the British government's listening post at GCHQ in Cheltenham involved itself under its

1 Beam me down, Alan! A proud Rupert Murdoch announces Sky as
Alan Sugar, the head of Amstrad which was to make the receiving
dishes, holds up a symbolic umbrella. (© *The Guardian*/Frank Martin)

2 It's smart to be square. The ill-fated
squarial which was to become the
symbol of BSB is launched on the
world from the roof of the IBA
building. The press failed to realise
that what it was looking at was just a
wooden dummy. (© Rex Features/
Clive Dixon)

3 Take your pick from round, squa
or oblong. A confident Anthony
Simonds-Gooding, BSB's chief
executive, shows off the various
permutations of aerials eventually
made available to customers. The
different shapes still did nothing to
boost sales. (© *Broadcast Magazine*

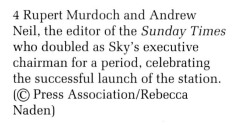

4 Rupert Murdoch and Andrew
Neil, the editor of the *Sunday Times*
who doubled as Sky's executive
chairman for a period, celebrating
the successful launch of the station.
(© Press Association/Rebecca
Naden)

5 Even his yellow cardy could not save Frank Bough, seen here in happier days when he was one of Sky's main stars. Bough's show was one of the casualties of the station's cost-cutting exercise. (Courtesy of *Today*)

6 His word was not his bond. Australian yachtsman and entrepreneur extraordinaire Alan Bond had the largest stake in BSB until his own empire crashed, he failed to stump up the extra capital needed and was diluted out of sight. (© Associated Press/Topham)

7 Hands-on operator. Rupert Murdoch took a close personal interest in every aspect of Sky's operation and moved to London to be full-time chairman during the crucial period when BSB was launching. Nick Ferrari was the first News Editor on Sky News. (Courtesy of *Today*)

8 John Stapleton, who joined Sky from the BBC as one of its principal presenters, was permanently amazed and fascinated by the way the whole operation seemed to teeter on the brink. (© John Stapleton)

9 Marcopolo House, the extraordinary post-modernist building in Battersea which BSB shared with the *Observer* newspaper and which made the staff feel like superstars overnight. (© Solo Syndication)

10 The Boss loses his dish. This satellite dish on the roof of Rupert Murdoch's penthouse flat in St. James' Place was ordered to be removed by Westminster City Council after falling victim to the rules about conservation areas. (© Press Association/Jim Janes)

11 Not a squarial in sight. The Sky drive to rope in C2 households produced what was known as 'pocketing', as on this council estate in South London, with the punters signing up on a 'me too' basis. (© Press Association/Rebecca Naden)

12 Hitting the opposition for six. Rupert Murdoch and the sports promotion mogul Mark McCormack show matching straight bats as the West Indies Test series early in 1990 goes to Sky to become one of its greatest successes. (© Press Association/Tony Harris)

May God bless all who sail in her
ASG and John Gau, BSB's director
programmes, lift their champagne
asses as they put a brave face on
e delayed launch of the Good Ship
BB. (© Press Association/Ian
cholson)

14 His bite was worse than his bark.
Sam Chisholm, already known as
the Most Feared Man in Australian
Television, was Rupert Murdoch's
choice to implement the drastic
economies at Sky and be chief
executive of the new BSkyB.
(© *Broadcast Magazine*)

15 The sultry presenter Selina Scott, recruited as BSB's highest paid star, was one of the few BSB people to survive in the new company of BSkyB. (© *Broadcast Magazine*)

16 The man who fell to earth. A shattered ASG huddles in his tracksuit at home after being ditched in the merger with Sky and banned from Marcopolo House. (© Times Newspapers)

remit that if anything was broadcast it needed to know what it was. If it was being scrambled GCHQ further needed to know how, so it could tune in to snoop whenever it felt like it. Eglise had first been made to sign the Official Secrets Act and then plunged into a bizarre series of negotiations after GCHQ informed him the security system for the movies was too secure and BSB could not use it.

Eglise had found the GCHQ lot extraordinary people, who were worried about the BSB system having the potential to carry terrorist messages on the DataVision operation planned to ride on the back of the programming. There was bizarre talk about air time being bought to give the 'the oxygen of publicity' Mrs Thatcher had talked about. As he talked to them they struck him as even more bizarre than in the movies. They were reluctant to speak on the phone, which they regarded as fatally insecure, and when they did occasionally use it he had to go through strange scenarios, reminiscent of a weird series of games, to establish they both knew they were talking to the right people.

Eglise had informed Grist, who hadn't been required to sign the Act, about these bizarre goings-on, saying: 'We must tell ASG.' But Grist again took the view that it was something that should be kept quiet. It was essentially a side-issue which had nothing to do with the project as such. 'Absolutely not,' he had ruled. Because of signing the Secrets Act, Eglise had found himself on the horns of a dilemma. He had a quiet word with sales director Chris Dickens, saying: 'I shouldn't be telling you this but . . .' to which Dickens replied with a practical suggestion – get ASG to sign the Act as well, then you'll be able to talk to him.

But Eglise had ignored this advice. Instead, after many restless nights, he had gone back to General Instruments, which had told him it already knew about the problem. The American secret service had said much the same and GI was now being told it would not be given an export licence for the stuff. The problem had been solved by a major redesign, which made the system less secure, and it had been presented in a way which had made the authorities happy.

But it wasn't just on the technology front that rapid repair work was needed. BSB had put a brave face on the delay débâcle by pointing out that it had not lost any of the expensive film rights. But behind the scenes it was acknowledged that this was a disaster because all the films which had been expensively bought would be old by the time they were shown. And there had been enormous public humiliation as BSB's advertising agency of BBH saw its first big campaign shot down in flames. One of the major embarrassments had been news of the delay leaking out as newspapers and hoardings all over the country were plastered with giants ads extolling BSB's virtues, backed up by more ads on terrestrial TV, all fatally beginning: FROM THIS SEPTEMBER . . .

The opening campaign had been worked out by Nigel Bogle, who despite the bonus of working with his old chums ASG and Peter Bell had found BSB a tricky enough brief to start with. Over and over again as the saga deepened Bogle was to rack his brains for an analogy to a previous product, but neither he nor his assistant Steve Kershaw ever found one. Quite apart from the massive size of its projected spend, Bogle had decided BSB was unique. The first question – whether there was a market – was relatively easy and straightforward. BBH was very confident on this front. Research proved that if you asked people if they wanted satellite TV, they said yes. Further refinement then narrowed down the type of people actually likely to buy as firstly what were known in marketing-speak as 'AB techno-buffs' – well-heeled people interested in state of the art equipment, like the ones currently buying CD players, who would go for the superior D-MAC picture. Behind them were the massed ranks of the C2s, with their highly disposable incomes and long hours spent slumped in front of the telly.

As the overall approach to hooking in these two markets Bogle had gone strongly for the 'branding' strategy both ASG and Peter Bell were so keen on. Bogle agreed completely that there was an enormous difference between BSB and conventional terrestrial TV. Now in his 40s and prematurely bald, he personally remembered the trouble there had been with Channel 4 in simply persuading the 'inheritance principle' viewers to retune their sets to receive it. The problem had been so acute that one evening the ordinary ITV programmes had been transmitted on the Channel 4 frequency in a desperate attempt to force people to find it on their sets. But BSB was facing a much bigger hurdle than that. As far as the GBP was concerned, watching ordinary TV was like turning on the lightswitch. BSB was about actually going out and buying something – which was more akin to having the whole room rewired.

Chris Dickens, as sales director, supported the same approach. The overall strategy started off being led by a corporate position, then moved rapidly into a product position. You had to create a perception of what BSB was by saying: 'Here is BSB and this is what it is. Here are the channels and this is what they are, and here are the programmes that you really want to watch.'

It was when you posed the question: 'What is BSB?' that the problems started. Bogle's main difficulty was that there were so many intangibles. BBH's job was to advertise something you could neither feel, touch nor see, and as he hunted for things tangible he found the company largely unable to help itself. Then there was constant opposition from programming people, who were continuing the original split with the marketing department. They wanted programme-led advertising, while from Bogle's point of view it would have been a start for him to have known what the different channels were going to be! But instead, at least before John Gau arrived, all he got was constant chopping and changing, so he dared not settle on anything in case it promptly altered. One supposed tangible he could grasp, however, was the squarial that had been such a publicity hit and he had determined this would be the 'umbrella' strategy under which the whole campaign would be run. Bogle's view was that BSB had seized 'square' as its property, and this allowed the company to brand itself on it on the rationale that 'it works for me and I feel good about it'.

The launch of Sky had served one useful purpose in cutting through the intangibles fog. The primary strategy behind the first campaign immediately reverted to the familiar bottom line always used in the ad business when one competitor stole a march on another. For once, instead of moving heaven and earth to persuade people to rush out and buy something, you urged them instead not to buy it, but to wait until your rival product came along. This in turn had led Bogle to the only other supposed BSB tangible apart from the squarial – the launch date. A campaign based on this would also give people the key information of how long you were asking them to hang on.

The result had been the giant FROM SEPTEMBER . . . ads: FROM SEPTEMBER . . . A STATION THAT SHOWS 6 FIRST RUN MOVIES A WEEK . . . A STATION WITH DIGITAL STEREO SOUND . . . A STATION WITH THE MOST LIFELIKE TELEVI-SION PICTURE EVER – the latter having a dig at Sky by tacking on the addendum 'Don't worry, Derek Jameson works for the opposition'. All were catchlined at the bottom with the squarial branding strategy, translated into the slogan: IT'S SMART TO BE SQUARE.

Now the campaign was hurriedly pulled, and as the posters were being torn down from hoardings and space cancelled in newspapers and on TV, a crisis 'awayday' meeting was called at ASG's country house near Dorking to hammer out how to cope with the disaster. As at the summer party, it was tipping down with rain.

Bogle was there, along with all the top execs, in line with ASG's belief that the agency should be a key player in the major decisions in the marketing process. The problem they were facing was now trickier than ever. BSB had to keep itself in the limelight, but at the same time not actually commit itself to anything, as the list of intangibles had now grown to the point where there was nothing tangible left. There would be a delay, but nobody knew for how long. Then, just as bad, Bogle was told the crucial squarial was being withdrawn from the ad equation.

The squarial, as the staff had suspected, had got into deep trouble, with the original arrangement with John Collins and his tiny Fortel company being dropped. Andy Coleman was instead starting to process one with the considerably larger company of STC, but as a technician he thought it wrong to brand yourself on a piece of technology, particularly one that wasn't yet working. He was also becoming aware of how squarial development sucked down people like Grist's former deputy Eglise, taking up too much of their time when they should have been concentrating on other things. There was enough to do without squarial development adding to the problems and Coleman was telling them he was in favour of ditching the thing altogether in favour of a simple round dish aerial. This would still be much smaller than a Sky mega-dish and easy to produce. Meanwhile, playing safe, he was proceeding with STC on the basis of first getting a squarial that worked before thinking about reducing its size to the much-trumpeted dinner plate 10″ across. But he could give no guarantees.

The full folly of branding on technology not yet in existence had by now come home to roost. With the chip iteration horror (although ITT was by now very bullish) fresh in its mind, the management now told Bogle various 'concerns' about the squarial meant it could no longer be featured in the advertising, although the new diamond-shaped company logo which had replaced the previous rounded effort was deemed to be irreversible.

As the execs settled down in ASG's comfy home the talk instead turned to press issues and how BSB could sustain a 'positive position' through a very 'negative period'. Bogle had already faced the fact that the climate in the press had turned against the company, not just in the News International papers where rubbishing and opposition was taken for granted. In more neutral papers BSB had been receiving 'not positive PR' which the delay announcement had now considerably exacerbated. The company, therefore, must be careful not to 'overpromise', a fault it had clearly been guilty of in the past.

Before the first ad campaign Bogle had looked at Sky and analysed its approach, reflected through its own ads. It was different to BSB's marketing-led strategy. Sky was not trying to market satellite as a new concept but going with its USP of simply offering 'more' of the sort of things already on terrestrial TV – more sport, more game shows, more movies. Its ads, made in-house, were blunt and crude – 'Tyson on Sky', 'Madonna on Sky' – that sort of thing. With sixteen channels on Astra, although only four were the Murdoch British service, BSB could never compete on that front. In terms of choice, if choice meant more of the same, it would always be Sky.

From this Bogle had identified a way forward for BSB. Sky appeared to be more of the same at the very time research showed people were worried about how much TV they watched – and especially how much their children watched. BSB, therefore, could sell the concept of additional TV – extra to what was already available, and worth having. It all fitted in with John

Gau's 'quality programming' idea, and the execs at the meeting then started further discussing the key elements of what BSB was about. There was much general talk about choice, offering more depth, scheduling, being distinctive, the proper balance for programmes, points of difference, the shape of the NOW channel, programmes by women for women, general interest for women, programmes for children (BSB had originally promised a channel dedicated to children), documentaries, the second set viewing issue, what they should do with music . . . The topics, naturally, were endless.

As one way for the company to sort itself out and get its aims clear, Bogle suggested a 'Mission Statement'. A Mission Statement is an American management concept by which you briefly summarise the aim you are intending to achieve, or 'go for'. The mission of the Starship Enterprise in the TV series Star Trek was 'to boldly go where no man has gone before', while the one for the giant American finance house of Merrill Lynch started: 'To be the world's foremost investment banking firm'. Following your Mission Statement people dealing with you can then nod sagely and reply: 'Right! Now I can see where you're coming from!'

Andreas Whittam-Smith had written one on a sheet of paper when he started the *Independent* newspaper. Bogle now wrote one for BSB, only to find it later amplified to cover five sheets of paper and contain a separate statement for each channel. Now he led on to the more practical problem of how you actually achieved your Mission Objective. Bogle had tabled a 'listening channels' concept as something worth developing. He started talking about talking to people, which he developed out of the question: 'What's our point of difference?' BSB's point of difference, he explained, was that it was giving viewers a new choice. It had gone out and talked to people about what they wanted and now it must say: 'We've listened to what you want and we've created five-channel TV to provide a range of things viewers have said they don't have currently.'

Bogle's thinking had been influenced by studying the print media and noticing how much more involved it was with its readers than TV. The approach had intensified recently with the new crop of women's magazines like *Bella* and *Prima*, locked in deadly rivalry for a finite market. Because the competition between them was so fierce, they were all trying to involve their individual readers as much as possible through constantly soliciting letters, viewpoints, recipes, shared experiences, competitions, and anything which could fall under the marketing-speak heading of 'interactive'. By always inviting feedback, the theory ran, the readers could say what they wanted and then be given it and consequently purchase the product.

Bogle had picked up another recent lesson with the launch of the Mission Statement-led *Independent*, which had attracted advertising buzzwords like 'more classic', 'younger' and 'fresher'. The *Independent* had changed people's perceptions of its rival the *Guardian* by making that seem, in Bogle's view, 'a bit '60s'. The result had been to tip it into a trendy redesign based round long headlines run in lower case type with lots of white space round them. But this had aroused varying reactions amongst its regular readers who, although traditionally liberal in their politics, were often deeply conservative in their personal lives.

BSB, Bogle explained, could do the same to terrestrial TV. Just like the *Independent* had done to the *Guardian*, it could make it seem old-fashioned. At the moment TV stations appeared to have little or no direct feedback apart from a smattering of phone calls to duty officers, the majority of them from nutters and people ringing in to complain. Only perennial topics like bad language or cruelty to animals got people at all excited, and in the normal run of things programme-makers would be delighted if they got more than a handful of calls. Some were not above ringing in themselves to make adulatory comments in disguised voices, knowing the gushing remarks would be written up in logs to be widely circulated internally and endlessly analysed.

Bogle pointed out that research showed, for example, that 44% of people questioned said they could never find anything they wanted to watch on TV. But BSB could blaze a trail by consulting the GBP to ask what it wanted to watch and then provide it, just like the women's magazines did for their readers. To begin with the GBP could be involved through questionnaires. Then, when broadcasting began, the association could be kept up through viewers being personally contacted. This was going to happen anyhow on the less altruistic level of sending them the monthly bill for their movie channel subscription, so the communication could be used as an opportunity to talk to them further. There were all kinds of possibilities for further personalising the interface by a combination of the D-MAC technology and modern computer programming. Lastly there would be the neat spin-off of building a comprehensive database, which could then be used for many purposes including attracting advertisers.

Bogle, speaking passionately, then gave the BSB execs a stern warning. If they were going to change strategy to this new direction and become a 'listening station', they had to be prepared for what it was going to develop into. You will have to answer people when they ask you things, he told them firmly, as well as demonstrating you have certain programmes which are either listening to people's views or are there because people want them. It was a long-term commitment, and they should think about that side of it seriously. But in the short term an advertising campaign could involve people by getting them to clip coupons out of newspapers or ringing one of the Freephone numbers introduced from America by British Telecom. Then they could be sent questionnaires to fill in. That would all take time, helping with the required objective they were all there for of keeping BSB in the public eye and building a bridge over the delay.

The awayday ended with a firm decision, as was becoming the norm at BSB, to hold more meetings. A regular O Group would now be started − a title lifted from the services where it denoted meetings at which commanding officers gathered their subordinates to tell them what to do. The Good Ship BSB's O Group would effectively continue the awayday by meeting every Monday morning, and sometimes twice a week, and be run by ASG with the key figures of Bogle, John Gau, Chris Dickens, Edward Bickham, Bob Hunter and Peter Bell on board. It was agreed a possible way forward had been found for the advertising. But at the same time everybody knew nothing would be done at the moment. No money was to be committed to anything until Coleman and the consultants had finished their trawl through the technology nightmare and they could all see where they were.

The question of staunching the financial outflow had been

featuring large in the life of Ian Clubb, a small, dour Scot from Aberdeen who had joined the company in April just as it became obvious there was going to be a delay. Clubb had been recruited after ASG realized the financial side of the company was getting so complex it needed a full-time finance director so they could all sleep more easily at night. Even by his standards he could see there was an awful lot of money sloshing about.

Clubb, now in his late 40s, had trained as accountant and gone into the media business in the mid-60s with the Thomson Group, rising to become finance director, first of *The Times* and then of the whole group. He had been personally involved in the sale of *The Times* to Murdoch, finding him 'a breath of fresh air' as an entrepreneur and businessman, before transferring across to the oil business through Thomson's North Sea interests. There he had arranged massive project loans and had later gone on to be MD at Carless, Britain's oldest oil company, which he was in the process of reviving when it fell victim to a hostile takeover. Clubb had registered with headhunters as wanting 'to do something complicated in the financial scene' and been offered the Spanish national oil company or BSB. Many of his contacts in the City had advised him against the satellite station, telling him it would be a disaster and never get off the ground, but he had still been unable to resist, seduced by the challenge of the massive fund-raising required.

Clubb had started at BSB with a characteristically low profile, tucking himself away in a small back office in Brompton Road to look at the books and get a feel for the company. His alarm level had immediately shot up. Never mind the fund-raising, he was first going to have to put in the kind of basic controls essential for any properly-run company – certainly one with such an enormous investment. Before he arrived he had already steeled himself for the age-old problem of applying financial disciplines to creative people. He knew all about that from his days at *The Times*. But what he was looking at in BSB was ridiculous. In terms of controls on people the place was a bloody zoo! There was zero financial discipline to stop these guys doing whatever they wanted – and when he talked about controls he didn't mean anything special, just simple, ordinary controls on senior executives and personnel.

Sorting through the mountain of bills he found the execs all putting their personal expenses on their company Barclaycards and then allowing the company to settle them. One member of staff had even used his company card to pay for a family wedding. Others were using them to buy their season tickets to and from work. The lack of control was not just at the top, but extending right down the hierarchy to the mundane level of the stationery cupboard. This was simply wide open and people were helping themselves to anything from gold top batteries for their Walkmans to crayons for their kids. Everywhere he looked it seemed to be the same.

Clubb recruited a junior from his oil industry days to sort it all out and kick things into a more Calvinistic mould. He found they all resented it like hell and squealed like stuck pigs, but he didn't give a bugger. To his great satisfaction one employee was caught red-handed cheating on his expenses and Chris Dickens, who agreed with Clubb about the free-spending mentality, fired him. The wedding man was hauled in and made to pay the money back, and the overall problem solved by stopping all the company credit cards and issuing new ones. Employees now had to settle bills themselves and then claim the money back afterwards on company expenses forms.

But it wasn't just the credit cards which were the problem. Clubb felt much the same as Robert Devereux had before Virgin pulled out, except things were now much further advanced. The company's attitude to spending money was wrong, more appropriate to a cash-generating business than a start-up project. From the top down there seemed to be lots of primadonnas feeling they could do as they wished on company money. The place had a party-type philosophy which needed to be got rid of. But then, Clubb soon decided, he would have set the whole thing up differently. The shareholders had the wrong structure, and he also wasn't at all sure ASG was the right person to be running it. BSB was a huge, hands-on control management exercise, which wasn't really ASG's bag. He was fine in a bull market for a cash-rich business, but at BSB Clubb thought he was the wrong person in the wrong job. Maybe a marketing person could be brought in and put in charge once the company was up and running, but what it desperately needed at the beginning was a project manager to start it up and make things happen. Clubb was having his toughest time with the marketing people. He knew the programming spend was unavoidable, especially on movies, and recognised there was a need to spend on promotion. But he wasn't at all sure that was being done properly with the lavish budgets, endless gizmos, huge promotions and 'best of everything' attitude. His view was more that it was out of control.

Clubb's typically Scottish attitude introduced a new idea to BSB – that of not spending money until you had to – which was remarked upon by Chris Akers, an analyst at Citibank who was monitoring the company's progress. Before Clubb arrived Akers had thought BSB's attitude to spending was similar to making the mistake of buying a family tube of toothpaste – a marketing trick which encouraged you to use more just because you had it. Then, putting it in a more appropriately media analogy, he likened the way the company was proceeding to the film Brewster's Millions, where the hero had to get rid of a mountain of money as quickly as possible, while whatever he did it just kept coming. Clubb's brisk approach had now got some basics under control, Akers saw, and Clubb himself felt things were beginning to improve. That was until he found out about the Canaveral jaunt.

The trip to Cape Canaveral in Florida was to celebrate, hopefully, BSB's first piece of really good news, the launch of the rocket taking its satellite, Marcopolo I, into orbit. At a board meeting ASG had asked the shareholders if he should have a party and invite them all over, but by now becoming more wary, most of them had firmly declined the invitation. Three marketing department minions had still flown over to America and organized a toned-down version which involved booking the penthouse in the hotel at Cocoa Beach and laying on essential marketing trappings, like little customized BSB bags to hold the binoculars they would each be given to watch through. In London a simultaneous modest staff celebration was being planned featuring, amongst other delicacies, quails' eggs.

Clubb then found out ASG had sent a memo to most of the execs inviting them to the celebration and, in accordance with BSB's happy families format, informing them the company would not just pay for them to go to Florida, but their wives and children as well. He hit the roof and went storming in to his CE to demand he at least pay for his children. ASG, who found Clubb 'a tiger – very fierce', dutifully wrote out a large cheque to the company's travel agents of Hogg Robinson. When Clubb then moved on to beard John Gau he discovered the programming chief obviously saw it the same way as him, as he had already paid for his children on his own initiative. Clubb then toured the other execs, telling them: 'I know what ASG has said you can do, but I think it's wrong. You should at least pay for your kids.' He left it at that and never went back to check whose consciences had been pricked. But he further underlined his point, together with his ally Chris Dickens, by refusing to attend himself.

The rocket that finally went up at 6.59 pm on 27 August was built by McDonnell Douglas Delta Space Systems of Huntington Beach in California. It broke new ground by giving BSB the distinction of being the first company to send up a privately owned rocket big enough to put a payload in orbit since the original Sputnik in 1957. All the thousands since then had previously been sent up by government agencies or government-owned companies, including the Ariane rocket launching Sky's Astra satellite which was owned by the 11 western European governments making up the European Space Agency. There was a slight hitch because the rocket was delayed, and the company representatives had to hang about for two weeks, but Florida was a pleasant place to be and the hotel was good. And for those who did go to Cape Canaveral, especially the technical people, it was an enormously dramatic moment as the 115-foot-long device – the same height as an 11-storey tower block – blasted off.

Even though the BSB party was two and a half miles away, perched on a temporary makeshift stand in the middle of a swamp, John Gau found it very dramatic. Peter Bell likened it to being present at the birth of his children, and it brought a lump to Andy Coleman's throat. (Coleman, wiser in these matters, had avoided hanging about for days by ringing his contacts to get constant updates, smoothly jetting in the day before.) Lord and Lady Thomson graced the occasion to represent the IBA, and ASG, sporting a white astronaut-style boiler suit, was on tremendous form, with Marjorie in glowing yellow positively ecstatic. Along with company representatives and the children, one of whom was wearing an American trucker's cap with cloth BSB squarials sticking up from it, they chanted the countdown before bursting into applause as the rocket took off. ASG, after tracking it into the ether with his BSB binoculars, commented on the success and the perfect weather by declaring: 'God must be a Brit!' before ladling out more bullish statements: 'I've always been known as an optimist, but now I'm an incurable optimist'. The launch was 'the biggest step in turning the dream into a reality'. There was more 'good news' coming on the technical front which would be announced shortly. 'I'm getting good reports from all around me,' he ended. 'It's not plain sailing, but plainer sailing – easier by the minute.' BSB was now going to continue 'the remorseless advance'.

Back in London Edward Bickham and Chris McLaughlin sat in the press office beside two piles of press releases – one announcing failure, the other success – and waited for the trans-Atlantic phonecall. When it came through they dutifully released the success version, along with a 'technical update' which proclaimed: 'All the element [sic] of BSB are on schedule for a Spring launch'. McLaughlin still found the rocket launch a non-event publicity-wise, as he had already known it would be. If the media was going to cover commercial events like this it had to be taken to them which was why Murdoch had flown out a planeload of hacks to French Guiana.

At BSB McLaughlin had first been informed that no hacks at all could go and then, at the last moment, allowed ten. He had declined, knowing he would never be able to sort out the ructions that would cause amongst the 300 or so who were jostling to enjoy such a glorious freebie. Snubbed, the hacks retaliated by virtually ignoring the event and the total result in England was one local radio interview. But over in America there was lots of publicity, delighting ASG, even though it was not so much for BSB as for McDonnell Douglas Delta and Hughes, who were expecting more customers.

Meanwhile, just as Rupert Murdoch had fully pressed the button on the Centaurs Business Park after the Ariane launch, now its own bird was in the air it was time for the terrestrial end of the Good Ship BSB to expand out of Brompton Road, moving to a berth which would triumphantly reflect its full corporate glory.

CHAPTER TEN

The Holes in the Mint

In its original plans BSB had envisaged having its complete operation based at the university park in Chilworth at Southampton, where the uplink to the satellite was already situated. But this had soon become a hot topic, leading to one of the first disputes on the executive board. Graham Grist had been heavily pro-Chilworth, where the company had already spent millions buying and equipping a large building. Grist said the company could have a head office presence in London, where the marketing operation could also be, but for the majority of the company Chilworth would be cheaper, staff could live there pleasantly and, he emphasized with the support of the engineers, they needed to have studios. But Grist had been fiercely opposed by both the original channel heads, Bob Hunter and Andy Birchall, who insisted there wasn't much point in their having large studios at the very time other ITV companies were trying to divest themselves of theirs. The argument had reached deadlock until ASG stepped in with one of his first positive decisions. It was a nonsense for the business to move to Southampton, he ruled. It obviously needed a London presence.

An official hunt then began for suitable premises, with the terrestrial TV stations not giving much in the way of clues. The BBC was marooned in Shepherd's Bush; Thames occupied a tower block at the top of Tottenham Court Road; Channel 4 was close by in Charlotte Street; and Granada, as they knew from the meetings before BSB won the franchise, was solidly ensconced in Golden Square in Soho. Only London Weekend broke the pattern,

THE HOLES IN THE MINT

going for the Thames tower block option but crossing the river to an area of wasteland next to the National Theatre, where its fatly paid staff contrasted sharply with the beggars of Cardboard City close by.

The BSB premises hunt, as usual, had galvanized armies of people and consultants, leading to a fresh level of noisy negotiations at the executive board as suggestions were bought in, with everybody chipping in that wasn't right, that was no good, or that was too expensive, until the arguments got nowhere and the full circle was completed by Chilworth being raised again. Eventually it had got to the point where a decision had to be made one way or the other, and attention had focused on Marcopolo House.

There had been a long debate about this option, with many points put forward as to why it shouldn't be taken. Chesterton's, the estate agency and property consultancy, had assessed about six premises and Marcopolo had not featured very highly, being described as remote, not ideal, and furthermore costed at about £15 million to convert. But it did have glamour, whereas in comparison the other options were quite mundane, and it was also big enough to get everyone into the same building. ASG was adamant this was crucial so communication could flow right through the company, and in demonstration of his point even penned little drawings for Graham Grist showing arrows like a weather chart indicating the flow between different departments.

Everybody was still dithering about the agonising choice when at one meeting ASG, exercising his full authority as CE, abruptly cut through the sea of corporate indecision. 'Right,' he said, 'we go to Marcopolo. Has anybody got any objections?' Nobody had, so Marcopolo it was. A sigh of relief ran round the execs that the thorny issue had finally been decided, for better or for worse.

One of the prime justifications for the building was that it was cheap by central London standards at £24 a square foot compared with a more normal £35, although the rent was still £2.5 million a year. But MPH was not in the centre of London. Instead it was located on the fringe of excited 80s activity in the dingy area of Battersea best know for its Dogs' Home and prime landmark of the old power station, which under pressure from keen conservationists had become a listed building.

The borough had been belatedly hauled on to the trendy circuit by an overflow of Sloanes, priced out of their traditional Chelsea and Fulham stamping grounds across the river and busy gentrifying its rundown terraces and mansion blocks. The quid pro quo for their lower prices, just as it was for BSB, was in being marooned by the transport nightmare south of the river, while Marcopolo had the additional factor of being sited in a rather desolate area. It was soon to become a grim joke that it would have been quicker and easier to reach central London from Chilworth.

The redundant Battersea Power Station which loomed nearby did nothing to cheer up spirits. This too had been sucked into the 80s excitement by John Broome, then owner of Alton Towers and one of the darlings of the decade's 'success story' – the tourist service industry. After Disney's decision to build its Euro Disney theme park in France rather than Britain, Broome had embarked on a hugely ambitious project to turn the power station into a massive rival attraction, with the eventual dream of packaged holidaymakers being transported from one to the other via the similarly exciting project of the Channel Tunnel. But even before BSB moved to Marcopolo the project had run out of funds and the old building now stood as a forlorn and gutted shell. Another wild scheme, Battersea Wharf, cloned on Chelsea Harbour across the river and designed to fill up the wasteland with a hotel, offices and designer shopping, had also failed to materialise. But, like BSB, Marcopolo had got in before the financial hatch came down.

As a building it was by any standards extraordinary, in the same vein as its creator, Ian Pollard. An extrovert character who had attracted attention in the past for driving his Ferrari down the M4 at 193mph during the 1973 oil crisis. Pollard, who sported a beard and long hair down over his shoulders, had already become a focus of attention for the chattering classes through his Homebase DIY store in Kensington which featured a mix and match of ancient Egypt and modern Stuttgart. The attention to detail had gone so far as mixing the paints in the authentic Egyptian manner, but the building had so upset Sir John Sainsbury that when he saw it he exploded, called it a 'fairground', and ordered some of its more outlandish features to be removed.

Pollard, who himself lived in a sixteenth century manor house outside Bath, had used another eclectic mishmash of past architectural styles at Marcopolo to create what had been described by the *Sunday Times* as 'the most spectacular essay in Post-Modernism yet built in Britain'. It had even received the dubious accolade of being pictured on the front of the London telephone directory. The building was spectacular – especially from the air – though what BSB had rented was in fact half a commercial semi-detached. The other half, Chelsea Bridge House, had been taken by the *Observer*, fleeing in the opposite direction from practically every other paper in the wholesale exodus from Fleet Street. (Lonrho, the paper's owner, was recouping some of the cost by assiduously renting it out as a location for ads and plays about newspapers.)

The building both now occupied was close to Chelsea Bridge and fronted on to the busy Queenstown Road. Passing members of the GBP gazed out of their vehicles in wonderment at the gleaming exterior of alternating vertical panels of black glass and a material called neo-paries, made in Japan and being used here for the first time in Britain. The material was manufactured like glass, but heated to a higher temperature so it crystallised to give a marble-like finish, and Pollard had used in alternating pale and dark bands, decorating the classical exterior pilasters and porticoes like a liquorice allsort.

In the prime position of honour at the entrance to the short slip road leading to the building was Ian Pollard's final jeu d'esprit, an oblong lump of granite 8' by 4'. This wasn't just any piece of rock, as nothing connected with Pollard was that mundane. It was, the story went, specifically chosen for its unique quality of having lain untouched in the natural flowing waters of the Scottish Highlands for something in the region of 600 million years. Pollard had had it delivered to the garden of his magnificent house, but decided it was not right and sent for another. The Rock, as it was known, was then repositioned outside Marcopolo, with the name inscribed on it in gold Italianate capital lettering.

Past The Rock, which initially tended to become confused with the debris of the building works, the main BSB entrance was found round the side, facing the uninspiring sight of the raised Network SouthEast line shuttling glum commuters backwards and forwards to Victoria. Automatic glass doors opened inwards, often startling the unsuspecting as they were leaving, to a small foyer. Here smart and friendly security guards occupied a desk manufactured from solid granite to BSB's specifications, while inside receptionists sat at a larger version of the same design. Between them the pair had cost £80,000. The reception side was permanently graced by 20 large and beautiful white lilies, religiously renewed every Monday afternoon.

The foyer was merely a preliminary to the space around which the whole building was designed – a huge and glorious atrium soaring up to the Third Floor as the ultimate expression of 80s triumphalism. Awed visitors parked themselves on the black leather sofas dotted round the large potted plants, whilst their gaze alternated from looking up at the sky above them to peering at the small and tasteful squarial placed alongside one of Astra's mega dishes for their delectation.

Towards the rear of the atrium two glass lifts occupied symmetrical positions, providing guests with a panoramic opportunity of taking in the sheer scale of the central area as they were sent gliding up to their appointments. Between them, Hollywood-style, were centred the stairs to the first floor. Members of the BSB staff, equally as gobsmacked as the GBP on their first visit, giggled that at any moment ASG would descend in full top hat and tails to entertain them all. It felt a bit like an Andy Howard Musical with Micky Rooney, they joked to each other. You started with a line like: 'Come on, guys, let's do a show – my dad's got a barn!' and the next thing you knew you were into a full MGM musical. No more slogging away at the BBC or one of the dull commercial companies to get to the top of this TV business – here was the dream that transported you into a charmed existence. When you walked into Marcopolo you felt like an overnight star. The building turned the image into reality. Here was a flamboyant and ambitious company, full of the best and the brightest, and pursuing its commitment to excellence through the 'remorseless advance' ASG had promised at Cape Canaveral. Meanwhile, as many people within the company were slowly beginning to realise, BSB was already falling apart.

The dourly Scottish Ian Clubb was especially horrified by the sheer opulence of the place. By the time he had joined it had been too late to change the relocation decision, but he had instantly seen how it would undermine all his efforts at economy and cost-cutting. It gave an inappropriately 'fat cat' impression. With the company in such a flash building, everyone would think it was flash – which as far as he was concerned gave entirely the wrong image. David Plowright of Granada was similarly appalled by it. It wasn't so much the cosmetic touches like the fresh flowers in the lavatories. Things like that didn't cost a great deal, and he might even have sanctioned them himself to motivate a group of people and make them think they were the Third Force in British broadcasting. But this grandiose building, with its extravagant atrium, was a different matter. Granada had always been a cost-conscious organisation.

It was the marketing department's brainwave of the mints which summed it all up for Clubb. The original germ of this idea had bubbled up from the fact that, as they were moving, everyone would need to inform their contacts of their new address. Then the marketing spin was added. Marcopolo House – so why not Marco Polo mints! With a flourish the department now produced its master-stroke as large packages thudded on to everyone's desks. 'What's all this?' Clubb screamed, breaking open a packet and trying one. It made him feel sick. The marketing department was puzzled by his reaction. Their clients all thought they were a wonderful idea! They had got a really good buzz going about BSB and everyone was talking about them all over London!

The mints themselves had grown considerably larger than the small ones normally proffered to the GBP and huge amounts of time and energy had gone into having them manufactured in a special one-off deal with the manufacturers of Rowntree. They had been tastefully packaged with a variation of the traditional green and white label and the new Marcopolo address in tiny writing. Finally they had been placed in chic black cardboard tubes. Clubb protested they were an outrageous waste of money and when someone told him what they would cost to post he started shouting and screaming even louder. Then it was realised that many people in the company had wide-ranging contacts abroad. They would have to airmail them if they were not going to take weeks to arrive and the postage cost soared even higher. Embarrassed employees pleading for simple change of address cards were brusquely told they were not available, leading to at least one member of staff having some made at his own expense to get over the embarrassment.

When he calmed down Clubb was able to write the mints off as just more marketing department profligacy, like the freebies the place was awash with. All departments had quotas of merchandise to distribute to clients, production companies, the press, and anyone else they thought might be useful or have any influence. These ranged through sweatshirts and T-shirts to plastic macs, hats, umbrellas, and all manner of gizmos. The merchandising cupboard on the second floor quickly emptied its stocks, with everybody walking around decked out in the latest gear, showing off the excellent jackets and carrying the convenient sports bags. Naturally everything was of the highest quality, with most legendary of all the superb leather jackets for the presenters of the Power Station music channel.

For Clubb what was of more significance with Marcopolo was a resurgence of the 'party philosophy' he had detected when he first got a feel for the company. Now it was back with a vengeance, destroying the mission he had been given by the shareholders to be the 'party pooper'. Parties, he soon discovered, were the order of the day at Marcopolo – as did *Observer* journalists. The *Observer* offices overlooked the atrium and the hacks inside pressed their noses to the windows with a mixture of envy and amusement as they watched the continuous circuit of cocktail dos and glossy presentations which were apparently the TV way of life.

To many of the staff ASG, permanently playing the jolly host, appeared to be enjoying the media-ness of it all, confirming their suspicions that it had been the glamour of TV which had been one of the aspects attracting him to his job in the first place. As well as positively blooming, ASG was also proving immensely popular with the new staff now coming on board who were blossoming under his charm and extraordinary ability to motivate them. When he held an introduction for the new employees they loved him immediately. The more lowly summed him up as 'a real gentleman', whilst he in turn fondly referred to them all as his 'boys and girls'.

ASG's wife Marjorie was also stepping up her activities, but arousing more mixed reactions than her husband. Marjorie had been in PR with Birds Eye when ASG first met her. He had left his first wife, by whom he had six children, for her and they had been married in 1982. She was blonde and pretty, but some BSB staff found her completely over the top with her gushing voice and posh accent. Others disagreed, saying she was friendly and warm and not at all snooty. There was the same disparity of viewpoints on the way she dressed. Some thought it casually chic but not overdone, whilst those less used to a privileged upbringing commented on how obviously expensive her clothes were. Many called her Lady Marjorie, and thought her a consummate Sloane Ranger who worked the floor, running ASG as an industry and making sure he was seen with all the right people and in the right places. Chris McLaughlin had once even joked that his earliest PR brief ought to be to get a knighthood for ASG – presumably automatically due from a grateful Premier if BSB succeeded whilst he was still at the helm.

What everybody did agree was that the couple were obviously very much in love. Marjorie was not only extremely supportive and loyal to her husband, but also determined to do her bit in building the family atmosphere ASG set so much store by. As well as organising him, she played her part by regularly attending the monthly staff meetings, pleasant affairs at which wine was served. Marjorie would watch her husband intently whilst he gave his blurb and quota of 'good news', seeming to the staff to be almost daring any of them to speak out or criticise him. Afterwards she would mingle with the gathering, tenderly inquiring after people's family and children, whom she always knew by name. Again opinion was divided, with some thinking her concern genuine, whilst others adversely likened it to her other good works which included being a prison visitor at Brixton.

Certainly although Marjorie had no official position she took an active part in all the company's activities, in return asking ASG's chauffeur to ferry her around, or his secretary to organise her voluntary work. She also enthusiastically joined the marketing department's drive to keep BSB on a high profile through lavish roadshows. Both ASG and Marjorie were great opera fans, so the company had four tickets every couple of weeks. Then, faithfully following the dictates of the social season, there was the box at Ascot and a high corporate presence at Queen's, the exclusive tennis tournament held just before Wimbledon, as well as Wimbledon itself.

Ian Clubb had no time for this end of the business which the marketing department set such store by. As far as he was concerned it was just more of the Canaveral rocket launch business. People had been hanging around then for two weeks when they should have been too busy to go in the first place. Now all he could see from the current activity was massive bills, people missing from the office for days, and infuriating incidents like Marjorie organising a hospitality tent at the Queens Club, then blithely sending the office car to Marcopolo House to pick up another couple of dozen BSB umbrellas to dish out.

The cars business was another thing that rankled. ASG now had the use of three machines – the chauffeur-driven Jag, officially no longer personally his but for the use of the company, a macho Shogun for out of town activity like going to Dorking, and a Vauxhall Cavalier whose exact purpose was unclear. This point was emphasised by the AA having to be called to start it when it was finally called upon. It had been so little used the battery had gone flat.

Motoring problems were also afflicting the staff. The car park was unfinished when they moved in and they had to leave the gleaming BMWs which were part of their contracts in Battersea Park across Queenstown Road. Then, when the nights started shortening, some women started worrying about walking there after dark. Demonstrating its caring attitude BSB soothed their concerns by laying on a minibus service to take them to their vehicles, as well as ferrying those using more egalitarian public transport to the lifeline of the tube station in Sloane Square across the river. When the car park was finally finished, women staff members were thoughtfully given priority in the race for spaces.

As more experienced hands were recruited they were astonished by what they could see. Susanna Capon, joining as head of drama and children's programmes after a long spell at the BBC and as an independent, thought she had never come across an outfit so preoccupied with status and how it was presented to the outside world, apart from the ill-fated Goldcrest Films. That just worried her even more. Oscar-winning Goldcrest had been the darling of the British film industry in the early 80s but titanic power struggles and wildly out-of-control finances had led to its rapid and painful downfall. Not only was Marcopolo House a showpiece, but Capon was amazed by events like the quails' eggs party celebrating the Canaveral launch, the lavish party in the Planetarium for the press, and the table at the Grosvenor House Ball, where she was hauled up to meet Prince Edward because of some idea that they would do something with the National Youth Theatre, which never happened in the end anyway. The newly started staff newsletter chimed in by reminding staff of small details like some of them forgetting to collect their free bottle of champagne (to celebrate the rocket launch), and advertising a two-bedroomed flat nearby for £94,000. 'Sounds like a bargain to me!' the editor commented enthusiastically.

The ground and first floors of Marcopolo housed the studios and transmission centres, all stuffed with gleaming rows of state of the art equipment. These in turn had been a real headache when the building was being converted, with constant muddle and confusion about how many studios would actually be needed as the great Chilworth dispute continued. As ever with BSB, it was not just the things which were actually done which cost a fortune, but the constant cul-de-sacs and alternatives which the company explored. The various changes had put the conversion cost up from the original £15 million to £26 million, with another £13 million for the equipment itself.

On the ground floor was the large and versatile Studio One, destined for heavy use in bigger productions like chat shows and musical events with studio audiences. Next to it were the other TV necessities such as the Green Room where the crucial hospitality (jokingly known as hostility in the BBC) would take place, dressing rooms, wardrobe, and all the other TV paraphernalia. Associated BSB companies, particularly New Era, instead of being impressed, constantly complained that the dressing rooms were too small, warning BSB it could not possibly expect stars like Selina Scott to work under such conditions.

On the first floor were the transmission control rooms and the small Studio 3 from where the daily JGP entertainment show was to be transmitted, and above them, on the second and third, the staff's offices and workplaces. Huge effort had gone into making these in keeping with the overall chrome and grey theme of the building. Before they moved, staff had been invited to a furniture exhibition to be proudly shown what they would be getting. They were also sternly informed they would not be allowed to bring their own useful pieces of furniture like bookcases as they would mar the colour co-ordinated look of the interior decor.

There was excited rumour about a visit to the Milan furniture exhibition, but the overall contract had been given to the substantial London firm of TSI. At £1.4 million it was its biggest ever and TSI had translated the building's overall grey theme into matching Olivetti furniture. Against a backdrop of blue-grey carpet tiles were open desks of silver birch stained grey, matching grey swivel chairs, grey filing cabinets, grey wooden bookcases and grey designer wastebaskets, with the obsessive attention to detail continuing right down to slimline grey telephones, grey coat stands, grey desk organisers, and, slightly confusingly, grey in and out trays. Execs on the Third Floor, which also housed finance and personnel, had the added bonus of grey wardrobes in which to hang the jackets of their grey suits.

The execs were considered well catered for in their big airy rooms, and the fact that the seat of power was located on the Third Floor gave Marcopolo immediate echoes of the BBC. The inner sanctum of the Director-General and his senior henchmen was on the same level at Broadcasting House in Portland Place near Oxford Circus, and the term 'Third Floor' now inspired the same reverential awe in both establishments.

Some of the exec offices looked over Queenstown Road on to the pleasant greenery of the park, but as CE ASG had an office looking inwards to the airy space of the atrium. It was flanked by those of his PA, Carol Goddard, on one side, with Edward Bickham on the other. The office was largely neutral. ASG's large desk, with a T-shaped extension used for meetings, was kept scrupulously clear, as he was a meticulous processor of paperwork, and he had only allowed himself one or two personal touches. On one wall hung a painting of the Yorkshire landscape of his schooldays, while a corner table had a small display featuring a modern Israeli sculpture given to him by Marjorie. A cuddly toy of a black stuffed cat came from his Saatchi days, and in a little joke ASG had placed it next to the latest craze of a mechanical pet fish in a tank.

Elsewhere on the Third Floor programme heads and others of equal status in the pecking order had decent-sized rooms. But the glories of the atrium and feeling of space at the top bore little resemblance to the majority of staff positions on the second floor. Most of the employees there were crammed into open plan offices which housed the various departments of press, marketing, research, programme commissioning, editing, presentation, computer technology and sales. Almost straight away it was clear there was not enough room. The company had outgrown the building almost as it moved in.

Prior to arrival floor plans had been issued at Brompton Road and people had devoured them avidly to ensure their status was adequately observed, with those who had got the grot starting Machiavellian manoeuvres to oust the more fortunate. The publicity manager on the Movie Channel threw a fit at working in an open plan office and defiantly occupied one of the meeting rooms, from which she was never to be ousted. The two acquisitions managers, allocated the smallest office of all, put into practice the same principle of occupancy being four-fifths of office law and purloined a larger office allocated to the DataVision operation. This had not yet arrived and was therefore in no position to fight its corner. Susanna Capon, consigned to a windowless interior box, simply walked out and refused to come back until she was found something better. After much head-scratching, the switchboard was evicted to a different part of the building and she consented to come back to occupy the room vacated by it.

The interior of Marcopolo was kept spotless by a troupe of cleaners whom staff members sniffily complained were always waving air fresheners about in the loos while at the same time stinking of BO. But dazzling though it all looked thanks to their endeavours, snags soon began to appear. The all-glass designer lifts got stuck, freeze-framing their embarrassingly visible occupants. There was constant grumbling that the air conditioning never seemed to work and in the heat of the summer the atrium heated up like a giant greenhouse. As the windows did not not open the staff could do nothing but seize gratefully on the fresh drinking water provided in cooled containers. At the IBA building in Brompton Road they had been given free non-stop perculator coffee and all the fresh orange juice they could drink, but this had now been discontinued in favour of vending machines which dispensed plastic cups containing free drinks labelled tea, coffee, and chocolate. Employees moaned they were almost undrinkable. For lunchtime meetings a small in-house kitchen facility provided sandwiches and snacks along with wine, orange juice and Perrier water. Coffee, tea and biscuits could be ordered for other meetings. But one of the most important factors in TV life – serious feeding – was completely uncatered for.

The *Observer*, recognising the need for both a communal eating and social space in such an isolated building, had installed a high-class canteen. But BSB had nothing indoors. Instead a grubby Portacabin, for the use of both staff and outside production companies, was positioned at the side entrance, overlooking the waste ground which by now was supposed to have been transformed into trendy Battersea Wharf. People complained that the food was expensive and inedible, but the only alternative was a fifteen-minute walk to the nearest sandwich joint. In an effort to solve the problem a long saga started rumbling round both the Board and the executive board about installing a canteen on the roof – the only place where there was room. When the cost eventually escalated to nearly £1 million the idea was dropped. Nothing else was ever provided.

The staff's answer was to take to the cabs, and some lunchtimes there were reports of up to 50 vehicles being ordered from the Delta minicab firm which had gratefully received the account. Its Ford Granadas and other vehicles rescued marooned employees to whisk them across the river to expensive restaurants like Zianni's in Chelsea, the Poule au Pot in Pimlico, Langan's in Mayfair, or Signor Sassi in Brompton Road. Desperate memos pleaded with staff to share as a constant series of single occupants emerged from the building, some jabbering into their portable phones, to leap into their individual vehicles and join a virtual BSB convoy. Thanks partly to the example of their seniors, but also due to the vast gulf between their extravagant surroundings and the reality immediately outside the door, cabs soon became the norm, with secretaries taking them as a matter of course to do their shopping at lunchtime.

Many of the staff were not, however, just idly fleeing to eat and drink. The main reason old hands like Gunnar Rugheimer of the Movie Channel had argued for London in the original Chilworth debate was because they knew the importance of being on the circuit. In the TV and film world things were often decided more by who, rather than what, you knew and it was vital to stay in the swim. That was what London was all about. But out in Battersea BSB was cut off from the tight Soho TV circuit revolving around Bertorelli's, Wheeler's, Villa Carlotta, Chez Gerard or L'Escargot and clubs like Groucho's. It was here, through casual meetings and constant rubbing up against other outfits and individuals, that you got deals done, picked up the latest buzz, exchanged the gossip, and generally established a presence on the scene for yourself and your outfit. Even the BBC in Shepherd's Bush was more fortunate. There were several good independent production companies in the area, along with go-ahead outfits like Chrysalis, and nearby were the Metropolitan and Central line tubes to take you direct to the right places.

There were two sides to that part of the equation, as BSB soon found out. It wasn't just a matter of members of staff going places themselves – there was the flip side that people thought twice about fighting their way through the traffic to Marcopolo, especially when the only place to eat was the Portacabin.

Catering was however laid on for the structured activity of ASG's Chief Executive lunches, to which carefully selected members of staff were invited. The idea behind these events was to bring together heads of departments and key personnel to 'interact' round the long table, with ASG in the middle orchestrating the conversation. After a bit of social banter the standard form echoed the meetings of the executive board. Each person introduced themself and gave an update on what they were doing, after which they ate, ASG gave a little spiel, and they all dispersed. The whole process took about an hour. Whilst the staff recognised these occasions as part of ASG's open management style of bringing people together – which they agreed was in theory a good thing – they still did not fight to attend and wriggled uncomfortably, furtively glancing at their watches, until they were released.

The principal reason for their embarrassment was that by the time BSB moved to Marcopolo the management style had become anything but open. Harrassed execs, realising gossip was the only way to keep tabs on what was going on, had by now become dependent on the effectiveness of their secretaries in keeping them informed. In the early days the company had always been political. But then it had been smaller and there had been such enormous joint enthusiasm for the venture it had been easy to feel part of the team. A great feeling of love thy fellow worker had been inspired from the top by ASG's charismatic leadership and his benevolent and caring attitude towards employees. The whole place had been very much like a big family with ASG as its confident and relaxed father, his door always open. Nowadays the stress of being captain of the Good Ship BSB on its increasingly tricky voyage seemed to be getting to him and he did not wear it well. He was becoming more remote and less friendly, and the door was often shut. The result had been hidden agendas springing up everywhere – partly, people felt, because the company had been growing too quickly and with not enough to focus its attention on. ASG had felt this himself and constantly worried about the difficulty of assimilating such a disparate group of people who had been individually headhunted into a team.

The hidden agendas found their focus in another of BSB's trendy decisions, designating Marcopolo a non-smoking building. A few rebels refused to conform and smoked in their offices, occasionally setting off the fire alarms, but there were so many fire drills nobody ever took any notice of them. The only person officially allowed to smoke was David Frost, one of the station's key celebs, and everybody would know when Frostie had been in because of the reek of his cigar along the corridor. ASG had offered to pay for any staff members wishing to quit the filthy habit, with the normal commitment to

THE HOLES IN THE MINT

excellence being demonstrated by choosing as the recommended hypnotherapist Alan Carr, the man who had written the definitive book on giving up.

For those unable or unwilling to do so a smoking room had been provided on the second floor. It was unfortunately located next to the office of Chris McLaughlin, who was a virulent anti-smoker and constantly lobbied to be moved, complaining the ventilation system allowed fumes to seep through to him. Small and sparsely furnished for its utilitarian purpose, it contained three small corner tables, each holding an ash tray, while a dozen chairs hugged the rapidly nicotine-stained walls. The ash trays, although large, were not big enough for the day's intake and always filled to overflowing before the room was cleaned out in the evening, only for late night partiers often to take it over for drinking sessions. The first smoker diving in the next morning would then be faced not just with the smell of stale tobacco but the reek of old beer cans. Even the most addicted and insensitive found the room so disgusting they went outside to light up, joining the group perpetually hanging round the side entrance sipping coffee purchased from TJ's Portcabin.

But horrible though the smoking room was, it soon became the nerve centre of the gossip and rumour machine. Execs with secretaries who smoked would collar them as they came back from their nicotine sorties to get the latest gen and thereby learn many a true story, from important matters like further launch disasters to the secretary who screwed one of the computer people on her desk. (This performance, according to the glossy BSB staff handbook, was deemed 'gross misconduct', and classified as an offence which could lead to summary dismissal without notice. In this particular instance, it was not detected.)

The move to Marcopolo took place in dribs and drabs over a number of weeks and was just starting as the launch delay was announced. Despite the nagging doubts which had gradually grown into certainty, the staff had still been working extremely hard, and their reaction to the announcement varied from relief they would have more time, to disappointment and anger about why, what was wrong, and whether it would ever be right. Now, as they settled into their glittering new surroundings, the summer dragged slowly. Nobody was allowed to spend any money until the techno-trawl was over, and execs found it hard keeping people motivated. Those employed to make or commission programmes, with their budgets now frozen, had little to do except make paper pilots and John Gau found himself bothered by the inactivity. Everything had to be renegotiated and people who had been brought in to work on programmes for independent companies such as his own suddenly had nothing to do. They had to be got rid of.

Every time he drove to work he saw more Sky dishes sprouting on the estates. BSB's job was getting harder by the day and he knew confidence was being lost. It reminded him of the terrible days at the start of Newsnight on BBC2, when union problems meant they all had to sit around for weeks in a basement hospitality room at the BBC Television Centre making pretend programmes. At the appointed hour each night everyone would rush around imitating a real live programme, but they weren't able to put their hearts into it, knowing all the time it was only make believe. The BSB delay had much the same implications, but on a much larger scale.

For Chris Dickens' sales force it was positively awful. There was nothing to say and no new date, except they knew it wouldn't be until after Christmas. Yet he had to sustain the go-getting team he had just put together. He tried to keep them busy in the hope of not losing anybody. The day before the delay announcement Dickens had given a presentation to the prime potential advertiser of Guinness. In the circumstances he hadn't had the heart to go back there, but he now started going through the motions of making pitches to other new clients without giving a start date.

Many of the staff took their holidays, whilst those remaining at work took advantage of being opposite the park. People could be seen wandering around at lunchtime in tennis gear before they departed for the municipal courts. Others just sunbathed. In the office they sat around watching a lot of TV. They rang people up. They lunched. They had to keep BSB high profile, yet there was no money. What else could they do? The answer was, hold meetings.

From its beginning BSB had been a great one for meetings

and now that tendency accelerated as the company grew. The meetings started at the top with the 18-person executive board, which Chris Dickens had quickly realised never decided anything important, and then spread both horizontally and vertically. The management, it now seemed to the more junior members of staff, seemed to spend all its time in continuous meetings, with many individuals apparently frightened of missing them as they were so vital to their power base. Women members of staff commented adversely on the macho attitude that had grown up on the Third Floor where there was great competition for who was wearing the most flamboyant and outrageous tie. The honour, naturally, usually went to ASG, although Andy Birchall neatly upstaged them all with his customary bow. But it was noticed there was one non-participant in these executive games. John Gau simply ignored the whole style contest, wearing dowdy suits and acting in meetings rather as if he was at home, taking off his shoes, putting his feet on the desk, and obviously not caring in the slightest whether he was in vogue or not. Amongst the minions this casual attitude only further served to confirm his guru status.

Many people thought the meetings pointless, and everybody complained about them, but as paranoia built up in the organisation they became a Catch 22. Nearly everybody now felt they had to go to them, and those not invited began to worry they might miss something or – even worse, and much more likely – somebody would take advantage of their absence to talk about them. The only exception was in the technical area, where there was simply so much work to do, involving huge amounts of travel as the different strands were pulled together, that there simply wasn't so much time to waste.

Each different department – operations, engineering, technical, marketing, finance, sales, press, PR, programming – had its own set of meetings with a bewildering array of names. Below these was a plethora of the sub-committees which tended to be formed when a new problem arose. Then there would be pre-meetings to discuss what one would be discussing in the actual meetings, with post-meetings discussing what had come out of them. This was usually nothing. Few things would be decided at the actual meeting itself, as another meeting would then be needed to make a decision about it.

That was just the official agenda. Heaped on top were a dizzying series of private lobbying meetings in which factions secretively met up to ensure they had enough support to carry the proposals they would put forward at the 'real' meetings. Unofficial meetings afterwards conducted endless post-mortems, exhaustively analysing why factions had failed or succeeded. Other furtive gatherings heralded regroupings as people jockeyed for position and realigned themselves. Staff wearily familiar with the labyrinthine organisation of the BBC remarked that even Auntie, with her formidable hierarchies and bureaucracy, could not compare with some of the shenanigans at Marcopolo House.

On top of this came a sea of paperwork. Memos, internal documents and vast tracts of market research about the interface with the GBP descended on desks like confetti. As the tide of meetings swelled, spawning yet more bumf, this was accompanied, BBC-style, by an increasing tendency to initialise. PB was head of the MD, ASG the CE, JG the DP, IC FD and CD SD; NB of BBH interfaced with the GBP to separate ABs and C1s from C2s, Ds and Es. ITT, GI, DBS, DTH, PAL and D-MAC were loaded in from the technical side while BSB itself, under the IBA, took on both the BBC and ITV. The result was a stream of communications in which it sometimes seemed the only words decipherable to an ordinary person would be 'Channel 4'.

The endless meetings put a strain on even the plethora of rooms provided for them which usually had to be booked days in advance. The biggies, along with the big lunches, were held in the third-floor Board Rooms One and Two, which had dividing doors to turn them into one room for the biggest of all. But it was on the second floor that the meetings activity was most concentrated. The most important room there was large, with a big central table and no windows, and called the War Room. Staff thought it felt appropriately like a bunker. According to legend its name sprang from its being where secret programme schedules and plans were kept under lock and key. But really, employees were prone to say, it was so-called because of the continuous violent power struggles which went on inside it.

Flanking the War Room were the other meeting rooms, each

named after the colour of the decor used to break up the otherwise uniform grey, with the natural exception of the Grey Room itself. There was the Blue Room, the Crimson Room, and the Yellow Room, though unfortunately none were marked as such. As they were all equipped with grey exterior doors, for weeks newly arrived lost souls could be seen wandering around vainly searching for the required colour-coding.

But by the beginning of autumn, when everybody was finally ensconced at their posts, the ennui which had been overtaking the organisation began to lift. The 13-week investigation by consultants finally ended. The operations and engineering side, crawling out from the bowels of the various technical operations, pronounced the technology back on an even keel, if not yet actually working. After Graham Grist's abrupt departure extreme caution had characterised the operation as everyone went into 'risk-averse' mode, and there was still no commitment to a firm new launch date. But everyone knew it looked like the spring.

The programmers and the rest of the organisation recognised things could at least start moving again. They settled down at their desks to get on with it, just as the first chills of autumn made them aware that, hot though Marcopolo might have been during the summer, the winter there looked like being a cold one.

CHAPTER ELEVEN

X Certificate

Over at Osterley the Sky executives sat glumly in their nondescript grey boardroom on a sweltering day in late July. In the five months Sky had been on air the initial dearth of dishes in the shops had long since been remedied. But that had only presented the more serious problem that hardly anyone was buying them. All the execs had found the principal reason for this when they embarked on soul-destroying missions to their local High Streets, posing as innocent customers for their new exciting service.

Before launch the advertising agency McCann-Erickson had conducted a survey amongst six retailers – Currys, DER, Dixons, Multi-Broadcast, Radio Rentals and Rumbelows – and concluded they were the biggest potential threat to Sky sales as the information given to potential customers by the retail staff had varied so wildly. One assistant had said a £63 licence fee would be needed, and half of them thought Sky dishes would also be able to receive BSB. Even more depressingly, after all the money spent in the techno-advertising war, four of the six had said they didn't know the difference between PAL and D-MAC. The two claiming they did had then come to the incorrect conclusion that it was PAL that was superior.

Even with Sky up and running, the execs' personal encounters of a retail kind made them want to hurl a dish at the assistants. As they were now moaning to each other, the trade was useless and obviously marooned in a state of hopeless ignorance. Few assistants even appeared to know how many channels Sky had and if the shops were that ignorant, how the hell could they expect a decent response from the public?

The only way out so far had been to give the bloody dishes away through promotions in the News International papers like *Today* and the *Sun*, which were tirelessly flogging Sky to the punters. Endless features plugged such delights as the soaps of General Hospital, the rehashed series The Sullivans, Love Boat, agony aunt Clare Rayner, the Nescafe UK Top 50 roadshow, Bob Warman's The Price is Right and Lifestyle, with a resuscitated David 'Diddy' Hamilton.

Pop DJs like Steve Wright and Kenny Everett chimed in under headlines such as WHY I LOVE MY TELLY DISH, while there was an hour by hour countdown of the lifestyle of Tony Blackburn 'star of Sky By Day'. Other attractions included Love At First Sight (cruelly described by a critic from the Big Papers as 'making Blind Date look like Omnibus'), Chris Tarrant's Secret Video Show, 'catching Britain with its trousers down through embarrassingly silly videos sent in by viewers', and Keith Chegwin's Star Search, a remake of the old Hughie Green Opportunity Knocks, which notably featured Alice Cark from Workington, Cumbria who had appeared unsuccessfully on that programme 25 years earlier. Dressed as a phantom, she performed equally unsuccessfully a song from Phantom of the Opera. Chris Tarrant had a talking budgie.

It was great stuff to beam down to C2land, but unless something was done about the shops it was all to no avail. Rupert Murdoch slipped into the room and took a seat as he listened to the continuing lament. Then he broke in: 'We should be in direct selling.' There was a general titter and one of the execs wisecracked back: 'You mean like brush salesmen?' Murdoch didn't smile back and as he now explained the position they were facing the execs began to realise he was deadly serious. The retail trade had failed them, Murdoch informed them. The shops were staffed by ignorant teenagers who couldn't sell a toaster. So it was up to the station to create its own audience – and the only way to do that was to go and sell itself to people on their doorsteps.

The new strategy which now swung into operation on the back of this was developed in great secrecy and codenamed

Project X after the sci-fi film which had launched the Sky Movie Channel. Pat Mastandrea, the joint managing director, proffered her experience of the States, where cable companies rented out decoder boxes, to suggest that the ideal route was for Sky to direct-sell a rental agreement. After lively discussion it was decided to offer a weekly package at the bargain price of only £4.49 on condition the punters signed up for a year, with the critical sweetener of a two-week free trial with no obligation. Sky's finance department was appalled at this last suggestion. Free trial combined with high incentives to doorstep salesmen would make credit control a nightmare, if it was possible at all.

A huge battle now raged inside the company as the accountants insisted they must have control. To start with their ruling that dishes could not just be given to anyone who asked for them was obeyed, but the resulting response was poor. In the first four weeks just under 200,000 punters expressed interest, but only a disappointing 5% actually signed up. The cautious money men were then overruled and the two-week free trial put into operation. Getting dishes on walls was critical, they were informed, both for subscription and ads, and that was what Project X was about, even if it did turn out to be expensive. It was quite simply a way of buying an audience. Money could either be spent on general advertising, like BSB, or what Sky considered the best form of advertising of all – personal experience – with the aim of reaching what BSB's advertising agency most feared: 'critical mass'. This meant installing dishes in 1 million homes, effectively translating down to one house in twenty, with a dish in every street. The lead up to Christmas was Sky's once and for all chance to achieve it whilst BSB was still floundering in a technological morass. Every Sky dish sold meant one squarial that wouldn't be.

Normally Sky managed its whole operation itself, but Project X was being set up on the run and needed short cuts. The logistics of the operation were enormous. Selling the dishes was just the start. They had to be supplied and, more importantly, properly installed. Although a newspaper story had shown an amateur techno-punter proudly pointing at a dustbin lid he had adapted as a dish, installation was not an activity for even the keenest C2 DIY hobbyist. The 60cm dishes, rising to 90cm in the far north, were unwieldy and heavy. Because planning regulations stipulated they must not show above the roofline they had to be securely screwed on to the brickwork using an industrial-specification angle bracket, with thick black cabling to be run inside the house. Most crucially, they had to be set at the correct angle to receive Astra signal. Maggie Brown, the media correspondent of the *Independent*, had been one of the first to get one and had already chronicled a long catalogue of woe for her Big Paper readers about the horrors of having it installed at her South London home.

So Sky turned to existing sales and installation companies to contract to do the job on its behalf. Companies with names like Startrak, Tele Aerials Satellite, Cranleigh Aerials, Sky Eastern, Caledonian and Nationwide were loaned money to employ staff, train engineers, purchase computers, vans and all the necessary hardware, and then expanded by a factor of ten or twenty times. Meanwhile strange advertisements sporting the Sky logo started appearing in regional papers: 'Teenagers wanted . . . no experience required', they read, promising: 'Full sales training, driving lessons, £3,000 pa . . . If you are aged 16–20 and free call this number . . .' Within days huge 'spotty youth' teams had been built up to hit the estates singing Sky's praises. The results were extraordinary.

Three weeks after the free trial offer began there were 1,000 salesmen on the streets selling Sky dishes, and eventually a waiting list of over 30,000 customers. Business then expanded to the point that Sky could not cope and the speed and success of the operation threatened to become overwhelming. A new office was hurriedly set up in Peterborough to deal with the detailed contractual side of checking the forms, issuing instructions to installers, and devising a whole subscriber management system on the hoof.

Sky had little realised what a Pandora's box it was opening and for the companies subcontracted to do the selling it was an unbelievable bonanza, with millions of pounds being made. Selling door to door contracts meant virtually no overheads to be deducted from the average of £50 commission on each sale, of which about £20 went to the self-employed salesmen. The double-glazing company StormSeal, well versed in the art of getting its foot in the door, set up a new division called 21st Century and moved straight over to selling dishes, so when the bottom dropped out of the double-glazing market the dish arm supported the whole group.

Monitoring this activity the *Independent* newspaper followed a sales team as it set off from The Eight Bells in Putney, fuelled up with Budweiser beer and packets of Silk Cut. The Putney command office, the paper explained, was like a military operation under the direction of area manager James Pringle, who had previously sold ranches in Colorado. His 25 men were now selling 1,000 Sky dishes a week. The individual office record of 216 dishes in one week – meaning over £4,000 in commission – was currently held by a dapper Frenchman, who had previously worked importing his father's wines from Provence. Pringle added that estate agents down on their luck with the crash of the property market were also making good recruits.

The Eight Bells team followed the normal sales policy of drawing up in a busy shopping area with the 'Skybus', a van fitted with a retractable roof-top dish to give on-the-spot demonstrations. When it was found the dish was not working and the screen was blank the team leader took a £10 note out of his wallet and sent one off of the salesmen to buy a video of Robocop at Woolworths. 'Something to put on the screen,' he explained. The *Independent* noted that those lured into the van were not told that they were watching Sky, but not told they were watching a video either. Punters were urged to sign on the dotted line immediately, without any need for credit checks or references, and the shopping area sweep was followed by an afternoon's door-knocking. The concentration was on council estates, searching for the 'me too' effect of other takers having placed their dish on the wall. The salesmen who went door-knocking in gentrified terraces complained they were 'too posh'.

By November an unsuspecting accountant from Bedford, Eric Walke, was being fêted in the *News of the World* and even *The Times* as supposedly Sky's 1 millionth customer in Britain. In actual fact because of the cable market, particularly the large numbers in Ireland, the lucky Mr Walke was more like the 200,000th person to acquire a Sky dish, according to a snide piece in the *Daily Telegraph* – which figure was correct was anybody's guess. But with installations climbing sharply to around 100,000 a month by Christmas, Project X, as BBH feared, was enabling Murdoch to start creeping towards the vital critical mass.

BSB in contrast, still with nothing to sell, had been thrown back on the 'listening station' concept tabled by Nigel Bogle on the soaking Awayday at ASG's house. A defensive memo from Peter Bell attempted to quell any more rebellion by warning: 'The idea is a non-starter if it is embarked on without the total and ongoing support of the programmers. If this is "just an advertising gimmick" it will be exposed as such and lambasted.' Bell tried to muster enthusiasm by informing staff of the marketing possibilities of BSB's advanced technology: 'Individual addressability of all our receiver boxes allows us in theory to wish a subscriber Happy Birthday on his TV only when he switches it on on the appropriate day', he told them brightly, adding that it was not 'the cynical involvement of the consumer in totally trivial issues merely to give us an advertising campaign'.

Instead Bell tried to give an idea of some of the things the GBP might come up with and how they would be dealt with – such as: 'Name your favourite three movies of all time and BSB will screen them (Not possible); During December we'll be screening these 30 great movies. Which would you like to see at 8pm on Christmas Day? (Possible); Which evening would you most like to see live football? (Not possible); Pick your favourite ending to our daily soap (Not possible); What were your favourite Galaxy moments from last week? (Possible) . . .

'Television you can talk to', the memo ended firmly, 'offers the PR man's dream'. Meanwhile Bell was asking the programmers to put forward suggestions that would meet the 'possible' criteria. He was looking forward to seeing some 'terrific ideas'.

The marketing spin had been increased by bringing in the direct marketing group of Christian Brann Ltd which reported under the heading INTERACTIVE POSITIONING that research showed 'customers respond very positively when a big organisation appears to recognise them as important individuals. As organisations get bigger, many of the traditional points of contact are disappearing. How many people know their Bank Manager today? What contact does a housewife have with a supermarket? As a result, when a normally distant and impersonal organisation starts to treat its customers as individuals the response is very positive indeed. You get improved perceptions on service dimensions and you get greater loyalty and higher frequency of purchase into the bargain.'

But when BSB did get in touch with people, Christian Brann warned, it was important who signed the letter and what tone of voice they adopted, as it was vital they had a distinctive BSB personality. 'It is an interesting challenge because this is neither Advertising nor Direct Marketing. It is a business-like communication aimed at forming a personal relationship.'

BBH had summarised what had now become the 'Television With Ears' campaign under flip sheets headed: THE CORE THOUGHT: INVITE THE BRITISH PUBLIC TO BE ACTIVE CONTRIBUTORS TO THE FINAL SHAPING OF BSB. 'We have a vision of a new kind of television station', the sheets read. 'But we want you to help us complete the jigsaw so that we can be sure we have exactly what the British viewer wants in the '90s.' The advertising, BBH stated, 'must bring the Mission Statement to life: innovative, accessible, intelligent, fun, British'. TV with Ears was:

* Interactive, like other media. But unlike television
* Relationship building
* Flattering
* British
* Never been done
* Flexible: consumer, trade, industry
* A long term property

The result was a series of press ads run under the strap YOU WATCH, WE LISTEN which invited the GBP to get in touch by ringing a Freephone number or clipping a newspaper ad. Ads were also run on ordinary TV, creating a new set of subproblems as the terrestrial stations were theoretically rivals and clearance for the content had to be obtained from the ITCA committee, which led to endless negotiation as they scrutinised them suspiciously. The ads fleshed out the old Awayday ideas by devices like listing the choice at 8 pm: BBC1 – Bergerac; BBC2 – Timewatch; ITV – The Best of Magic; Channel 4 – Brookside. 'If you want to watch live sport at 8 pm on a weekday who do you turn to?' it asked.

BBH were pleased with the advertising. Bogle thought it 'high awareness, impactful TV' which stressed what was different about BSB. But inside the company feelings were more mixed. Chris McLaughlin, the press officer, was not a fan and when he had first seen some prototype 'dancing boxes' ads (which never reached the GBP) remarked loudly: 'What wanker produced that?', only to be shushed into silence by anxious juniors reminding him he was standing in an open plan office and that Peter Bell was just across the way.

John Gau was also not happy with them, after being very enthusiastic about the first batch, which BBH thought a shame. The agency had more time for Gau than the other people on the programming side, quite apart from Bogle finding him a very nice man. He knew about the importance of aspects like scheduling which were being stressed by the ads and seemed to be the one programmer who understood marketing and was constructive, rather than feeling threatened or suspicious. Bogle often felt that otherwise he seemed to be dealing with two sets of people – those in marketing who knew nothing about programming, and those in programming who appeared to understand nothing about marketing.

Chris Dickens was equally unimpressed. He felt the role of advertising had never been fully enough debated at the executive board but had become a territorial, strategic and philosophical argument all at once. No long-term communications strategy was ever worked out and there were just kneejerk reactions to both the opposition and changing circumstances. As Dickens saw it, the advertising had developed out of confused briefs and he was bitter that the sales department had not been allowed to take part in the discussions. After a major row with ASG he had it bluntly minuted at an executive board meeting that he did not support the direction it had taken.

Ian Clubb, with his down to earth and aggressive attitude, kept telling ASG the ads should be more brash, vulgar and raucous. They aimed much too high and were much too complicated.

'Maybe', he suggested, 'those writing the copy are too close to us. It's too BBC1ish, drifting even to BBC2.' Privately ASG agreed. Even with his natural flair for the medium he was finding they were struggling. They were always talking about a product that wasn't there – they had to address how to cope with being different, communicating better quality when you couldn't talk about the programming, couldn't say when you were coming, and even what the receiver cost. It was a very difficult journey, he felt, and he was never very happy with the advertising because it kept changing. 'Television With Ears' was a nice idea, but at the same time it was wrong. It should have been run by someone like the BBC. Not that the problem was with BBH – it was with BSB. ASG was a great believer in the old adage that a client gets the advertising he deserves.

BBH was very bullish about the response from the GBP. There were over 100,000 inquiries, and over 20,000 questionnaires sent back. But the results did not contribute much to the sum of either BSB or television knowledge, apart from huge enthusiasm for the BSB trump card of parental control. This device would enable parents to programme the station's output according to cinema classifications so their television blacked out those deemed unsuitable, which 80% of respondents said was important to them. Otherwise, unstartlingly, the GBP confirmed such mundane facts as the most popular time for it to watch a movie was 8pm (40%), followed by 9pm (25%), while first run films were important to 93% and sport to 73%.

On the core idea of getting themselves personally involved with BSB people were more lukewarm. The most interest was shown in participating in a movie quiz, with a 50/50 split. But only 34% of the questionnaire respondents, who were by their very nature more responsive than the rest of the GBP, were interested in sending in questions. On sport 80% not surprisingly agreed it was most exciting and interesting when it was live, but only just over 50% welcomed the Bell-inspired idea of fans joining the experts to commentate. Then only 29% said they would like to be involved personally. More – 39% – were interested in being a contestant on a game show.

As for BSB coming to see them, only 20% were 'very interested' in hosting a BSB roadshow in their street/workplace/school/pub, with an equal 20% 'not at all interested'. There was a subsidary blow for arts programmes on theatre, opera and ballet, which ASG was so bullish about as one of BSB's quality cards. Only 30% were 'very interested'.

While 'TV With Ears' struggled through the autumn to maintain a public façade of convincing activity and build up database facts for the computers to do the real work of communicating with the GBP, Ian Clubb was grappling with a more fundamental problem. Even if no one yet knew when it would launch, the Good Ship BSB must now raise a huge amount more money just to stay afloat financially as the second planned round of financing had been put on ice following the launch delay. The money-raising show was put back on the road.

Until this point BSB's funds of £423.5 million had been raised in a conventional fashion, with each shareholder chipping in their percentage. First there had been the initial expected amounts and then the extra needed because of the escalation in the price of the films, meaning Round 1 financing being complemented first by Round 1b and then Round 1c. These extra calls had only exacerbated the difficulties arising from the worsening position of the major shareholder, Alan Bond, whose stake had risen to 36.9% when he had bought Virgin's shares at the start of the year. The IBA, bending over backwards to help, had temporarily waived the rule limiting holdings in BSB to 20% for non-EEC nationals. The chairman, Sir Trevor Holdsworth, described Bond as a 'bright sign-writer', referring to his origins as a Perth sign painter, but bright or not he was slipping further and further into trouble. His financial crisis in Australia had become public knowledge mainly as a result of an attempt to take over Lonrho, owners of the *Observer*, BSB's next-door neighbour at Marcopolo, who then brought it to the attention of the world. The head of Lonrho, Tiny Rowland, had fought Bond off by investigating his affairs and producing a damning report which described him as 'the South Sea Bubble of Debt'. Despite his glorious facade he owed A$14,000 million and was what accountants describe as 'technically insolvent'. Rather than the reported profits of A$400 million in the past year, Lonrho's estimate was a A$300 million loss.

Bond had spent little time on BSB, making only rare appearances at the Board, and usually sending a sidekick instead. On one occasion his pleasant daughter, Jody, attended in his place, much to the interest of the other Board members. But the first time he did come himself he had an electrifying effect. In April 1989, not long after Sky had started, he showed up at the New Connaught Rooms where the Board was meeting that day and when discussion turned to strategies for dealing with the competition, made a bold proposal. BSB should announce that when it launched it would give away its dishes and receiving equipment for nothing. That, he declared, would kill the opposition. It was a daring idea, but rather too adventurous for his fellow directors.

(As some of them were to observe ruefully rather later on, with the amount spent on marketing they could have given away the dishes and still had plenty of cash to spare.)

After that intervention Bond had hurriedly disappeared Down Under to deal with a crisis in his media affairs there, soon made worse for him and BSB by the Australian Broadcasting Tribunal ruling him unfit to hold a broadcasting licence and calling into question his ownership of the prestigious Channel Nine. Two unfortunate skeletons emerged concerning an alleged pay off to the Premier of Queensland, Sir Joh Bjelke-Petersen, and an incident where Bond had threatened to use Channel Nine journalists to dig up dirt on a business opponent. The fabulous house of cards he had constructed with other people's money was collapsing and although he might have achieved fame by paying $54 million for Van Gogh's painting Irises, like every other purchase of his it had been made with borrowed money, this time from the auctioneers, Sotheby's. When the accounts to June 1989 were published Lonhro's estimate was proved more than correct. Bond had made a loss of A$980 million, while his annual interest bill had doubled to around A$1,000 million.

Bond's financial chaos was alarming the rest of the BSB Board. Every time his payments were due his people were ready with excuses, yet it now looked inconceivable he would be coughing up the serious money demanded by Round 2. But every penny that did not come from him would have to be found from somewhere else and the shareholders well knew if they failed to find other investors to replace him they would have no choice

– severally or jointly they would have to take the extra burden upon themselves.

Before Clubb arrived there had been much grand talk about the Good Ship BSB being floated on the Stock Exchange, as a major British institution with parallels being drawn with the Channel Tunnel. Senior execs were offered share options on joining which had the potential of being very lucrative on the great day, like ASG's theoretical possibility of becoming a virtual millionaire overnight. Drawing once again on the good offices of Sir Trevor Holdsworth, the company had already persuaded the Stock Exchange to waive the normal rule which forbade a listing until a company had been formed for more than five years. In September 1988 it had then announced it intended to go public before the end of 1989 and some of the Big Papers had speculated that Clubb's appointment confirmed this. But in fact he was thinking exactly the opposite and that the equity funding idea was lunacy as it would dilute the shareholders' current control.

Clubb was now proposing a quite different route to fund BSB's future. His experience in his oil days had convinced him of the advantages of raising money from banks against specific projects. He had used this highly specialised route to raise vast sums, starting with £100 million for Thomson's North Sea Claymore field in the late 70s through to Australian $1.65 billion for Woodside Petroleum in the early 80s. BSB, he now thought, should ideally opt for the same approach. Clubb had no illusions about what he was doing. As the banks would be taking a risk, they would lend the money at a higher rate of interest than normal, with myriad clauses and conditions attached. As ASG said, they'd only lend you an umbrella on a sunny day. But the quid pro quo was that they would have limited recourse against BSB's assets, or those of the shareholders' main companies, if it all went wrong. It was easier with oil and gas because technical people could scientifically agree on the size of a strike and the likely yield, but the huge amounts of market research on BSB and its theoretical audience provided a substitute.

Asking about in the company Clubb found nobody who knew anything about the idea, mainly because they had been so fixated on equity funding. So to test his theory he went back to the City and explained what he had in mind to his old project loan contacts. Their initial reaction was to tell him they thought he was mad. But as Clubb used to tell people, it wasn't his bonny blue eyes that got them to commit, but his record built up during successful past deals. By the time he had shown his contacts at Barclays the business plan plus optimistic financial projections based on the market research and talked them through it, they had decided it was perhaps not such a wild idea after all. Convinced, Barclays then agreed to take the lead in finding other banks to form the first stage of the group which would eventually underwrite the loan.

Clubb produced a memorandum outlining BSB's requirements and organised a series of presentations to persuade other bankers to part with their money. Large numbers of them, along with teams of consultants, now started turning up at Marcopolo House to crawl all over the company. The consultancy firm Arthur D Little, on behalf of their client Barclays, made lengthy enquiries and concluded that although the business plan was a little over-optimistic, basically it was a sound and worthwhile project. Clubb himself, feeling like a commercial traveller in the City, went round drumming up more interest. After Barclays had looked the scheme over he knew he needed some others pretty quickly to make the approach more credible to the financial community. Again he leant on old contacts and soon pulled in two more banks he had worked with in the past, NatWest and the Industrial Bank of Japan. By the end of the underwriting process the total had risen to six.

These banks were in turn looking to share the risk and commitment, and in addition to specifying a series of conditions and crucial performance targets they insisted BSB must match pound for pound the £450 million of the loan. Clubb, reluctant to turn again to the long-suffering shareholders, decided to explore a quite different route. Looking once again to his old City contacts he went to the American investment bank Shearson Lehman, proposing that the remaining funding should be raised in the US through high yielding securities, otherwise known as junk bonds, the market pioneered by the notorious Michael Milken, operating out of the Beverly Hills office of Drexel Burnham.

As their name implied, high yielding securities were a form of borrowing where the lender accepted greater than normal risks in exchange for better interest rates. In the 80s they were most spectacularly used by corporate raiders like Sir James Goldsmith or Asher Edelman who, pledging the assets of their prey, raised junk bonds to finance their attack. But originally they were devised as a means of financing risky expansion and investment which could not attract more conventional sources of funding. Rupert Murdoch had successfully used this route to raise more than $1 billion to expand Fox TV, with an offer document for the issue believed to have been the longest ever issued on Wall Street.

That had been back in March 1986, just as the junk bond market was taking off, and by 1987 Milken's success meant junk bonds represented a quarter of the entire US corporate bond market and he personally earned $550 million. But as with so many events, starting with ASG's arrival on Black Monday, BSB had got its timing wrong. By the autumn of 1989, when Clubb hired Shearson's on a retainer of £100,000 a month, the greed decade was drawing to its close and the junk bond market giving its final gasp. Within a few months Michael Milken was under arrest and Drexel Burnham in the doldrums.

Anyhow, by then the shareholders decided there was no longer any point in side-stepping the issue. Why not bite the bullet and take the alternative way to obtain the matching funds by agreeing to a guaranteed facility? Standing down Shearsons and the junk bond option, Clubb suggested the shareholders pledged the assets of their own companies in the form of guarantees as security. That way the shareholders would underwrite the second £450 million, each receiving proportionately more BSB shares in exchange. They readily accepted and on 23 January, 1990 BSB publicly announced it had raised the money to fund Round 2.

There was one further hiccup. Because of the extraordinary size of the commitment the Stock Exchange imposed its rule that shareholder approval must be sought, as the aggregate potential liabilities exceeded 25% of the companies' average net profits over the last three years. Pearson, Reed and Granada all had to hold extraordinary general meetings, with only Chargeurs, being French, not subject to the ruling. Jangling nerves were not improved by Graham Grist, the company's first employee, appearing in person at the Granada meeting. He rose to his feet to challenge the statement that there was no material legal action pending by pointing out he was currently in pursuit of a claim for breach of contract which was to be successful after he claimed assurances given to him had not been honoured.

But Reed and the others still managed to write reassuringly to their largely unaware shareholders outlining their corporate wisdom: 'Your board has concluded that BSB is an investment with potential for high growth and for the creation of significant value,' Chairman Peter Davis informed them. Reed's participation in the further funding of BSB is in the best interests of Reed shareholders.' Old ladies in Harrogate and retired colonels in Bognor were mightily reassured, and Reed's potential exposure of £112.5 million smoothly endorsed. Naturally if all the various shareholders came in to share the load Reed's liability would lighten to only £45 million, but that was looking less and less likely – especially in Alan Bond's case. As the moment of commitment passed BSB was rapidly shaking down to the Big Four of Pearson, Granada, Reed and Chargeurs.

On 28 February the loan was finally agreed, with Clubb and his team working through the night at the City offices of Warburgs, who were advising the shareholders. They preferred working there to the offices of Lazards, BSB's merchant bank, as the food was better. Lazards, who also came under the Pearson umbrella, were not offended. They were anticipating a cool £3 million fee for their efforts in arranging the funding.

But the work was still not over. With the shareholders safely on board the bank loan now had to be syndicated so the load could be shared between a greater number of banks. Waves of more presentations and consultations followed. Over 200 bankers from all over the world came to a special two day session during which they were taken by coach to visit the Chilworth uplink. Then, in batches of ten, they toured the wonders of Marcopolo and inspected the impressive studios. On day two, with Clubb in the chair, there were a series of presentations by the senior executives at the Cumberland Hotel.

The 'dog and pony show', as ASG called it, using a popular American expression, went on and on. The five senior executives of ASG, Gau, Clubb, Bell and Dickens toured the City endlessly talking to shareholders' boards, bankers and investors. Gau said his presentation on BSB's programming plans was so familiar he could do it in his sleep. He had long since given up using notes. Even when the loan was completed the nightmare was not over. Clubb was warning that presentations would have to continue as the backers needed continuous reassurance.

Occasionally the roadshow had its lighter moments. Travelling to the City for a lunchtime presentation to a Japanese bank, Bell mused to the others that at least there was the enticing prospect of dining on delicious sushi. But when they arrived he found to his dismay that the Japanese had gone to great lengths to honour their Western television guests by laying on roast beef and Yorkshire pudding. Bell rolled his eyes at his colleagues as he tucked in.

Unfortunately when the loan was finally syndicated once again the Good Ship BSB was found to have been left high and dry by the tide of events. By then it was the turn of the regular banking sector to be in the doldrums and only a disappointing ten further banks agreed to enter the syndication. Neverthless City types and analysts looked on in awe. To sustain the confidence to raise such a loan had been an astonishing achievement by Clubb and his team given all BSB's other difficulties – never mind the tricky matter of Bond wanting out which hung over everything and, as ASG said, made him like a loose cannon.

In Marcopolo House too there was a growing sense of confidence in the future. Now with £1.3 billion in committed funds, and the shareholders in it up to their necks, BSB had the financial muscle to last for three years. By that time, the charts and research proved, it would be in profit. The shareholders, despite now contemplating the second largest private financing ever raised in Britain, remained hands-off.

CHAPTER TWELVE

Chicken Noodle

John Stapleton turned off the A4 at Gillette corner, drove past the untidy sign proclaiming the wares of the Centaurs Business Park, and swept down what he called 'Osterley's Avenue of the Stars'. Passing the nondescript warehouses which contained a mixed selection of light industry he caught the familiar whiff of the hot dog stand as he approached the Sky barrier, or Checkpoint Charlie as he knew it. Stapleton always joked that the legendary security guards had come as a job lot with the fall of Eastern Europe and they were known to everyone in the office as a branch of the dreaded Wapping Securitate. Spoof memos, with a fake signature 'Ken Crouch – Securitate Manager', regularly sprang up on the office noticeboards saying things like: 'On Thursday units of the Osterley Securitate carried out a controlled explosion on a vehicle that was parked in the red zone of the Sky Car Park. Let this be a lesson to those members of staff who are preventing us from carrying out our task of making Sky a pleasant place to work in.'

Once into the compact car park there was further evidence of the heavy hand of the Securitate with the 'sleeping policemen' speed bumps. These had been constructed to such height and ferocity they frequently tore the exhaust pipes off crew cars loaded down with equipment. Even ordinary private cars had been damaged, leading to a spate of heavy claims, and financial and security interests were at present in conflict over their fate.

Easing his way over the sleeping Securitate, Stapleton parked his black Jaguar XJ6 and made for the building called Unit 6, which he knew as Cell Block 6. In the year since he had first entered the chaotic muddy site things had much improved. There were now chairs, desks and proper phones and no longer did the buildings, now resplendent in bright primary school colours, remind him of a local DHSS Office. Even the robot canteen had been supplemented by the occasional human being from a contract catering service. There had been changes right at the top as well. Since the New Year Murdoch himself had come across from America to move into the driving set of the Skyship Enterprise. To the relief of the other execs, the company's chief loudmouth Andrew Neil had gone back to his day job editing the *Sunday Times*. It was an indication of the serious drain Sky was making on the Empire's resources that the Boss wanted to be there for the period when BSB would finally hit the airwaves. And, as Stapleton noticed, he was very hands-on, even making regular morale-boosting appearances in the canteen, where he liked mucking in with the rest of the blokes.

But Stapleton still shuddered whenever he thought back to his first programme, which had appropriately gone out live on 1 April. After finally accepting Ben Hawke's offer to present Newsline, the job Andrew Neil had offered to Jeremy Paxman, he had started work on that date. Scheduled as a thrice weekly half-hour current affairs programme, in true Sky style it was to go live the same evening with no pilot or rehearsal. An hour before transmission Stapleton had looked round the studio to see men with plugs crawling across the floor, still building it. The set itself reminded him of the inside of a Samsonite suitcase and the whole place had an unreal toytown atmosphere. Everyone was rushing round to get the show on air, whilst nobody knew if a single person out there was actually watching. If his audience got any smaller, Stapleton used to tell people, he'd be locked up for talking to himself.

But whether anyone was watching or not, what had never ceased to fascinate and terrify him was the way the operation seemed permanently to teeter on the brink. On that first evening about a third of the programme was to be a live interview with the Health Secretary, Kenneth Clarke. But there had then been last-minute confusion. Even though he was a highly experienced broadcaster, Stapleton had begun to suffer creeping anxiety and chain-smoke even more furiously than usual. Here he was, presenting the first programme of a new show on a new station, yet if Clarke did not show he would have an eight-minute hole and nothing to fill it. Clarke's appearance was finally confirmed ten minutes before they went on air.

The Clarke drama had been only the start of it. Night after night there had been excruciating moments as communications failed, sound disappeared, or guests never made it. The overall effect of Newsline was supposed to be like BBC2's Newsnight. But although the production team was young and ambitious the programme was made on less than a fifth of the BBC's staffing levels and resources, and inevitably it showed. Still Stapleton had to admire the dedication and hard work that went into it – made even more remarkable by its being believed that the audience across the whole country was sometimes only in three figures.

But occasionally he winced as the whole fragile edifice fell apart, like the memorable four-way foreign affairs discussion between Glasgow, Westminster, Washington and Bonn. First the sound from George Robertson MP in the Glasgow studio failed and never returned, reducing the discussion to tripartite talks. Then Defence Secretary George Younger in Westminster suddenly wafted off into the ether. Stapleton, watching him disappear without even a chance to say goodbye, was now left with an American Senator in Washington and a German academic in Bonn, both of whom totally agreed with each other on every single point. Meanwhile he had 12 more minutes to spin out. 'Could you just expand a little on that . . .' he heard himself endlessly repeating.

Then there had been the agonising countdown to transmission as they all waited for the former Treasury Minister, Lord Bruce-Gardyne, to turn up for a live interview. An enterprising cabbie had refused to believe the shabby Centaurs industrial estate could house something as important as a television station and instead dropped his distinguished fare at a place called Osterley House several miles away. Just as they were going on air the veteran politician rang in from a phonebox demanding to know what was happening. A rescue mission was mounted and Bruce-Gardyne was quietly eased into the studio with the programme already going out.

Stapleton recognised that in any outfit live television was subject to cock-ups, but other systems had slack built in to cope with it, like a stand-by film which could always be relied on as a filler. At Sky there was no slack at all. Every evening he could sense the show going live on a wing and a prayer and when it finished at 10pm would always heave a deep sigh of relief before discretely inviting his studio guests into a small nearby room for a surreptitious drink. After a 12-hour working day, with its inevitable stomach-churning moments, he felt it was much deserved.

The problem Stapleton had formerly faced was that Sky did not believe in the customary television hospitality because it cost money, and anyhow the standard Murdoch drinking ban positively forbade it. When he first arrived Stapleton had been amazed that guests who made the arduous journey to Osterley were not even offered the equivalent of a glass of BBC plonk. Persuading anyone to appear was difficult enough anyhow without being inhospitable into the bargain. Sometimes all they could get was a succession of junior MPs using Sky as a cheap form of television training. Eventually Ben Hawke, as his boss, had agreed something must be done and obtained an unofficial blind eye towards Newsline drinking, providing it was tightly controlled. Once the guests had left, the glasses and cheap wine had to be returned to a locked cupboard in the Newsline office. But, as officially drinking did not take place there were no waiters to do the job and, night after night, Stapleton found himself carrying dirty glasses and empty and recorked bottles back from the studio area to Cell Block 6.

In spite of all this, though, he was enjoying himself. Sometimes the ambitious plans came off, the output was not at all bad, and there was an atmosphere of youthful optimism and energy, as if the spirit of Neighbours stalked the corridors. He liked the intimacy of the station and the way that decisions which in the BBC would require endless meetings, committees, and referrals were here made almost instantly. Sky gave no sign of containing a celestial Sun but seemed to be making a serious attempt to be a Europeanised version of CNN in America. When it had been launched as a 24-hour news channel in the early 80s CNN had been derisively nicknamed 'Chicken Noodle News', but over the years had matured into a relatively serious news operation.

Stapleton's misgivings about working for Murdoch had also been allayed. There was no heavy editorial hand and they had even attempted subjects disparaging of the Empire. After the Hillsborough stadium football disaster at which 95 Liverpool fans had been tragically crushed to death the *Sun* had run an outrageous smear story, but Newsline had covered the story of Liverpool's outrage without the Boss intervening. When Stapleton looked at the overall output it seemed surprisingly free from bias. Murdoch, especially now that he was around more, might ring up the newsdesk to criticise and complain, but not to exert unwarranted editorial pressure. During the violent London poll tax riots smoke billowed round the window of his St James's flat and he called the newsroom demanding to know why Sky News was not screening live coverage from Trafalgar Square, then he might send a note to Norman Tebbit telling him to be nastier on the Target show, but that was all perfectly understandable and far from heavy-handed.

Stapleton had the impression that somehow Murdoch was running the News channel to settle a few old scores. It was designed to lay the ghost of the *Sun*, although occasionally youth and enthusiasm overcame sound judgement. Screechy-voiced secretaries from ITN became reporters, leading to an abundance of clichés and solecisms. There was neither the time nor the manpower to write decent prose across all the 24 hours of the day. More seriously, when Salman Rushdie had gone into hiding after being sentenced to death by Muslim fundamentalists for his book, *The Satanic Verses*, Sky stupidly showed his young son playing in a street which was easily identifiable. The Cable Authority feebly berated such irresponsible behaviour. Some of the lightweight presenters made regular and sometimes excruciating errors and alert viewers could watch them listening as the producer shouted each question into their ear-piece, presumably because they were regarded as incapable of conducting an interview without this sort of heavy prompting.

Stapleton had also watched with some amusement the gradual overcoming in the newsroom of what the more sensible ex-BBC and ITN types knew as 'the Wapping tendency'. This had been personified by Nick Ferrari, one of the brighter sparks brought across from the Sun, with a family background in enterprising print journalism. Not fully conversant with television, Ferrari had been full of ideas for stories of a Sun-type nature, unaware that some bollocks which could be flammed up for a tabloid would look pathetically thin on television. Eventually he had begun to grasp that in television news editing was all about meticulous planning and organisation. On a tabloid someone would manufacture in their head the sort of scam story the editor liked and then brief a reporter to get it one way or another. At the Sun Kelvin MacKenzie had called all copy 'crap' and 'bollocks', and constantly driven reporters and sub-editors to increase 'the spin' on actual events. But in television, even if you wanted to act like that, to cover anything you had to consider how you got pictures. That meant you needed a camera crew and all their equipment. Unless there was time to return to base the story had to be edited somewhere on location. Then it had to be 'fed' from a suitable 'feed point' along Telecom lines, which needed specially booking in advance. And if there was to be any live broadcasting the right satellite gear and other communications equipment had to be taken along as well. It might all look effortless when it hit the screen, but Ferrari soon began to realise the logistics of television were often a nightmare.

When he had arrived at Sky he had decided it needed plenty of the Sun staple of crime and hired a succession of specialist crime reporters, traditionally the pits even by Fleet Street standards. Some had only lasted a week as Ferrari's visions of dramatic reconstructions and live footage of villains and coppers on the job faded into the reality of lengthy pieces to camera outside the Law Courts or the visual bottom line of the revolving Scotland Yard sign. Over the months he became increasingly frustrated with the endless nitty-gritty of television journalism. Trying to sort out a story about a charity concert, he complained to a colleague it was all such a bore. If he'd been on the Sun he would have made it all up and written it by the time the crew had got out of the door – or at least over the sleeping Securitate in the car park. The TV hacks were not impressed by such sentiments. As relationships soured they wrote memos complaining about his incompetent news editing, whilst Ferrari retaliated by calling them 'lovies' as he sneered at their ignorance of the harder end of Fleet Street.

The irony of the Sun input into Sky News was not lost on TV hacks aware of how the roles of newspapers and television had switched over the last 20 years. The switch was one Rupert Murdoch himself had accurately forseen and capitalised on when he started the Sun. At that point people still used to look to their newspapers for news, and their television for entertainment. Now, at least in C2land, and mainly thanks to Murdoch's papers, that position had been reversed. Sun readers called their paper 'The Comic', whilst the comedian Jasper Carrott thrived on endless jokes about them. Ferrari, firmly on the entertainment side of the fence, had tried items on Barbie Dolls and singing AA men before falling back helplessly on the old standby of animal stories, which supposedly straddled both ends of the business. (An animal story – a film of a skate-boarding duck – was already legendary within the industry for doing for BBC Nationwide's claim to be a serious current affairs show.) As a result one hapless cameraman spent what he later decided was the silliest moment of his professional life when Ferrari sent him to cover National Pet Week and he arrived at a stills photocall to find it consisting of two dogs, a rabbit and a hedgehog. Ferrari had more success when he arranged for a Rottweiler to appear live in the studio.

Classic tabloid techniques also gave him a moment of glory when he persuaded the comedian Ken Dodd to do an exclusive interview after being acquitted on tax evasion charges. After Dodd had been hunted down to the Liverpool hotel he was hiding out in Ferrari phoned him and told him he represented the US network NBC. The interview would be broadcast across the States, he told him. When the King of the Diddymen then agreed to an exclusive Ferrari slammed down the phone triumphantly, announcing: 'We turned that one over!' Eventually he was moved upstairs until Murdoch offered him the job of vice-president of the Fox station in New York. Well chuffed, he flew off to become, with his blond good looks, what a colleague described as 'the Dan Quayle of Fox TV'.

Stapleton had shared the general relief at his departure and with the tabloid influence erased Sky News was now delivering a standard, workmanlike product on a fraction of the resources of the BBC or ITN. The comparisons were extraordinary. At major structured news events like summits and conferences the BBC would turn up with hordes of correspondents, producers, camera crews and assorted fixers. Sky personnel always came at the last moment with the absolute minimum of people, who then proceeded to work all hours feeding the neverending cycle of bulletins. During the June 1989 disturbances in China and the Tiannamen massacre most of the networks sent at least a dozen people. Sky sent just two – one responsible for producing, directing and reporting while the other quadrupled up as cameraman, sound recordist, picture editor, and engineer. At Westminster, where the BBC and ITN employed large teams of journalists in series of offices for their lobby activity, Sky originally had four representatives, who for a long time operated from a couple of regional ITV editing booths.

As a result the station sometimes spread itself so thin it was unable to deliver. But on other occasions lean and mean translated into small and unencumbered by bureaucracy, combined with the winning card of flexible scheduling and light footwork. John O'Loan, the Head of News, used to liken getting the BBC to respond to trying to turn the *Queen Mary*, whereas Sky News was sometimes in a better position to react quickly. The point was proved by the release from prison of Nelson Mandela. Both BBC and ITN had cleared their Sunday schedules to cover the story live at the appointed time of 1pm. But it was late and after spending an hour filling in with insignificant interviews and studio discussion by talking heads they gave up and went back to their normal Sunday afternoon fare. When Mandela did eventually emerge a major internal row in ITV finally ended with a brief news flash being inserted into the feature film, which had started. Sky News simply cleared the whole afternoon and returned to South Africa for extended live coverage of the entire story.

It was on occasions like these, when it came up trumps, that Murdoch was proud of his fledgling service and grateful for it. Its audience might be below 5% of Sky's already modest total and therefore scarcely measurable; it might be costing a fortune; but it was playing a vital role in the Sky's four channel constellation.

John Carmody, the distinguished TV critic of the *Washington*

Post, had observed about Murdoch's American operation: 'Fox won't be taken seriously until it has its own news and current affairs. News is an expensive, low-profit business but it distinguishes one network from another'. In Britain, as some outsiders had realised, Sky News did more, drawing the fire of the critics and giving the overall station an entirely different perspective. News was the clothes on the nude. Without it the station was barely more than some films, a few tired old soaps, turgid sport and yards of American rubbish.

The result showed in Sky News' relationship with the Labour Party, where things had moved on from the sacking of Austin Mitchell and a Shadow Cabinet discussion at which even the respectable and moderate Labour MP John Smith had advocated non-cooperation. Officially there was still a determination to seek a referral to the Monopolies and Mergers Commission, but on a day-to-day basis party members had no problem in co-operating. A few hardcore left-wingers like Arthur Scargill and Dennis Skinner still refused to appear, but their number was diminishing. There had also been an amusing conversion at the 1989 Labour Party Conference in Brighton when a Sky reporter asked Tony Benn for an interview, but was refused. An enterprising young sound recordist had then run after Benn to explain she had been one of the TV-am strikers who had been locked out for months. The launch of Sky had given her a job. 'You talk to TV-am these days, so why won't you talk to Sky?' she asked, posing a comradely dilemma. Benn had thought for a moment and then changed his mind and agreed to the interview.

In the media feeling against Murdoch was much stronger in newspapers than in television. Opprobrium had reached a high point with the move of News International's titles to Wapping in January 1986, abruptly ending 5,000 print workers' jobs. Although there was scant sympathy for the printers, who had shamelessly held newspaper managements to ransom for years, there had still been widespread shock at the brutal and ruthless way the operation had been carried out. Not just journalists, but others concerned about standards, had also bemoaned the way papers like *The Times* and the *Sunday Times* had been degraded after Murdoch had taken them over, leading to a wholesale exit of talented staff.

There were many things to complain of about Murdoch, including the Sun's coarse enthusiasm for the lager lout culture evinced by Harry Enfield's yobbish 'Loadsamoney' and general support for the nasty and brutal side of Thatcherism. Currently most anger was being directed at the Sun and the News of the World for their leading role in the new 'bonk' journalism which crucified celebs and public figures by printing searing details of their sexual peccadillos. But on this front again, when Sky's overall output was analysed, there did not seem to be undue cause for alarm.

Before Sky had been announced the 1987 Edinburgh Television Festival had considered the theme 'Television Fights Back', with one speaker ominously warning: 'The changing ecology of television means the furry woodland beasts may have to become lizards'. Leading luminaries like Melvyn Bragg and Michael Grade had then warned of the end of the 'golden age' of British TV. In October 1988, four months after the announcement of Sky, the terrestrial station of TVS had raised an even more ghastly spectre with newspaper adverts headed: ITALIAN HOUSEWIVES DO IT ON TV. These explained how standards had dived since Italian television had been effectively deregulated in 1981. As always advertising revenue had been spread more thinly, so each channel had less money to spend on programmes, whilst at the same time good programming sparked off furious auctions, with prices spiralling. Pointing out that the biggest savings could be made by scrapping the highest quality material, it asked what could be cheaper than home-made videos of saucy housewives stripping off?

(The ad, did however fail to mention another consequence of deregulation, the Vatican channel of Lumen 2000, created to transmit Papal messages, spiritual exercises for bishops and priests, sermons to the faithful, and evangelical programmes for the unconverted.)

The satellite broadcaster Filmnet which broadcast steamy stuff, scrambled, had sparked off an enterprising trade in pirate decoders. Meanwhile the Home Office and the Whitehall committee on broadcasting were flinching at this unwanted example of the new freedom of the airwaves they were supposedly in favour of. Much agonising about how to combine the light regulatory touch with keeping this stuff out had reached no satisfactory solution beyond thinking of ways to penalise advertisers. There was now increasing fear amongst the bureaucrats that it would inevitably arrive here sooner or later.

But on this front Murdoch was giving them no worries. Rather the reverse – he was positively leaning over to help and abide by as many regulations and codes as he could find, setting an example to all. Sky Movies had gone so far as screening the comparatively mild Emmanuelle IV, against the prurient wishes of him as Boss, before he ordered withdrawal from the brink; he had made sure Sky offered to let the British Board of Film Classification review its output; he had even voluntarily agreed the station would abide by the code of Lord Rees-Mogg's Broadcasting Standards Council, in contrast to many mainstream broadcasters who deeply resented it as an interference with their freedom and grumbled about it loudly.

On the porn front it was in fact BSB, with the help of the Murdoch media, that got into trouble after it picked up on a 30 minute magazine show being launched in America, which, the buzz said, was very sexy. It was based on purporting to show what went on in France – 'We go to a French nightclub ... we meet a man who used to make personalised chairs by taking plastic moulds of people's bottoms ...' To illustrate this point the naked bottom of an extremely attractive model then appeared on screen. Execs who saw it judged it crass but not excessive, and not porn, just titillating. Negotiations started to do a deal with the American company of IBS, which then disclosed what was going on to Fleet Street. PORN FROM SPACE, Murdoch's *Today* newspaper splashed gleefully, and BSB withdrew.

Murdoch had always shown a great interest in Christianity though he denied being born again. Harking back to his strong Presbyterian genes, his paternal grandfather had been Moderator-General of the Church in Australia, while his maternal grandmother had been a great gambler, both pointed to as keys to his character by those seeking the motivation that drove him. One of his contributions when he took over the mantle of chief executive from Andrew Neil had been to introduce a religious programme. Sky One already featured each Sunday 'The Hour of Power', broadcast from the church of the Protestant Reverend

Schuller, broadcasting from his crystal cathedral in Orange County, California. Eager for more of this sort of thing the Boss called Clifford Longley, the distinguished and very serious *Times* religious correspondent, into his Wapping office for a chat. Murdoch's first plan was for something along the lines of the tele-evangelism which was so popular in the States, but Longley argued this was inappropriate for Britain. Instead a discussion programme with an ethical and religious emphasis was devised in which a protagonist put forward a case and two opponents then tried to knock it down. Called Challenge, it would be hosted by Longley once a month and feature controversial topics like women priests or animal rights which were much discussed in the Big Papers. Initially rather nervous of Sky's trite tabloid stereotype, Longley found himself pleasantly surprised when he actually started at Osterley. He was not even discouraged from using long words or expressing complicated ideas. No one, he thought, could call Challenge tabloid telly.

There was also little sign of that other horror currently being decried by the Big Papers, the new American phenomenon of Trash TV. David Frost, revolted by it and not fitting into its raunchy format, had been fired from his £500,000 a year job as anchorman of the show Inside Edition, one of the so-called 'current affairs' shows descending to gruesome depths of titillation. Trash, labelled in the trade 'reality programming' or 'non-fiction TV', was a straightforward plunge into re-enactments of deaths and murders, death row interviews with mass murderers, and 'investigations' into sleazy subjects like transexual clubs, devil worship, lesbian mothers and sex surrogates. The consequent public uproar had been so strong it had merited cover features in both *Time* and *Newsweek*.

Murdoch's Fox had been sucked in through its programme A Current Affair, an unashamedly televised tabloid in a tradition going back to the Victorian penny dreadfuls. Its most famous episode had shown a home-made video of a murderer just before his conviction for strangling his victim in Central Park in which he had joked about the death and twisted the head off a doll as he spoke. Fox also produced The Reporters and America's Most Wanted, a lurid recreation of rapes, murders and stabbings using freeze frames and 'slo-mo'.

The trash phenomenon, blamed on the short-term scrambling for audience figures, had thrown up personalites such as Geraldo Rivera, a former investigative reporter who had made a new name for himself with a live film of the opening of Al Capone's vault. Even though it was found to be empty, it had sent the ratings through the roof.

Rivera had since gone undercover to take part in a drugs deal, stripped off to interview nudists, and most famously had his nose broken with a chair when a fight erupted in the studio during a live programme he was chairing, entitled Young Hate-Mongers. Joining him in the trash stable was Morton Downey Jr, who ran his shows iike prizefights with the audience baying for blood, and chain-smoked as he spat sarcasm at guests. Downey had been hauled into court for slapping a gay activist on his show and shouting at him: 'Keep your bodily fluids to yourself!' Other personalities like Phil Donahue and Oprah Winfrey weighed in by interminably interviewing people about their fears, fantasies, and sex lives, with the psychic and paranormal cards thrown into the mix to keep the gory pot boiling.

But none of this had arrived with Sky. To find much of its output just mindless, banal, low grade, rubbish, crap, pap, moron fodder, junk food for the masses, or whatever else you wanted to call it, was hardly surprising or anything new for the chattering classes. They had traditionally resisted the medium from its early days, when women had covered the set before undressing because they thought it could see them. Later people had worried about the technology side with wild talk of the 'rays' that emanated from the sets. Viewers had carefully placed themselves the recommended distance away so as not to damage their eyes. Then, in the days when there were hours of the test card and strange wallpaper footage, with 'Interlude' superimposed over it in flowery lettering, they joked about being 'square-eyed'. After that they called it 'the dreaded goggle box' and started sneering at the majority of its output. Many of the middle classes had held out for years before they could bring themselves to watch it. The arrival of the more worthy Channel 4 had cheered them up, but the answer to Sky, as almost always with the box, was to try to ignore it, even though many had a sinking feeling when they remembered that once they had had the same attitude to McDonalds' hamburgers.

And for those at BSB with longer memories there was another uncomfortable fact. A condition of the original DBS franchise had been the winner providing an effective news service. After the ITN negotiations had aborted, BSB had moved those goalposts with the help of the IBA and commissioned the alternative skeleton service of two minute 'rip'n'read's' illustrated by still photographs. In the office it had already been decided this 'radio with pictures' would be less interesting than watching the washing machine. However much you criticised the quality of Sky News, you couldn't deny it was the kind of service the IBA had been looking for.

Stymied on the main front, BSB now turned to its second line of attack.

CHAPTER THIRTEEN

Cross Eyed

While BSB had been scrutinising the Sky output for moral or political transgressions the European Institute of the Media had been painstakingly poring over the newspapers and in May 1989 published the study BSB had commissioned on the reporting of satellite TV. Its conclusion: that there was 'a significant body of material promoting Sky Television, and unfavourable to BSB in the editorial content of News International papers'. BSB triumphantly pounced on this as vindication of its case, along with the attached statistical proof that News International papers had devoted seven times more space than the others to coverage of satellite.

ASG was especially pleased. For him this issue of cross-promotion had been of paramount importance. It had not been just the incessant puffing of Sky and the harping at BSB itself. Even the BSB shareholders had seemed to be in the firing line, especially on the business pages of the *Times* and *Sunday Times*. ASG felt himself learning things about the media he had never dreamt of. Once he had been a man who opened the newspapers to read the news, but not any longer. For a start lots of it seemed to be all about him. At Whitbread and Saatchi ASG had had moderately successful careers, yet the pile of cuttings on him had remained small. Now he was heading BSB they were mound thick. Worse still, newspapers now appeared little more than the mouthpiece of the proprietor.

Facing a competitor who owned a third of the press was a debilitating and head banging experience and trying to deal with the problem seemed to have been taking up more and more of his time. This official recognition of the outrage gave huge satisfaction to him and all the boys and girls. Take stories like the one about a man with a satellite dish who was acquitted of not paying his TV licence fee on the grounds he only watched Sky: henceforth no one would be able to pretend it made the splash in the *Sun* on sheer news value.

Unfortunately there was a slight problem. The EIM, as an independent body, had also taken issue with the *Daily Mail*'s glowing reporting of BSB. That was a tricky one. New Era Television had been picked to make BSB's shows for women which were to be broadcast on the NOW channel precisely because it held the crucial carrot of the backing of the *Daily Mail*. Sir David English and his organ had since indeed been an invaluable source of support, even if at the cost of attracting heavy fall-out in the rival *Daily Express*. ASG tried to reason on practical grounds that the *Mail* represented less than 10% of newspaper readership, while Edward Bickham added his three ha'pence worth by being at pains to underline that when *Mail* reporters had pestered him for inside information, claiming a 'special relationship', he had honourably given them short shrift.

Nevertheless it had to be admitted that the *Mail* business was a bit of an own goal, and ASG's and BSB's irritation at the problem was compounded by the standard rubbishing and counterclaims about the report itself. News International hired a statistician from the London School of Economics to join in the fun, sparking off the usual high-profile mudslinging between the two organisations. As the noisy row continued in the Big Papers, ASG worried it was only further contributing to the grubby image satellite was getting.

But a month after the EIM report the BSB argument received a substantial boost from inside the Empire. Sky had taken the unusual step of sponsoring Harvey Goldsmith's staging of Bizet's *Carmen* at Earl's Court – an involvement planned in anticipation of the much-vaunted Sky Arts channel, of which rather less was being heard these days. *Carmen* at Earl's Court was unashamedly opera for the masses on a grandiose scale, full of fabulous effects and featuring a cast of thousands and, as *Today* newspaper told its yuppie readers, 'not just a load of old libretti' but containing 'passion, nudity and violence'. In the eyes of true cognoscenti like Tim de Lisle, the arts editor of *The Times*, a performance such as this barely rated the name of opera. But the News International's plugging machine thought otherwise. One evening after de Lisle had left Wapping, his page was remade without his being consulted. The next morning he opened the paper to see the arts page now leading with a substantial promotion for the Carmen extravaganza – to be shown, naturally, exclusively on Sky Television. The promotion took the form of a competition: 'Roll up for the Great Carmen' it cried, promising an outstanding chance to 'Win a Night at the Opera'. De Lisle resigned in protest, saying giving such prominence to a promotion for Sky undermined the credibility of the arts page.

The Times' NUJ chapel then took up the issue by complaining to the Office of Fair Trading over the promotion of Sky in the paper's editorial columns, introducing a new element by claiming it breached the undertaking of editorial independence Murdoch had given to the Trade Secretary when he had taken the paper over. BSB was delighted, especially as the Office of Fair Trading had changed its mind following the EIM report and agreed to look at cross-promotion. By late summer BSB was confident it was generally perceived to have a reasonable case, despite having shot itself slightly in the foot over the *Mail*, – an impression confirmed when *Private Eye* extended its 'Eye Sky' column, inviting readers to send in prime examples of Sky puffery in News International papers, to incorporate BSB puffs in the *Mail*.

The News International response was to concede nothing, while at the same time gently toning down the more blatant cross-promotion. All the free publicity had been calculated by BBH, counting column inches of copy as advertisement space, as being worth over £30 million to buy, but by now cross-promotion was becoming a sideshow to the much more important issue of cross-ownership.

The Empire had first marshalled its troops to seize the moral high ground on this front at the end of August 1989, two days before the BSB rocket launch from Cape Canaveral. To the surprise of that year's chairperson, Janet Street-Porter, Rupert Murdoch had accepted an invitation to give the keynote McTaggart lecture at the Edinburgh Television Festival, the annual jamboree for the great and the good. He had used the platform he had been handed to deliver a blistering attack under the title 'Freedom in Broadcasting'.

'Much of what passes for quality on British television,' he said, 'is no more than a reflection of the values of the narrow elite which controls it and has always thought that its tastes are synonymous with quality'. The system produced 'costume soap operas in which strangulated English accents dominate, dramas which are played out in rigid class structured settings', and pandered to an American desire 'to portray and freeze Britain as a museum'.

'Is it really healthy for British society to be served up a diet of television which constantly looks backwards?' Murdoch had asked, dismissing British public service attitudes by pointing to the virtues of multi-channel free market television on the American model. Amongst other things, he argued, a multiplicity of channels would ensure more independent and less muted television journalism. Cynics noted he chose to avoid mentioning the role of his own papers in undermining television journalism – in particular through hysterical *Sun*-style support for the ban on interviews with elected representatives of Sinn Fein.

But the crucial sub-text of the speech very much involved his newspapers. For the real message was not an attack on its opponents, but a defence of the Empire, which Murdoch stressed in the climax of his lecture through an enterprising defence of cross-media ownership. 'Were it not for the strength of our newspaper group and our human and capital resources,' he stated, 'we surely could not have afforded to have doubled the number of television channels available in Britain.'

As the cross-promotion issue faded BSB had also been limbering up for the bigger fight by calling in Chris Bellamy QC, a leading competition lawyer. In June Bellamy had duly produced an opinion arguing that the government's proposals, to be included in the forthcoming Broadcasting Bill, were inconsistent. Newspaper owners were to be limited to 20% ownership of an ITV franchise or a UK satellite, but satellite services 'not on UK broadcasting frequencies' were to be excluded. This, Bellamy contended in a legalistic version of the argument Edward

Bickham had put to the officials at the Home Office, lacked any rational basis. If the programme service beamed from the satellite could be received in the UK, and have a significant impact on UK viewers in terms of sources of information and formation of attitudes, it was irrelevant whether the piece of metal in the sky had a Luxembourg owner. The principle should be the same. ASG's simpler way of putting across the BSB argument to people was to explain it was like moving the printing of The Times to Amsterdam and saying that made it a foreign paper. Bellamy's solution was legislation across the board, just as in Australia, to subject both UK and foreign satellite services to identical controls.

This now became the thrust of BSB's high profile strategy, which seemed for a time to have struck a nerve amongst the concerned classes. A head of steam was building up over the issue of concentration of media power, and there were worried letters to the editor from Important People. There was another disturbing factor for News International in November 1989 being the twentieth anniversary of the Sun, which it knew would provide a focus for media criticism. On Channel 4 a new TV series called Hard News had already started regularly exposing its appalling journalistic standards.

Uncharacteristically, as Murdoch's McTaggart lecture had shown, the Empire had decided it was time to fight back after years of simply ignoring outside criticism. The Boss himself had announced he was writing a book to set the record straight and Jane Reed, a former features editor on Today, had been appointed News International's first Director of Corporate Affairs. But BSB's campaign not only disturbed the News International fight-back team, it also angered it. Many outside observers shared the same view. It seemed an extraordinary and cowardly route for BSB to take. It was accused of being too frightened to take on its competitor in the market place, and being anti-enterprise by seeking to close its rival down rather than engage in a fair fight. The feeling extended to Downing Street, where Mrs Thatcher had already made it clear to the country as a whole that Moaning Minnies and Whining Jimmies were not appreciated. The Prime Minister was a Sky-watcher, and approved of Sky News and the way it was so proud of what it did. Not personally experienced in big business, she did not see the struggle as a fight to the death by both sides, but rather that they complemented each other in the same way as the BBC and ITV. When ASG, on one of his rare visits, complained about bias in favour of Murdoch, which he usually referred to by talking about 'level playing fields', she curtly instructed him to stop whining and told him he was being 'wet'.

In contrast was the close axis between the Prime Minister and the Boss, which the Wapping move had helped to cement through Murdoch doing the government's job for it by bashing the unions so successfully. But this was only one aspect of the governmental appraisal of the two sides. Other Whitehall officials were very sceptical, feeling BSB was using the issue as just a way of handling a competitor, rather than making a serious charge. Whenever they met ASG at receptions there would be endless snide remarks. Frankly, they felt, BSB was 'just talking its own book'. This feeling that it should be protected was part of its mindset that it was a monopoly. It was not living in the real world. One official, echoing Thatcher herself, had told ASG to his face to stop taking on Sky so obsessively. If he had been trying to set something up, he preached, the last thing he would do was to knock his competitors all the time. He would concentrate on getting on with his own job. But it got him nowhere. Simonds-Gooding seemed to be in the grip of an obsession to rid the world of Sky and Murdoch, as if he was dealing with a monster, whereas, the official reminded him, the BBC and ITV were in the same boat. They were all affected.

Murdoch believed his personal good standing at Number 10 would see him through, coupled with his veiled threat to move the whole Sky operation offshore to Luxembourg, losing a supposed 2,000 jobs in Britain. When the Broadcasting Bill was finally published in December 1989, it duly confirmed satellite services not on UK frequencies were to be excluded from cross-media controls. But with the Parliamentary passage of the bill still ahead, Murdoch's advisers were nervous. BSB's vigorous campaign had already led to an Early Day Motion in the Commons calling for 'new safeguards against the control of televison . . . by those who already own large sections of the Press'. 'No one should be able to avoid existing or future safeguards against media concentration by broadcasting from outside the United Kingdom,' it declared. The motion had collected nearly 100 signatures. More worryingly 60, including the sponsor, Mike Woodcock MP, had been Conservatives.

The Early Day Motion had delighted Edward Bickham, BSB's Director of External Affairs, who had been largely responsible for the whole cross-media argument. Bickham now threw himself wholeheartedly into heading the campaign, which took off at a formidable pace with no expense or effort spared. As its main weapon BSB used a large glossy brochure entitled 'Raising Kane?', designed to evoke echoes of the notorious American media mogul, supposedly based on William Randolph Hearst, who had been immortalised by Orson Wells in the film Citizen Kane. Written by Bickham in a hotel room in Paris during an annual media conference, 'Raising Kane?' was ponderously sub-titled 'Media ownership in a free society – diversity, fair competition and the public interest'. Pontificating from on high, it led off with a quote from the philosopher Edmund Burke: 'The greater the power the more dangerous the abuse'. 'Concentration of media power is against the interests of a free society,' it then began: 'The idea that too much power in too few hands risks distortion, corruption and the peddling of self-interest is long established. This belief is neither controversial nor narrowly held. . . ' Pages of weighty and convoluted copy, stylishly printed on expensive paper, amplified the same didactic message before the 'end of the world as we know it' conclusion: 'This is not merely a tiresome row between satellite stations. It is an issue which is at the centre of the future [sic] and of the ethics and freedom of broadcasting in the 1990s.'

Having composed this imposing document, the next problem was deciding to whom it should be sent. The BBH philosophy of involving the GBP, albeit on a higher and more corporate level, now swung into place as direct mail companies were contacted and special lists bought of the sort of top people ASG regarded as 'resonsible for the fabric of Britain'. All over the country a copy of 'Raising Kane?' then thudded on to 10,000 influential desks in an unsolicited direct mailshot aimed at selected 'opinion formers'.

At the weekly and sometimes twice weekly meetings of the O Group Bickham reported to his colleagues on the progress of the campaign. Only Chris Dickens, was openly critical. Once again unhappy with the advertising strategy, he was uneasy about the way the campaign was increasingly developing into a personal attack on Murdoch. After an encouraging response from the opinion-forming 10,000, some of whom had written in to ask what they could do, Bickham had done them a second mailing of a series of dummy newspaper advertisements which asked things like: 'Who do you think will be the most influential person in Britain in the nineties?', below pictures of Thatcher and Murdoch. Dickens thought this outrageous. He told the executive board he bore in mind that every media business in the country Murdoch had become involved in had gone from nowhere to success. The campaign might have taken Murdoch's eye off the ball, but it had done the same for BSB. They didn't have time for all the lunches and meeting people and the stuff being produced by BBH. They were trying to start a TV station. And there was another aspect. 'Do you realise,' he asked them, 'you are trying to undermine a man the ad industry believes is providing communications vehicles that are great, and where it spends a lot of its money?'

Elsewhere in the company however there was praise for the all-singing, all-dancing campaign. The Chairman, Sir Trevor Holdsworth, was dutifully eating his way through both Houses of Parliament and although ASG did recognise deep down that he was becoming obsessive, he also knew the Broadcasting Bill was BSB's window of opportunity to challenge Murdoch's power. As Bickham kept pointing out, Murdoch had been forced to divest in Australia and the US. The Broadcasting Bill would go through several stages and they only needed to win once for the same to happen here. News International, meanwhile, had to win every time.

The frenetic political activity also served another purpose by helping to fill the vacuum at the new headquarters of Marcopolo House, where an awful lot of people were sitting around with nothing to do. With the aid of colleagues, a lobbying company and BBH, Bickham now directed a combination of more mailings, advertisements, letter writing and entertaining. Key personalities like Michael Grade, Melvyn Bragg, the ballerina Dame Beryl Grey, Sir John Harvey-Jones, and a host of former distinguished civil servants were persuaded to sign letters or address meetings. The Bickham strategy, as with 'Raising Kane?' which had pointedly avoided telling the opinion-formers to do anything, was always to light the touch paper and retire. Large newspaper ads plugging the cause did not have BSB's imprimatur on them but were credited to the unknown outfit 'Checks & Balances – The Campaign Against Concentration of Media Control'.

But as the campaign progressed Bickham also became more and more convinced he was fighting a just cause. Although there was widespread support, he frequently came across people who told him confidentially that they were in favour of stopping Murdoch, but were reluctant to be named publicly. A famous actor declined to sign a letter, explaining he had once been turned over by the Murdoch press and was frightened of it happening again. Bickham realised the overwhelming perception of the power of the Wapping press as Tory MPs who claimed to be with him at the same time muttered that, with the party behind in the polls, it was dangerous to risk annoying Murdoch. ASG had had the same experience at the Tory Party conference, when he was bearded by a dyed-in-the-wool supporter, telling him crossly: 'Don't you realise he's going to get us in?'

Bickham knew anyhow that BSB's best chance of success lay in the Lords rather than the Commons, where a three figure Tory majority allied to a three line whip would mean no chance of overturning the Government. The House of Lords had a greater tradition of independence and as a strong protagonist there he could choose between Baroness Birk, a former Labour Minister who was now its spokesperson in the Lords, and Lord Mark Bonham-Carter, the distinguished ex-BBC governor, both of whom were keen BSB supporters. Even better would be a Tory, whom he then found in the person of the present Earl of Stockton, grandson of the former Prime Minister Harold Macmillan. Bickham knew Stockton from the days he had worked as PA to his father, who was then chairman of Macmillan's, and found him extremely sympathetic. Macmillan's had been caught up in the difficulties facing all small publishers now that the industry was dominated by conglomerates like Murdoch's massive HarperCollins, able to offer serialisation and promotion through News International newspapers and magazines, and the implications in his own field were something Stockton had long talked about. When Bickham invited him to lunch at Marcopolo House he positively sparkled.

Bickham now set about briefing his key people in the Lords. The intention was to insert into the Broadcasting Bill a clause bringing non-domestic satellites under the same rules as domestic, which would force Murdoch to divest his Sky holdings down to 20%. But Bickham found it was not always easy to agree exactly how this should be achieved and at one point Lord Stockton, Baroness Birk and Lord Bonham-Carter, all wanting to propose their own version of the amendment, fell out amongst themselves. Baroness Birk's version was used in the Committee stage of the bill because she represented the official opposition. Its snag was that it was also the toughest attack on cross-media interests, which defeated Bickham's object of encouraging Conservative support through proposing a milder, Conservative-sponsored amendment. So after the Committee stage, he employed his best diplomatic skills to bring his various cross-party supporters together before the final Report stage, and after he had smoothed feathers ensured that this time the Stockton version he favoured would be used.

Sky had no inkling of such inner tensions in what looked to them like a highly polished and effective campaign. At News International the uneasy feeling had been growing that Murdoch's tea and chats at Number 10 might not be sufficient to save their bacon. He and his wife Anna might have been honoured guests at the dinner celebrating Mrs Thatcher's tenth anniversary as Prime Minister in May but it was also clear her own star was on the wane. Jane Reed had therefore already taken the unusual step for an organisation normally doing everything in-house of recruiting the lobbying company of Sallingbury Casey. This was a lobbyist in Sky's own mould, operating on the principle of hard work rather than boozy lunches, as well as refuting the common practice of having an MP on the board, to avoid any suggestion of buying influence. The company blurb stated it 'works ethically at source, aiming to provide the maximum benefit for its clients without unnecessary publicity or disruption of the public policy process'. The company's managing director, Leighton Andrews, had once been a lobbyist for the housing charity Shelter and had worked for Lord Scarman on his report into the 1981 Brixton riots, while the chairman, Michael Casey, had drafted the original Fair Trading Act as a civil servant – which meant they were particularly well placed to handle what was a competition issue.

Leighton Andrews perceived his industry had a generally sleazy image in Britain. There was a lot of cant about it here, with periodic rows about MPs declaring their business interests and a seeming inability to decide how much it should be officially allowed. In America by contrast it was big business, with companies openly employing vast teams to win politicians over to their argument, and Andrews agreed with this approach, regarding it as an honourable and entirely upfront activity. Now he applied this no-nonsense approach to mounting the case for Sky. The research department of keen young graduates set to work scouring Hansard, consulting the archives on broadcasting matters, examining Commons Order papers and searching for writings in the media so as to bracket and cross-reference all politicians showing up as having an interest in the subject. These were then targeted in a methodical approach completely different to the BSB random spraying about of 'Raising Kane?' to the 10,000 'opinion formers'. Such had been the depth of research behind that exercise that Michael Casey himself, after showing up on one of the lists, had received a copy.

Instead concentration was to be solely on the few dozen key people who needed to be won over. Jonathan Miller, Sky's PR man, moved into an office below the Sallingbury Casey headquarters at 25 Victoria Street just round the corner from Parliament, where three floors up Michael Heseltine was simultaneously working on his campaign to take over the leadership of the Conservative Party. Once the Broadcasting Bill had begun in earnest fortnightly planning meetings were held there to discuss strategy and compare notes. Lobbyists, lawyers and News International representatives all attended, with Jane Reed reporting back on discussions with Ministers or Home Office officials.

Meanwhile Sallingbury Casey took crucial MPs and peers on the long trail out to Osterley where, one by one, they were given a guided tour of the facilities, introduced to key staff and taken to the boardroom for a general chat. Large receptions and even drinks parties were rejected, as Sallingbury Casey believed they gave no opportunity for serious, detailed briefing. Other targeted politicians were seen individually within Westminister or invited over to Victoria Street for a small demonstration and to be told about the issue over a sandwich. Follow-up came with tightly focused selective mailings and telephone calls. By MPs' standards it was all very austere. Occasionally there were wilder ideas, such as Leighton Andrews wondering if Sky might cross-reference all dish owners by constituency and then write to them asking them to contact their local MP, perhaps with an enclosed postcard. The message would indicate concern that the customer's proud investment would be wasted if Sky were to be hampered by cross-media controls. The idea was briefly considered, but dropped when it was decided the effort and computer work involved would be too demanding.

To Westminster and Whitehall insiders it was an interesting campaign which cut right across party lines as Sallingbury Casey worked hard to get support wherever they could. Leighton Andrews even tried to persuade Lord Bonham-Carter on a trip out to Osterley, but without success. He was however pleased when he won over Ted Willis, the Labour peer and award-winning playwright who had created the seminal police series of Dixon of Dock Green, as well as Lord Annan, author of the respected report into broadcasting which had led to the establishment of Channel 4. Andrews was also amused to see that the issue divided not only parties but also families when the venerable TV mogul Lord Grade spoke out for Sky, in disagreement with his nephew Michael.

There was another lighter moment amongst the serious leg-work when Lord Hailsham, the former Lord Chancellor, was approached by Jonathan Miller after being identified as a likely Sky supporter. Bearding him shortly before a key vote, instead of a promise of support Miller got an angry complaint. Hailsham had appeared on the Mitchell-Tebbit Target programme on Sky News some weeks previously and submitted an invoice for his fee, but the Sky accounts department had neglected to pay his VAT. Many letters had gone to and fro, with the accounts department maintaining the VAT would only be paid if an invoice with the registration number was submitted. Although the amount was less than £20 Hailsham had assiduously pursued the correspondence, even threatening to report the matter to Customs and Excise, but the accounts department still would not budge. A furious Miller shot back to his office, faxes flew to Osterley, mountains of red tape were moved and a cheque written and despatched within hours. His Lordship was suitably mollified.

The scale of support for the original Early Day Motion on cross-ownership, now known as the BSB motion, had originally caused Leighton Andrews some concern. He thought it a strong marker. The 60 Tory MPs gave BSB a wide base to trawl. Yet as the Broadcasting Bill lumbered on he felt somehow BSB was not capitalising on its advantage. Its high-profile campaign of cleverly timed announcements, letters to the papers, and the multiple mailings to the 10,000 seemed to be more about creating lots of noise. Michael Casey had studied the copy of 'Raising Kane?' he had been mailed and decided it was over the top. He thought it would only serve to alienate people who did not usually like taking sides in a commercial dispute. Sallingbury Casey's more low-key approach, on the other hand, appeared to be yielding results and by the time the Broadcasting Bill started its final passage through the Lords, although there was much more foot-slogging to be done, he and Leighton Andrews were quietly confident Sky was on the winning side.

CHAPTER FOURTEEN

A Licence to Burn Money

It had been Lord Thomson who famously described the original TV franchises as 'a licence to print money', but more and more the shareholders of BSB were looking at a financial equation adding up to a licence to burn it. This was intentional, as the marketing-led philosophy of 'fast burn', officially adopted as company policy after Murdoch's announcement of Sky, came into its own. The shareholders' money was to be thrown at 'ramping up' the market through pushing the aspects Peter Bell had laid out in his original beer analogy – satellite as a concept, BSB as a brand, and the individual channels as sub-brands. The success of Ian Clubb's massive fund-raising exercise had enabled ASG to hold a triumphant press conference at which he told the media hacks he wanted them to send Sky the message that it was now 'looking down the barrel of a fully-funded gun'.

There was a sharp intake of breath at the Centaurs Business Park as exactly what that meant sunk in. BSB, ASG announced, was to follow the £30 million it had spent on advertising over the previous 18 months with a budget of £33 million for the year 1990 alone. That meant, the Big Papers noted, that the company was poised to break an advertising record by spending more on promoting itself than any other brand in Britain. The sum was £10 million more than the Abbey National building society the previous year, two and a half times the spend on McDonald's hamburgers, and three times that on Pedigree Chum. It would also make BSB the seventh largest corporate advertiser in the country, above even companies like Vauxhall with an entire model range to plug. The vast firepower of the Murdoch press was at last to be met shell for shell. And that was not all, as ASG revealed by firing BSB's second financial salvo. The company was also to spend another £200 million over the next three years in subsidising rental equipment and subscriptions.

The climate for both the Good Ship BSB and the Skyship Enterprise was not, however, looking promising. Although the government had yet to admit a recession was inevitable, the annual survey of the British consumer electronics industry by Ferguson revealed over half the population saying it would have less to spend that year on leisure goods. The survey also pinpointed a separate and disturbing factor for the satellite market. The GBP was becoming wise to the dust-up between the two protagonists and resisting their blandishments for fear it could get locked into one operator's system 'that could go down the drain next year'. Only 14% of the population was interested in buying, a figure scarcely changed from the previous year despite the millions of pounds spent on hype. More ominously, only a quarter of those were actually thinking of making their purchase that year. Interest also dropped off markedly in the older age ranges, with nearly 30% of 18–24 year olds interested, but only 7% of those over 44. Ferguson calculated that in 1989 the total number of dishes 'either sold or given away' had been 450,000, which it rated as 'respectable, rather than either a triumph or a disaster', and forecast 1 million more customers for 1990, which would take the market as a whole well over critical mass. The question now was which they would be boarding – the Skyship Enterprise or the Good Ship BSB.

ASG kicked off the New Year in January by staging for the benefit of the press the first public link-up between the Marcopolo satellite and a functioning squarial at Marcopolo House. Clutching a portable phone, he ostentatiously dialled the Customer Management Centre at Leeds, which was being run up to its full complement of 400 people to take sales inquiries, process subscriptions and generally interact with the GBP in translation of Bogle's 'listening channel' concept. To prove its commitment it was to be open from 8am to 10pm, seven days a week. The media hacks heard the phone dutifully answered by the disembodied broad Yorkshire voice of Jackie, who mechanically offered Mr Anthony Simonds-Gooding a three month free trial of the Movie Channel, 'as he had been told in the shop', if he consented to join the Launch Club – a device dreamt up by the marketing department to ensnare members of the GBP by persuading them to pay £10 in advance in return for various discounts and incentives. After watching ASG's sterling performance as he laid on the customary dollops of 'good news', Jane Thynne, media correspondent of the *Daily Telegraph*, reported to her readers: 'At times like this, some members of the press reflected, there are no lengths to which the satellite men will not go, no television programmes they will not appear on, no stunts they will not perform, to win the advertising war of words.'

On the programming side at Marcopolo the attitude became distinctly brisker. Not only was the staff cheered that after months of hanging around at last there was something to do, but for the first time its side of the business was coming to the fore. The period immediately before the launch was a welcome whirl of activity after sitting around for so many months. Programmes were at last being made and there was a sense of nervousness and excitement as the whole enterprise started pulling together in preparation. Recruitment had also been continuing apace for celebs and well-known faces for viewers to identify with, who were now arriving along with the remainder of the staff. The money was good, both for individuals and across the board, as the *Express* gleefully reported under the headline 'BSB sky high in TV pay wars'. The paper quoted a survey in *Broadcast* magazine which said ASG, thanks to his various perks and bonuses, was paid £430,000 a year, while BSB employees had an average salary of £34,659 pa – £6,000 a year more than the next highest payer, ITN. More significantly in the battle between the two sides, Sky was staying true to the concept of lean and mean by paying a paltry average of £17,033 a year, making it bottom of the pay league. Edward Bickham countered lamely by saying the survey did not take into account that many BSB staff had joined since the survey and had been recruited into lower paid jobs. ASG had been particularly annoyed by what he called 'a lot of scuttlebutt' about management salaries. All the talk and the stories in the paper made people see them as a lot of profligate lounge lizards! Not that he was saying the money was that poor. Graham Grist, for example, had started on £108,000 a year, which had rolled up to £180,000 when all the perks were added in, and none of the other headhunted execs had been exactly cheap. Then there had been all the fuss over the John Gau Productions deal. The only salary out of line was his own – as he freely admitted. But then, as chief executive he had a unique job to do.

Average pay was anyhow now increasingly irrelevant in an industry where union rates were being replaced by salaries which individuals negotiated for themselves. This had led to huge wages for top personalities and celebs, including supposedly impartial figures like newsreaders whose only job was to read out scripts prepared by others. The ultimate example of this cult of personality rather than content was said to be Dan Rather, the anchorman for CBS in America. Rather's behaviour was reported to have become more and more eccentric as his salary soared to a dizzy $3 million a year. He had begun developing strange quirks, signing off one programme with 'Courage!' and then changing it the next day to the Spanish 'Coraje!'. Next, angered by a live tennis broadcast which ran into his news slot, he had walked off the set, leaving the screen blank for seven minutes. In the latest development he had taken to reading the news from a podium. TV executives justified the huge salaries with buzz words like 'authority', 'credibility', and 'unflappability', but John Humphreys, the veteran BBC newsreader, replied that it was all a myth. 'You could put a blue-faced baboon on the news and in ten years he would become top of the list as a national celebrity,' he commented.

BSB could not match the salary paid to Michael Aspel, shown by a survey to be the highest-paid celeb with £500,000 a year from ITV, followed by Terry Wogan at £375,000. But it was still prepared to wield the big cheque-book for its two key stars, the recently knighted Sir Robin Day, who merited £150,000, and Selina Scott who topped him with £200,000. Sir Robin was very much a last-minute coup for BSB's line up. After honourably retiring from the BBC, where he had become a national institution without ever receiving much financial recompense, his talents had been sought by both Sky and BSB. When he received Sky's measly offer he had no trouble deciding which satellite station to climb aboard!

The arrival of Sir Robin and Selina Scott fitted well with the increasingly BBCish tone of BSB. Its programming head John Gau used unconsciously to underline this by being prone to the Freudian slip of using 'BBC' instead of 'BSB' at presentations, but there was more to it than that. At the beginning of 1990 Gau had appointed his former colleague Hugh Williams to take charge of the NOW channel. Williams had none of Gau's schooling in the commercial realities of the independent sector. Instead he came straight out of the BBC, where he had worked all his life. His wife, the presenter Sue Lawley, was still working there. Williams, as editor, had once been responsible for Nationwide's famous skate-boarding duck. Taking up the reins at BSB, his preferred and safe strategy was to rope in a few chums from his BBC days to fill the various programming holes. Calling up several former BBC types who had ventured into the independent sector, he hastily offered them commissions to organise a few dependable series like Sir Robin Day's Now Sir Robin show. The BBC feel became so strong that Bernard Falk, whose company had been awarded a travel programme, joked as he looked round the room at a pre-launch meeting: 'It looks just like a gathering of the old Nationwide team.'

The original decision to delay the launch until some time in the spring had been made on the strict understanding that above all BSB must avoid the Sky error of setting off with no kit in the shops. Yet while the shareholders' energies and perceptions had been concentrated on the nail-biting business of the fund-raising, it now became horribly clear there had been a terminal spin-off into the technical area. Andy Coleman, trying to get things back on course, found himself spending a great deal of time not talking to manufacturers about the technical problems, but trying to give them confidence in BSB. People were nervous, which was landing him in a Catch 22. It was very difficult to push any manufacturer to technical commitment while the company was not fully funded, yet the funding would not come through until the technology itself had reached some sort of milestone. It had not been until nearly the end of February, when BSB had at last officially got its project loan, that all the manufacturers had been confident enough finally to press their various buttons to get production moving.

This confusion and uncertainty had had a knock-on effect in the High Street shops, where satellite as a product was anyhow a highly unpopular topic with the retailers. It was only a tiny part of their business and they had been hugely antagonised by Sky who at first dithered around with various factors like the film encryption then started the direct-sell Project X which undercut them. This made them less inclined than ever to make an effort. Remarks like Murdoch's ignorant-teenager-couldn't sell a toaster jibe had hardly improved their attitude.

Looking at this situation Peter Bell, in charge of distribution as part of the marketing department empire, had decided to put all BSB's eggs in one basket by pursuing a deliberate strategy of trying to win the retailers' co-operation through publicly eschewing direct-sell. This chimed in neatly with BSB's overall approach as direct-sell did not in any case fit its more upmarket image. But with the satellite market as a whole not coming up to expectations, many retailers were still as suspicious and uninformed about it as the GBP itself. And after the difficulties of wrapping their heads round Sky they now saw a new nightmare looming. Earnest techno-punters would pester them with questions about the relative merits of the two different systems and make things even more complicated. Furthermore the hanging-back by BSB's manufacturers had meant pricing deals for both rental and sales were still being postponed in February, bemusing trade observers who knew all the equipment should have been sold in by then.

To test things out for Big Paper readers the *Sunday Telegraph* called on Rod Allen, the chief executive of Television Entertainment Ltd, which distributed programmes to both Sky and BSB. On a trip down the High Street shopping for dishes, Allen discovered things had not improved much since the days of Project X. At the Curry's branch in Camden Town, North London the salesman showing him a Sky dish told him: 'You get lots of programmes broadcasted [sic] from America', adding that you needed planning permission to put it up and it 'might' be able to pick up BSB. 'BSB is a bit shaky at the moment – it's had lots of breakdowns,' he said helpfully. The assistant at Dixon's hadn't heard from BSB and neither had DER, although it was taking the names of people who made inquiries. As a last resort Allen trawled Britain's electronics Mecca of the Tottenham Court Road, but only came across one salesman who seemed to know anything. 'We want to sell them, but BSB hasn't contacted us yet,' he explained.

As the various elements compounded and built on each other the retailers were belatedly offered what small amount of equipment there was. But they then decided not to take the inventory risk of stocking up before launch, with the result that the figure of 50,000 units originally promised to be in the marketplace was gradually translated down until it finally bottomed out at 2,000. Even then most of these had not actually been sold, but just placed in the shops as demonstration models to solicit firm orders. The very thing Chris Dickens had hammered on about, and which everybody had feared most, had happened. All that marketing, all those extra millions of pounds spent, yet there was still to be nothing there to sell! Over at Sky Australian eyes popped in disbelief.

Now beyond caring, and anyhow locked in by events, the Good Ship BSB fell back on the novel concept of a staggered launch. On 25 March it slid halfway down the slipway by piping its signal to a theoretical 270,000 cable viewers in what was euphemistically described as a 'service launch'. This merely served to deepen the rift between the marketing department and the programming people. John Gau, desperate to get the service up and running, insisted on treating the 'service launch' as the launch proper, while the marketing men tried to pretend BSB hadn't really launched yet to hold things back for the DTH (direct to home) or dish launch, which was to be a month later.

BBH, still groping to locate a tangible to hang its ad campaign on, was kept as much in the dark about the launch as everybody else. Nigel Bogle, along with his equally bemused assistant Steve Kershaw, found the date 'on wheels'. Behind the scenes it had first been brought forward, then put back as far as June, then brought forward again as the company juggled the various problems of pleasing the banks as potential backers, the correct season, and equipment being in the shops. When it was finally clear that it was the equipment end which had been caught in the mangle, the first leg of the £13 million campaign, designed to establish BSB as a brand, was simply pulled.

None of this really surprised Chris McLaughlin. When he had been told in February about the staggered March/April launch – a PR nightmare – his reply had been that he didn't think they could make it. McLaughlin was in the middle of an odd situation. All the execs seemed wrapped up in their own thoughts about how well they were doing, yet he had become a conduit by which he kept hearing the exact opposite. People would walk into his office and refer to aspects of the technology by saying things like: 'Y'know, SCOPE doesn't work', or 'ALPS doesn't work'. Then someone from Philips would ring and say: 'You do realise this doesn't work either?' or: 'You do know our first production line isn't really working at full pace?' Someone else would then ask him if he knew they were getting a lot of chip failures. As these various reports plunged him into deep gloom McLaughlin found himself getting a reputation for always looking on the black side of things. He didn't see it like that. He just saw a company that was drifting.

Now, tasked by the marketing department with making the 'real' launch a major media event, McLaughlin faced yet another PR disaster. Failure to announce the date in good time had meant the company losing almost all the magazines because of their lead times, including the crucial women's ones which had originally inspired Bogle's 'listening channel' concept. And when the press officers rang newspapers and the mags with shorter lead times they encountered a hugely negative response.

As with Sky, the BSB launch had been scheduled for a Sunday. The inevitable party, laid on by the marketing department and based round the glorious atrium, went on all day and turned into a jolly and very relaxed affair which grew so large it spilled out into the car park, where champagne glasses were perched perilously on the bonnets of gleaming BMWs. A robot from one of the programmes circulated amongst the guests, who were also treated to waitress service, champagne, giant prawns, a buffet of finger food, and a squarial cake as a centrepiece. The minor glitterati included BSB's major stars, Selina Scott and Sir Robin Day, and a smattering of other VIPs such as mid-ranking politicians and England footballer Gary Lineker, who explained he was present 'because BSB is a friend of football'. All the execs and programme heads had been invited, with everybody naturally encouraged to bring their families, leading David Jessel, the presenter of Crown's VIP show, to tell people it was the first time in his career that his family had been invited to a 'do' and it was the best he had ever been to.

Yet despite all the money previously spent on partying it was decreed humble BSB rank and file should not attend, causing massive internal resentment. Many of the staff had been working towards this big day for more than two years, yet officially as far as they were concerned it was to pass unnoticed. Some likened the consequent crushing disappointment to a dud firework which had failed to go off, while one described it as 'like having sex but never reaching orgasm'. In an organisation so devoted to outward show it was a blow to the morale for some from which they never really recovered. It had been a rough winter anyhow in Marcopolo, with people getting continuous colds and using fan heaters in their offices to keep warm. There had been constant headaches from the fluorescent lighting and excited rumours that the place had the buzz complaint of 'sick building syndrome'. Now summer was coming it was going to get boiling in there again. The only consolation was financial. The promised launch bonus of 12–15% of salary across the board, with 25% for senior execs, formerly deferred, was now deemed to be payable.

The deflated reaction was much the same in the press department, where McLaughlin had been allocated a PR spend of less than £20,000 because of all the money committed to advertising which had then been canned at the last moment. The media hacks McLaughlin knew well could not believe BSB had finally gone out like that. Afterwards he and the others had sat around in the press office thinking, Is that it? It was such a huge letdown – the first time, and that was as good as it got. Chris Dickens disapproved so much he didn't even go to the party. As far as he was concerned the company didn't have the money to spend on the frills. What it needed was something to bring in people like advertisers who would spend money with them, rather than the other way round.

An ebullient host as ever, ASG was undeterred by these sour grapes and, with Marjorie at his side, radiated bonhomie. In a short speech from the Hollywood-style staircase he announced the guests were attending 'a "celebration". On the scale of things is it lethal, or irritating, or irrelevant, that people can't buy the equipment yet?' he asked, answering his own rhetorical question by replying: 'I would say it was irritating, but that's all.' He promised that between 100,000 and 200,000 dishes and decoders would be in the shops by the end of June, although of course the real need was to build up stocks for the autumn 'when people want to buy'. Sir Robin Day, not fully aware of the realities of the situation, chipped in by telling the thin smattering of press: 'It's a wonderful revolution in broadcasting. In the 1950s we had an audience of fewer than 200,000 homes. Now millions of people can tune in!'

As the station switched on with a flourish the handful of customers both able and bothered to watch were treated by the Movie Channel to the James Bond film The Living Daylights, Beverley Hills Cop II and, what was to have been the launch highpoint, Scandal, the British-made film about the Profumo Affair. Andy Birchall had previously paid £1 million for this in a special deal which 'closed the video window' by allowing it to be screened simultaneously with its video release. But the screening date had originally been set for the previous September and the video trade, naturally, had not waited. There were wry grimaces, apart from the shame of it all, at copies of a promotional pamphlet being used by the retailers which was handed round. It was headed: 'BSB Five Channel TV: A Guide to What You're Missing'.

A spokesman for Sky, which was showing the B movie High Anxiety on the Movie Channel, said it was not planning a spoiler. 'We don't need to,' he added contemptuously, a point proved by the coverage in Monday's papers. Even with the normal lack of news on Sunday this was muted, with the most-used phrase describing the launch as 'purely symbolic'. The Daily Mail dutifully rowed in under the headline 'Now, that's real TV', with a full-page article praising the Galaxy light entertainment channel for 'distilling the essence' of BBC and ITV with old favourites like The Best of Steptoe and Son, Bewitched, Hart to Hart, and Hill Street Blues. It did however slam a game show called Wife of the Week, which had Christopher Biggins in 'holiday camp style' cross-examining elderly couples about their married lives. The new soap, Jupiter Moon, supposedly set aboard a space ship and described as a cross between Neighbours and Star Trek, was summarised as 'looking and sounding more like an undisciplined school party running riot on a cross-Channel ferry'. The greatest plaudits were awarded to Hugh Williams' NOW channel, which the *Mail* called 'the jewel in BSB's crown'. It had captured the art which had previously eluded television of translating a general interest magazine on to the screen and was 'a brilliant example of the programmer's art'. Highest praise of all was reserved for the daily hour-long magazine-format First Edition presented by Selina Scott, which the *Mail* said had echoes of the BBC's old Tonight programme. The only real criticism was for the lack of a decent news service.

The Express meanwhile put the boot in by pointing out on its news pages there had probably been more guests at the launch party than people who'd bought dishes. The 40,000 hapless members of the Launch Club, it announced with great relish, were going to have to wait. But on the TV page its critic was more supportive, saying he wouldn't mind betting BSB would prove to be 'more agreeable' in his household. With his customary openness ASG even agreed to enter Sky's lions' den and subject himself to a mild savaging by Austin Mitchell and Norman Tebbit on Target. Ben Hawke watched in amazement as ASG ducked questions like why there was no kit in the shops. As far as Hawke was concerned BSB was a modern South Sea Bubble.

The lack of equipment and viewers did not deter BSB from its market research obsession and a huge operation swung into action after the 'service launch' on the back of a tiny sample of 200 cable viewers in Tredegar, Medway, Hull, Nottingham and Southampton. The study warned allowance should be made for the 'downmarket bias of the sample', which contained 63% DEs. It was 'more typical of the Sky audience . . . through exhibiting a greater propensity to view than other types of television households', which translated into between 3.55 and 4.65 hours a day stuck in front of the telly. A further clue to DE lifestyle could be glimpsed by audiences being 'particularly buoyant from Sunday through Thursday, falling away significantly on Friday and Saturday – the two most popular evenings for out-of-home entertainment'.

The viewers in the sample were given 'self-completion diaries' and then interviewed by telephone the next day to find out what they had watched. The first test, to indicate 'spontaneous awareness levels', asked them to name what they remembered without any prompting. Then they were prompted and asked again, at which point twice as many often remembered that 12 hours earlier they had watched Sky's Eurosport, BSB's Sports Channel or Sky News. There was scant comfort for the BBC or ITV, who fared little better in the prompted v unprompted stakes, leading the researchers to comment 'it indicates the extent to which television viewing is an habitual behaviour'.

More detailed questioning revealed many cable viewers could remember the correct name of a film unprompted, particularly if it was Rocky IV. Otherwise there was a string of depressing answers – 'Sylvester Stallone movie', 'all films', 'sports round-up type programme', 'pop videos', 'don't know [the name] as I didn't catch the beginning', 'football', 'quiz show', 'can't remember the name as it was on when we were decorating and some sport we watched later on', 'can't remember', 'cannot recall the names of the programmes', 'cannot recall movies', ending with the bottom line of 'don't know'. The research, spattered with phrases like 'conscious decision to view', 'channel-specific', 'normative data', produced reams of spidery graphs, rows of figures and block graphics for the chartists to get their calculators into as they built up profiles of viewers on paper. 'Audience appreciation scores' asking the cable people how much they had enjoyed their fare then scored them out of 10, provided a whole new area of chart activity. Most appeared to react mildly uncritically, varying almost without exception between 7 and 8.5.

The research, which started on day one of the 'service' launch, could be exceptionally cruel, as when it revealed the NOW channel, despite the *Mail*'s mid-market approval, had gone down like a lead balloon with the DE cable people. It had failed to get any audience whatsoever for its first week until the last day, when it climbed to a minute share by gaining one person in its 'reach', defined as those who 'viewed for three consecutive minutes or more'. The solitary NOW viewer then gave the channel a spectacularly low 4 out of 10 appreciation rating. More paperwork activity followed to build 'audience appreciation indices', with ASG informing everyone meetings were being arranged with the channel heads to go through the figures in greater detail. Meanwhile the programme heads below them received screeds of 'top-line' results weekly, and major surveys were summarised in long memos to all staff, with ASG adding supportive little remarks about the results like 'they make very good reading'.

John Gau didn't think this research of much significance. Instead his reaction to the whole launch fiasco was what he described as his 'moment of truth'. Of all the people in BSB Gau had been the one pushing hardest for the earliest possible launch. Until then he had thought they would be okay and Sky's 15-month head start wouldn't matter. Now he saw things differently. This was the second time the technology had let them down, and while he had never been in such a marketing-led company, all the marketing was obviously not working. If you were the new kid on the block, Gau thought, you could either do it big and say you were important – or you could say, Let's wait until we have something to show. BSB had banged the drum so often, always announcing things and then not delivering – from the squarial to the launch itself – that it had lost all credibility. Gau had anyhow always found BSB's presentations too exuberant. He knew that was because those responsible came mainly from Whitbread where that was the way it was done. But in BSB's case he thought it inappropriate, stylish though it all might be. It was too rich. It had led to too many false dawns.

Whatever the programmes were like, with no equipment in the shops to provide an initial surge of sales Gau now saw no alternative. Sitting down at his desk he composed a long memo to ASG, telling him they ought to seek a merger with Sky and outlining how he thought it could best be achieved. But in proposing this he was miles behind many of his colleagues, some of whom had been nursing the same idea since that fateful day, now approaching two years ago, when Murdoch had first stood up in the dry ice smoke to announce Sky.

PART THREE

CHAPTER FIFTEEN

Midsummer Madness

There are times when even businesses can feel that God is not on their side, and the long hot summer of 1990 was to prove exactly that for both satellite players. The correct seasonal window to open a new television venture, as BSB had always planned, is the autumn, when shortening days and changing clocks drag the GBP back to its fireside, to be bombarded by the terrestrial companies hyping their autumn schedules. Sky, launching in February, had at least a few months to bed in before the C2s donned their shorts and plunged into their summertime pursuits. But by the end of April, when BSB started transmitting, it was already theoretically too late and a cruel freak of nature now made the timing error terminal. In stark contrast to the rain traditionally accompanying visits to ASG's country house, the glorious weather on launch day was followed by a record-breaking week of brilliant sunshine and high temperatures, sending the population streaming outdoors and sparking off more excited chatter in the Big Papers about the current end of the world scenario of global warming.

Looking at the bigger picture there was also gloomy news from America, where the first quarter of the year had brought an unprecedented 4% slump in television viewing figures across the country. In a country where Cagney and Lacey had won the Emmy for Best Drama, Hill Street Blues had been axed for being popular but not popular enough, and casting for minor parts was done literally by computer, Howard Stringer, a Welshman who was President of CBS, warned of a new generation of 'unhappy wanderers, forever unfulfilled, the undead of the media age . . . a media-jaded audience that wanders restlessly from one channel to another in search of that endangered species – originality'.

More evidence, this time suggesting TV's pre-eminence was on the decline in Britain, came from Steven Barnett, the director of the Media Futures Group at the Henley Centre for Forecasting. Barnett reported the figures showed that from 1960 onwards the time the GBP spent each week watching television had increased from around 13 hours to just over 26. But it had peaked in 1985, and by 1989 dropped back to 24 hours 44 minutes – a decrease of 5%. The social contrast was also marked. ABs spent just under 18 hours a week watching and DEs, at just under 32 hours, almost twice as long. TV was also playing to an aging audience. The over 65s were watching twice as much as those aged between 16 and 24.

Choice could be one of the reasons, Barnett suggested. Television was now overwhelming people by breaking existing viewing patterns and, deprived of a simple solution to the problem of what to watch, viewers were resorting to avoidance. Exactly the same had happened with the launch of Channel 4 in 1982, when viewing had temporarily decreased by ten minutes a week. Viewing in satellite homes had risen overall by 5%, but Barnett considered that low, and in any case partly due to novelty value. All the evidence pointed to the fact that television as a medium was becoming more peripheral to people, with a growing aversion to 'an evening stuck in front of the box'. The BBC challenged the figures, countering that video timeshifting (recording programmes to view later) was not included, but nonetheless could only go as far as maintaining viewing was 'static'.

But initially the change in climate both in the weather and the attitude to TV, made little difference to BSB. The squarials had grown in size from their original dinner plate 25cm to 40 cm because the Marcopolo signal was feebler on five channels than the original three. But they continued to remain virtually invisible because there simply weren't many out there. ASG's bullish launch predictions had turned out to be more 'good news' misinformation. Production delays had continued throughout the early summer. With the first 40,000 sets of receiving equipment already presold to the members of the Launch Club there was no chance of getting sizeable numbers into the shops and the optimism which continuously surrounded forecasts at BSB now led to a fresh disaster.

At some stage the marketing push to establish BSB as a brand had to be unleashed through reviving the advertising campaign which had been postponed at launch. But this had to be booked weeks in advance, with the additional problem that much of the money committed to the first campaign had only been reclaimed in the form of credit notes against future ads in the papers and on TV. So this time, once the commitment had been made and the ads booked, they would have to run whether there was any equipment in the shops or not. Having got ASG-style positive feedback, BBH therefore booked space for May and June. But by then the BSB forecasts had been revised downwards, and there were only dribs and drabs of kit in the shops, leading to the new horror BBH had already forseen and warned about. When you pushed satellite at people, research showed they took between four and six weeks to make what was classified as the 'lifestyle decision' to buy it. Then they went into the shop. By now they were locked into their personal equation and if, despite being triggered by a BSB ad, they found only Sky stuff, they were likely to walk out with that instead. That was a double disaster, as it meant BSB money had both deprived BSB of a certain sale and sold a Sky dish. Ill-informed toaster-selling shop assistants keen to shift anything only added to this likelihood.

Nigel Bogle and Steve Kershaw were now finding BSB a very fraught scenario, and in the circumstances the ads they had designed could not have been much worse. Bogle had first attempted to revive the squarial branding concept to bring the advertising back to where it had first started. But he had been told there was a new complication. The flight on the technical side of the company away from reliance on squarials had led to the parallel production of small parabolic reflectors like mini-Sky dishes, archly dubbed 'compact dishes' by the marketing department. Ads featuring squarials might therefore only serve to confuse the already confused GBP even more. Anyway, Bogle grasped, BSB had been too burnt by past squarial events to have the nerve to go back to it. So instead BBH devised ads which took their tone from Steven Spielberg's film Close

Encounters of a Third Kind. Cameras swept down empty streets
to a backdrop of scudding clouds whilst a dramatic voice-over
intoned: 'Something strange and wonderful is happening. BSB is
beaming down its five channels . . . If you're not connected you
won't ever know it's there . . .' As everybody ruefully remarked
when they saw them, connected was the one thing you could
not be.

The concept of the seamless, invisible squarial versus the Sky
dish had always been crucial to the different approaches of the
two companies. Murdoch saw Alan Sugar's prominent white
dishes as a free advertisement and wherever possible installers
persuaded punters to allow them to be fixed to the front of
their houses to make them more visible. The result had been
'pocketing', with high dish concentration building up in certain
areas, as a Sun hack out pointed out to his office when he phoned
in from a monstering job on a vile council estate in South London.
It was the worst place he'd ever been in his life, he moaned. He
knew this to be true as he had never seen so many dishes.

The success of Project X in getting dishes bolted to walls
had also put more heat into the great dish grumble led by the
Big Papers, with the *Guardian* describing them as 'identified
non-flying objects, staring motionlessly south-east like pilgrims
at an electronic Mecca . . . to reassure us of the benefits of being
a nation of consumers rather than producers'. The BSB squarials
had won both sympathisers and the high moral ground amongst
the chattering classes in the controversy. Some boroughs, and not
even the 'Loony Left' ones pilloried by the *Sun*, had gone on a
campaign against Sky dishes. Liberal-controlled Sutton, holder
of the Greenest Borough in Britain award, had denounced them
as architectural vandalism and forbidden council tenants from
having them on their walls on penalty of eviction. They were
however allowed to receive Sky on SMATV (satellite master
antenna television) installations, which had one aerial for a block
of buildings with cables running to each individual house or flat.
There had been more rows about designated conservation areas,
where they were not allowed to be visible. In gentrified areas of
inner London like trendy Islington – which was definitely Loony
Left – vigilant preservation associations roamed the streets on
dish-spotting expeditions, noisily lobbying the local authority

to have the culprits removed. Then there was huge merriment in the Big Papers when Rupert Murdoch himself was ordered to remove the dish from his penthouse flat in a conservation area in St James's Place overlooking Green Park.

As coverage increased about how the Sky dishes were changing the architectural face of Britain, the waspish Auberon Waugh, the chattering classes' prime Thatcherite, told Thames Television's Thames Report: 'I'd certainly think twice about buying a house if the next door neighbour had one of those filthy little carbuncles stuck up. Because what he's telling me is that he's the sort of incurious moron who lives on 24 hours a day drivel, because that's what he wants.' For balance the programme inserted an old black and white newsreel clip reporting the row about 'the ugly crop of television aerials, like demented hatstands' covering the country in the 1950s.

To dampen down the fuss Sky introduced a more environmentally-friendly dish made of black mesh, and there was talk of transparent ones and even ones painted to look like bricks. But a further dish problem had now loomed for both sides as it was realised current regulations stipulated planning permission was needed to erect the two aerials needed for both services. As Sky had generally got to homes first this problem was more squarely in the BSB camp and it had been fed into the bureaucratic labyrinth of the Department of the Environment for a ruling. The answer was expected in months, rather than weeks.

A new joke now started circulating Marcopolo linked to the current media scare about mad cow disease: 'What's the difference between BSE and BSB? – You can catch BSE!' while the old 'Where's Salman Rushdie/Lord Lucan/presenter on Sky?' jokes were recycled for the new station. Cynics weighed in by adding the correct observation that it would have been cheaper for BSB to bike its programmes on cassette to each viewer, no matter where they lived, or even send round the delectable Selina Scott to make each a personal programme. Meanwhile a trail of minor celebs like Lord David Sutch of the Official Monster Raving Loony Party, always keen to appear on any media to plug their act, dutifully turned up at Marcopolo for the standard interview and then vainly sifted through their friends for somewhere to watch the finished result. After a fruitless week of searching, during which he was bombarded by helpful letters and phone calls from BSB about when the interview would be screened, Sutch commented drily that more people appeared to vote for him than watch the station. The situation was just as bad for people making the programmes. Many of the young researchers, who included Terry Wogan's son, Alan, were in their first job in television. They found it both demoralising and humiliating when neither they nor anyone else they knew could watch what they had made and resorted to videoing programmes to play back proudly to their mothers and close friends.

When the full extent of the equipment disaster became apparent a programming decision was taken to screen what was arguably the world's longest repeat. The first ten weeks of transmission on the NOW channel were simply shown all over again. The sensible grounds for this were that virtually no one had seen the originals, and only a few more would anyhow be able to see them second time around. The most vulnerable to time, editions of a few programmes had to be canned, like West of Moscow, which carried stories on the fast changing situation in the Russian satellite states. But First Edition, the topical magazine programme made by New Era and praised by the *Mail* at launch, was simply repackaged with timeless old features and refronted by Selina Scott and the other presenters, who had amongst their number Peter Smith, the son-in-law of the *Mail*'s editor Sir David English. Just as with the launch delay the repeat decision caused a subsequent fallout in the independent production sector relying on making BSB programmes for its bread and butter as production teams were laid off for the duration. Management fees, however, remained intact.

Meanwhile the final painful steps in putting together Ian Clubb's refinancing deal were being taken in a very different atmosphere to the wild days of 1987 when the company had raised its first funds. The last froth of the 80s had evaporated and the advertising and media sectors of the Stock Market had crashed. ASG's former employers, Saatchi and Saatchi, were so far from contemplating bidding for the Midland Bank they were now officially classified as one of Britain's smaller companies, with a share price which had collapsed from the 700p plus of his days to below 50p. Other trendy 80s stocks which had been a triumph of marketing, from the BSB minor shareholder of Next to vogue companies of Filofax and Sock Shop, had either gone bust or seen their share price reduced to pence.

The crash of the 80s had produced even heavier fall-out in Australia, where the froth on the market had been higher than the Bondi surf, and the problems of BSB's major shareholder Alan Bond, had stopped rumbling away in the background. Instead they had become terminal, and worse than BSB's not being able to attract any new backers was the fact that nobody could be found to buy his share and at least take some of the heat off the other shareholders. As a heroic worldwide trawl continued the Big Papers speculated about interest from Disney, which had settled Murdoch's $1.5 billion writ out of court and was supplying the Sky Movie Channel with films from Touchstone. The speculation, unfortunately, proved to be just that. CBS in America was approached, as was the Hughes Aircraft company which had built the Marcopolo satellites, but the advances came to nothing.

Robert Maxwell, another potential buyer who was inevitably being courted, announced he was attracted by the prospect of buying Bond's full 36.9% stake. But when he was told he could only have 19.9% to keep him below the sacred 20% laid down in the cross-media regulations, his interest waned. BSB's old rival from the original franchise application, Michael Green of Carlton Communications, expressed serious interest but only, as before, on the condition he had managerial control. Green had been astonished by the way BSB had been acting and especially by Marcopolo House, which he saw as the height of extravagance. 'Have you seen their building?' he asked people indignantly, informing them he had started off in a crummy place in North London. Conrad Black, the Canadian owner of the *Daily Telegraph*, also wanted in, but only on the back of Green. When the condition of managerial control was not conceded both parties went away.

The deadline of 31 May for Bond either to take up or sell his stake was re-extended and extended as he pleaded for time to find a buyer, until finally at the end of July the other shareholders reluctantly accepted the reality of the situation and ended the period of grace. Granada, Pearson, Reed and Chargeurs between between them took up the newly-issued shares, leaving Bond with only 7.5%. They were able to dilute his stake so low because the overall value of the company had declined – the initial value of the investment was now worth much less – even if that had not been officially written off in their individual accounts. The Big Four between them now owned 90% of the company's equity or equity equivalent which totalled £882 million. Such a huge exposure was frightening for all. From an interesting seedcorn project which had seemed a long-term stake in the future, BSB had grown into a monster threatening to overwhelm them. The ramifications were spreading through their own core operations, draining cash from businesses varying from china manufacturing and magazine publishing to oil rigs, textiles and motorway service stations. The Bond business resolved, the new Big Four moved in to take over control.

Until then in all his experience of joint ventures Ian Clubb had never met a more supportive group of shareholders. Neither had Peter Bell. After all, BSB had taken a business plan put together by Granada and Virgin which was relatively conservative and low spend, and then made radical changes. Bell thought the shareholders had been good about that, not minding when BSB asked for more money. But now he detected a change. They were obviously much more nervous. Clubb could easily imagine what was going on back at the boards of their parent companies. The other directors would obviously be pressurising the BSB representatives, saying that with another £450 million in guarantees going out to match the Barclay's project loan they needed to get control and start managing things properly. Sir Trevor Holdsworth could see from their pained expressions that they had been back to their parent boards once too often. They had borne the pain of Bond, but any more hiccups and it would be the end.

ASG also had the picture. He knew that if you ran a public company and then had a sideshow like BSB which didn't go well it became an albatross around your neck. It had been the same with Whitbread USA. Every time you had an AGM and talked to your shareholders it was always the albatross which came up. It became a terribly debilitating distraction and very bad for morale because it wasn't the main line of business. He realised the shareholders were probably thinking: God! I wish we could get rid of it! It had been an arduous journey from the original £100 million stake but nevertheless he had been much heartened by their courage and remarkably sustained belief in the project. As he wrote to the staff in a round robin in July: 'I cannot overstress the magnificent way in which these four great companies have maintained faith in BSB and its mission despite a media that was generally sceptical and an economic environment that is less than helpful. May their faith be properly rewarded.'

As the refinancing had effectively diluted the other shareholders out of sight, Sir Trevor Holdsworth, whose contract expired in July anyway, had informed the Board that as the company was now effectively being run by the four main shareholders it would be better if they chose a chairman from themselves. He had been asked to stay on until things were sorted out. As a post-mortem started on why things had been allowed to get to this stage there was a dawning realisation that with four main shareholders – Alan Bond had scarcely ever been there – no-one had really taken charge. The hands-off Board members had allowed themselves to be reassured and seduced by the very presentation skills they had hired the management for.

Now they were removed, to be replaced by new hard men with both the time and temperament to be tough. Reed, which was panicking the most, led the charge by putting in its deputy chief executive Ian Irvine who, wearing his other hat as part-time Chairman of TV-am, had successfully sat out the strike there. Derek Lewis, with his background at Ford, came to bolster Alec Bernstein for Granada, while for Chargeurs Jean-Pierre Le Grand was replaced by his boss, Eric Guilly. Until then Chargeurs had been extremely laid back, with Jean-Pierre never saying anything but just smiling a great deal at the meetings and returning to France. Eric Guilly arrived not just to inspect Marcopolo, but Leeds and Chilworth as well, and then started coming aross the Channel every week.

The new attitude was most graphically illustrated by Frank Barlow, who took over from the gangling old Etonian Mark Burrell for Pearson. Burrell, famous within the group for once turning up at company senior management course in full hunting gear, had been very supportive of the project. Barlow was quite different, miles away from the standard Pearson uppercrust family types. As Ian Clubb instantly saw, here was a gritty bugger from up North – the provincial newspaper general manager par excellence.

Barlow, who had previously managed the *Financial Times*, used to like taking home journalists' expenses claims to peruse on his chauffeur-driven ride such was his attention to detail. He was respected in Fleet Street as a fair but very tough operator. After Murdoch had moved to Wapping and derisively offered the old *Sunday Times* building to the print workers to produce their own paper on the old technology, Barlow had been chosen by the unions to conduct a feasibility study, sensibly coming down against it. Not initially in favour of Pearson's investment in BSB, he had only been convinced by John Gau's presentation to its board.

Carol Goddard, ASG's secretary, had never heard of him before, but as he moved in as fulltime sceptic suddenly he was there all the time, not just at meetings but always on the phone, wanting all kinds of papers and details about BSB operations. Derek Lewis was repeatedly on the line as well along with Alex Bernstein, who was desperately concerned about the promotion of squarials. Apart from the sudden barrage of calls Goddard found ASG's schedule was changing rapidly. Within a day he was abruptly called to meetings at Granada and then asked to report continuously on sales figures and marketing.

So the new team could get a tighter grip on day to day affairs the existing large and unwieldy Board was sidelined by being rescheduled to meet only quarterly. Effectively it was replaced by the weekly strategy group which previously had been run on an informal and somewhat vague basis. Now it started meeting at Marcopolo every Friday at 8am, bringing together the new shareholders' representatives and the management trio of ASG, John Gau and Ian Clubb. To signal its new importance it was also renamed as the Standing Committee, leading one exec to mutter that it had been typically BSB to have a strategy meeting a week. ASG, given an ultimatum to give a report on each occasion, at first baulked. Then he buckled under to the new tighter control.

The management roadshow was over. The new shareholders' representatives wanted to know everything, and within weeks BSB was to be transformed into an entirely different company.

There had already been one major crisis when the production delays meant failure to meet the June performance targets set by the banks. As a condition of releasing money they had stipulated BSB must achieve pre-agreed levels of production and market penetration by particular dates, and the painfully-raised loan had therefore gone into default. In a heroic last-ditch effort Ian Clubb had renegotiated the June target by moving the goalposts into the future, meaning BSB had to reach 600,000 homes and produce 230,000 receivers by the end of September.

The new shareholders' representatives, making an overriding resolution to go all out to meet this target, now put the pressure on the production side, where the equipment delays had mainly been caused by water contamination problems with the complex ITT chip. Throughout July and August, as the technical people worked flat out to meet targets they anyhow thought almost impossible, this continued to cause trouble. People were being persuaded to work over their holidays and at week-ends to make the receiver boxes when there were not enough chips to put in them. But in the new harder climate the panic behind the scenes was kept extremely quiet. Very few people inside the company even knew anything about the drama. The 'need to know' philosophy the long-departed Graham Grist had originally espoused was now back with a vengeance, and there was another indication of how things had changed when nothing about the problem appeared in the newspapers. As far as leaks to the press were concerned BSB had at last become a tight ship.

By now the GBP had receded into the far distance. All the brave talk about interacting with it, or even thinking about it at all, had vanished out of the window as company policy was subjugated to the banks, which had become all that mattered. As the chip horror continued it was realised the only way to meet the target they were demanding was by switching the focus from DTH – selling dishes to individual homes – to SMATV installations like the ones the London Borough of Sutton was stipulating for its council tenants. Concentration on deals which put one aerial on a whole block of flats enormously bumped up the total number of people 'available to view', as the market research people put it. Effectively this was narrowband cabling rather than sales but fortunately the bankers, not personally avid cable viewers, had not fully grasped the distinction. SMATV bulk viewing in flats and hotels gave the opportunity to produce the convincing figures they wanted.

Coupled with the desperate new SMATV sales direction came a dramatic change in the marketing department. Control of distribution was taken away from Peter Bell and handed to Peter Symes, whom Bell had recruited from Whitbread and had previously operated under him. Symes, with his own distribution department now bypassing Bell and reporting directly to ASG, started giving much-needed attention to the nuts and bolts of the operation. At the retail end Granada pitched in its TV rental expertise, carving up the country in a joint operation by which BSB covered some cities, whilst it did others. The retail shop toaster assistants started on their long learning curve.

The lead up to the end of the September banking target was so nerve-racking that ASG held a special meeting with the IBA on the 23rd to warn that if it was not achieved BSB would be in serious difficulties. But the meeting proved to be alarmist as to everyone's huge relief the massive Symes' SMATV operation got the company there at the last second. But no sooner had everyone drawn a breath than the next target was relentlessly bearing down on them and this time nobody believed it would be feasible. The banks had belatedly caught up with the SMATV point and next time a captive semi-cable audience would not save them. The banking target was BSB having 400,000 squarials sold by the end of the year. With some arm-twisting that figure had been reduced to 275,000, but even so it was just three months away. In its first six months BSB had sold only 68,000, mostly to the long-suffering members of the Launch Club. The current sales of no more than 6,000 a week had to be trebled.

As the outlook grew more gloomy people began to fall off the sledge. The head of the Movie Channel, Andy Birchall, who had always wanted each channel to have its own autonomous identity – in opposition to John Gau's overall scheme for the station – officially resigned and said he would be leaving in December. David Eglise had already gone, and now he was followed out of the door of Marcopolo House by Chris Dickens. Dickens had projected to have pulled in about £4 million in ad revenue by the end of the year, which he did not think bad when spots were being sold at £50 and the whole thing was being done on a wing and a prayer. BSB was a real act of faith by the advertisers, but the station had still carried 300 brands in its first six months. Five significant ad agencies and six major companies had committed themselves to some form of business arrangement. But Dickens had soon found his range of hypotheses about viewers over-optimistic. On the advertising side the SMATV installations had done little to help as they often only carried two of the five BSB channels. Both the advertisers and media buyers, more aware than the bankers, knew full well the difference between proper sales and piping the signal to bottom of the barrel semi-cable viewers. In the bigger picture too they had seen that with the country moving into a deeper recession than had been forecast, BSB's figures lacked logic. So much had changed in the general economic environment the forward projection of costs had gone all wrong. When Dickens' old company of Young & Rubicam made him an offer, he didn't refuse.

Then it was the turn of the architect of fastburn to resign. Peter Bell had by now accepted that BSB was so far behind it would never become the brand leader against Sky. But with patience he still thought it could win through. Bell had never stopped believing in BSB. The programming which catered for the 'discrete' viewer' was great, the scheduling thoughtful, and there was the British attention to quality. To Bell BSB looked like real television, not satellite television, and gave him more of what he liked at times that he could watch it. But with distribution taken away from him, and the long-term commitment to fastburn abandoned, he was pissed off. When endless rows with ASG got him nowhere he left.

For the first time BSB had come up against the novelty of a bottom line and the new hardline attitude from the shareholders was slashing forward budgets. Behind the scenes Frank Barlow was using his newspaper management skills to draw up a series of contingency plans carrying redundancies of up to 40%. Rumours abounded that ASG's head would be offered on a plate as part of the changes that were to come. For the staff in general there were also painful daily reminders of how the heady days were over. Money, as Ian Clubb put it, was 'tighter than a tick's arse', and Hugh Williams of the NOW channel, paralleling Barlow's contingency plans, was even contemplating a worst-case scenario of repeating the entire first year of broadcasting. With no money for new programming inside Marcopolo, world events had taken on a new perspective. A series of desperate conferences and meetings called after Saddam Hussein invaded Kuwait at the beginning of August concluded helplessly that there had better not be a war in the Gulf as BSB simply couldn't afford to send anyone to cover it.

Williams decided the company would have to cut more losses by abandoning its planned coverage of the political parties' autumn conferences, even though Crown Communications had already committed substantial amounts to booking facilities. As BSB was going to have to meet these bills anyway the Crown staff still attended, only to sit round glumly with no programmes to make while their colleagues from other stations beavered away excitedly. But the hospitality side was kept up as part of the public façade, with lavish conference parties hosted by ASG, John Gau and Hugh Williams. At Bournemouth, where a marquee had been hired in the hotel grounds, ASG made a short speech to the Tories, telling them: 'I hope you've enjoyed your champagne and thanks for making BSB possible.' But the line was drawn when the second D-MAC satellite, required by the franchise conditions as a backup, was launched from Cape Canaveral. This time only one person was sent to watch and there were no emotional tears of joy.

After the company had scraped through the September banking target Andy Coleman had spoken out strongly on behalf of the technical side against any more. 'For Christ's sake,' he had said, 'don't give ourselves consumer targets for Christmas. If we don't do as our plans say we've got no time to react and change anything through the retail trade. If you can't sell enough you can't do anything immediately – you just have to sweat it out.' Coleman was overruled, but he knew from the moment the new targets were put in place they would not be met and there was bound to be some sort of financial crisis. In that he was not alone. But now the shareholders had seized the helm from the management, and unknown to him and most others, the Good Ship BSB had already altered course. With the storm now upon it, far from sailing towards being the Third Force in British broadcasting, the new crew had already abandoned the banking targets and was heading for the only available port. And to get there they now screwed the ship's engines up to full power.

The start of the autumn sales offensive had already been flagged by commentators as the final showdown between the two sides. ASG kicked things off by pronouncing to the press that BSB had been 'limbering up' over the summer. John Gau thought that was at least true of the programming side. He had always been more aware than most people in the company that success would not come overnight and believed the real BSB would not start until October. The station was bedding down well, he thought. He knew instinctively some changes would be required, such as simplifying the Galaxy general entertainment channel, but overall he was pleased with the way BSB had got it about right. It had stayed true to the BBC1 line which would eventually deliver the right types for the advertisers and his close connections with the BBC had also paid off on the programming – even though the two bureaucracies struggling to close their deal had been a cliffhanger lasting almost up to the cable viewers' 'service' launch. They had lost Miss Marple and were not happy about the substitute of The Big Deal, a mid-80s low life comedy drama about a gambling man, but they had got all the reliable old chestnuts like Dr. Who, Shoestring, Dad's Army, Steptoe, The Young Ones, The Goodies, Are You Being Served?, Grange Hill and Porridge. A separate deal had secured Gardener's World and an assortment of documentary programmes.

The negotiations with Equity had been officially solved, although some individual members did not think so, as was made plain by angry letters coming from The Goodies' agent saying they had never been repeated on the BBC and BSB had no right to transmit them. Even the much-maligned cosmic soap, Jupiter Moon, had acquired a minor cult following. Gau liked it, especially as the £7 million contract bought three different thirty minute episodes a week, when by normal drama costings you would expect one. The IBA and the Big Papers had been warmly approving of the wall to wall weekend arts programmings, likening it to a televised Radio 3. The only major disaster had been the loss of 200 hours of the Survival wildlife series – one programme the satellite family could definitely watch together. Even though Anglia was a minor BSB shareholder, it had still pulled out of negotiations less than eight weeks before launch because of worries that it would jeopardise its position with the whole ITV network.

Now Gau could parade his Christmas offerings, which at least showed where some of the money had gone. The £70 million 'exciting Yuletide package', entitled The 12 Days of Christmas, certainly made the terrestrial companies sit up and take notice. The Movie Channel, its monthly subscription held at £12.99 and now with free trial for new takers, had four of the top five films of 1988 and was to offer box-office hits like Midnight Run, Scrooged, My Stepmother is an Alien, Rain Man, Personal Services, Crocodile Dundee II, A Fish Called Wanda and The Adventures of Baron Munchausen. 'Classics' to back these up included Oliver! and An American In Paris. The Power Station had New Kids on the Block, Phil Collins, Van Morrison, the Stranglers, and Eric Clapton, along with America's leading country rock show, Austin City Limits, and highlights from Jazz '90 at Montreux. Sport had annual reviews of motor racing, tennis, and cricket, live football matches from Scotland and Italy, live American football, live coverage of the Stone's Bitter Rugby League championship and two days of darts from the British Open. NOW had 100 hours of arts programming, including actor Anthony Hopkins' debut as a TV director with a one-man play called Dylan Thomas, Placido Domingo, the recently retired Dame Joan Sutherland, Dame Kiri Te Kanawa, the Bolshoi Ballet and a performance of Beethoven's ninth live from Leipzig. Galaxy added in Wonder Woman, Ian McShane in a trio of Dick Francis adventure movies, Till Death Us Do Part and The Kids in the Hall, billed as 'a fresh, hip and freak gang of five hailed as America's Monty Pythons of the 90s'.

Best of all BSB had the Teenage Mutant Ninja Turtles, the biggest marketing operation aimed at children ever to come out of America. Seeing what a lead-in they provided to the bottom line of the kiddie market everybody had been chasing them. ITV had then decided they were too violent, but the BBC thought the problem was surmountable and was still keen. Neither Sky nor BSB was offering enough. But the Gau-led combination of BSB plus BBC once again equalled success. The Turtles were repackaged to be less violent and the Japanese connection severed by retitling them 'Hero' rather than 'Ninja', and BSB obtained all the available episodes for a mere £250,000. They were being stripped in twice a day seven days a week and pushed by an advertising poster campaign which promised 'A turtle on the menu every day'.

The ad campaign had also changed under the new leadership. Nigel Bogle, establishing BSB as 'a big brand I could warm to', had moved on to a series of TV ads featuring a typical household where famous people kept ringing the bell and dropping in on various pretexts so they could really watch BSB. The celebs ranged from Paul 'Gazza' Gascoigne and Jason Donovan to David Frost and Gary Lineker, with Superman arriving at the end to ask if he could borrow some sugar, at which point the lady of the house fainted. 'Are you as well connected?' the strapline had asked. Bogle had then been told to produce simple Sky-type programme advertising, only to find that now the programmers were finally having their day what excited them did not always have the same effect on him. A huge amount of money, for example, had been spent on a run through Britain called The Great Race, which Bogle just thought made for boring television. And as far as he was concerned there was another fault with the new approach. It no longer differentiated BSB from Sky but just meant both sides were spending money to cancel each other out. Nevertheless Bogle had followed the new dictates and the ads leading the Christmas push were now blip-types featuring black and white cut-outs of the stars against a lurid yellow background, with a linking commentary by the popular BBC Radio One disc jockey and personality, Adrian Just.

Another pointer to how the two sides were mirroring each other occurred in distribution. Under Peter Symes the high-flown principles which had originally rubbished Murdoch's Project X had been abandoned as BSB followed Sky down the door-to-door road. The company did its best to distance itself from the inevitable hard-sell connotations by officially referring to the new approach internally by the coy euphemism of 'bringing the retailer to the customer'. Publicly it distanced itself from the Sky 'spotty youth' brigade by announcing that the 3,000 strong sales force it would be hiring both to knock on doors and approach people in the street would be largely female, 'adopting an "Avon Lady" style of approach instead of foot in the door tactics'. Pay for the 'BSB ladies' would be £25 a day, with £15 commission on each squarial sold. Going one step further down the Sky road BSB then announced it was going into installation, although typically instead of just backing an existing company it had actually bought Startrak, which had done such sterling work for Sky.

There was however still one significant difference beween the two sides. BSB's marketing contribution, set up before Peter Bell had left, was being retained in the last desperate attempt to 'ramp up awareness' and 'kick start the market'. The massive sum of £50 million was to be spent before Christmas – £16 million was to go on the direct programme-led advertising campaign and £35 million on incentive schemes – £20 million of it on pushing dish sales through the lures of interest-free credit and free installation, £9 million on marketing to cable subscribers and between £5 and £6 million on free trials for the film channel.

As far as ASG was concerned this was the first time BSB had been in a position to communicate its proposition to the public. There had been one unfortunate moment when he had unwisely remarked that he was having great fun spending other people's money, which had got into the papers, but he knew what he meant. The technology was at last working and the equipment being produced. All the company's ducks were in a row and the season had arrived. The traditional brown goods curve meant new consumer electronics were slow to take off, but Sky had already bucked it by three or four to one. It had failed to strangle BSB at birth and now was the moment for BSB to follow its lead with everybody landing running. It was punchy stuff. Sky was going to throw lots of money about as well in the massive marketing battle which was about to commence. But that was what they were all there for. 'The show,' he announced confidently to the media hacks, 'happens now'. Some thought wearily that they had heard that somewhere before.

CHAPTER SIXTEEN

Tie Me Kangaroo Down Sport

In March 1989 ASG had gone on record as saying: 'The business and programming approaches of ourselves and Sky are fundamentally different. Although there may be room for both, we cannot both be right.' So far, with its virtually clear run, Sky had surged ahead on the business side. Now the verdict came in on its programming.

The official Big Paper view was pronounced by Chris Dunkley, the respected TV critic of the *Financial Times*. After scrupulously watching Sky for more than a year it was summed up on the famous 'no comment' pages by the headline 'A dish of Muddle and mediocrity'. To make his point Dunkley took readers through the 16-channel Astra output one Friday evening, starting with Eurosport's Prime Time Wrestling from the US. 'The commentator was saying: "Yuh have tuh admire the cheek of Demolition, incredible that they're willing tuh put those belts on the line, and drop a toe hold! And some nice fluid moves there! And another tag! Taking advantage of the five seconds there! If Santana gets a flying hammer on one of these that title could go right now! And lookee here Krusch trying to counter but Santana quick to . . ."'

'I swear I am not making any of this up,' Dunkley reassured his readers, observing the commentator might as well be speaking Serbo-Croat. 'Perhaps he is,' he added helpfully before zapping across to Sky News where Angela Rippon was topping and tailing ancient newsreel clips in Those Were the Days. The MTV music channel was screening The Coca-Cola Report – 'pop music news presented by a girl speaking American' –

and for the £9.92 a month it cost to unscramble Sky Movies, that evening he could have watched Odd Jobs, Weeds, and The Dead Zone. 'Well, yes, quite,' Dunkley added, pointing out the uncomfortable fact, which the government was dimly becoming aware of, that for £90 you could buy one of the pirate decoders which were openly advertised in the satellite magazines to unscramble not the movies, but Filmnet and notably its late night porn. Dunkley's advice was it was probably more fun to watch it scrambled 'where men with purple faces and green legs remove the underwear from co-operative ladies whose outsize bosoms in centre screen suddenly bifurcate to reappear in two parts, screen left and screen right'.

Dunkley said he had bent over backwards to let Sky One impress him, zapping into Frank Bough's World, which he thought sounded promising. He found an Australian-made film about an attempt on the world speedboat record which had nothing to do with Bough, who merely appeared in the studio at the end to look up from a video recorder and bid him goodnight. Beyond 2000, billed as a 'round up of the latest developments in the fields of science, technology, and medicine' was revealed to be a two-year-old Australian current affairs programme about Expo '88 in Brisbane. It was followed by an episode of the American series Moonlighting, which had previously been shown on BBC2, and then another American import, Wiseguy, which had not. You soon found out why, Dunkley explained, describing it as 'like an attempt by children with a video camera to make their own episode of Hill Street Blues'. Commercial breaks took up 15 minutes in every hour, station promos were sung in American, and Dunkley's overall conclusion was that Astra and Sky were overwhelmingly foreign television. 'The fraction which is comprehensible to a British audience seems to be aimed – unsurprisingly, perhaps – straight at readers of the Sun,' he ended.

Sky had retaliated to this type of criticism by counting the number of American hours on both stations and pronouncing them virtually level-pegging. There was also perceived to be a considerable amount of cant in the sneering when terrestrial television itself was reaching new depths, with the chattering classes latching on to cult programmes like the Australian

Prisoner, Cell Block H, and all manner of horrors laid on for late and all-night audiences. Programmes like The Hitman and Her had started appearing. Hitman was an appalling tour of dire downmarket Northern discotheques fronted by a wrinkly Pete Waterman, during which girls turned out the contents of their handbags for the camera (hairbrush, packet of Mates, chewing gum, packet of Mates . . .). Then there was the loathsome James Whale Radio Show, broadcast from Radio Aire in Leeds, which specialised in general abuse and tacky novelty acts, like a man in a fluorescent green jumpsuit who farted popular tunes while the microphone was obligingly held in full view of the camera inches from the sounding-off orifice. Ageing TV star Robert Stack, once Elliot Ness in the popular Untouchables, fronted up Unsolved Mysteries, Hughie Green-clone Casey Kasem presented America's Top Ten, and insomniac viewers could tune into American college football and the US-made Murphy's Law (no second series planned).

The audiences for some of these programmes were sometimes tiny, but the regular in depth research carried out by BARB (Broadcasters' Audience Research Board) was also showing that Sky News in particular was paying an even heavier penalty for broadcasting throughout 24 hours. In a week when 15.47 million people watched Coronation Street, 14.23 million Neighbours, 68,000 Welsh persons Dros/Nghwm Rhymni and 62,000 Dyddiau Da on S4C, 208,000 Sky punters might have tuned into The Return of the Killer Tomatoes on the Movie Channel, but chunks of Sky News, The Frank Bough Interview, and the repeat of the Tebbit-Mitchell Target show before breakfast were on occasion failing to attract an audience large enough even to register.

Whilst all this was only to be expected, Rupert Murdoch also perceived a rapid need to tidy up the bottom line. In the August results Sky reported losses of £95 million for the ten months it had been treated as a fully operating unit of News International, and Murdoch took the decision to write off £121 million of investment at one stroke, demolishing the profits of the world-wide News Corporation from £211.3 million to £120.1 million. The loss for News International, covering the British operation, soared from £55 million in 1989 to £257 million.

On the plus side by now 750,000 homes were paying for the Movie Channel, which would ultimately generate £90 million in revenue.

Attention now turned to mopping up the debris left by the 'spotty youth' Project X. The direct-sell operation's bad debt rate – the number of customers signing on and then either changing their minds or failing to pay the bill – had been horrific. In some parts of the country it had run as high as 30% and the dish installers now turned reclaimers in the hazardous work of braving the lands of Rottweilers and dead cars to retrieve their equipment. As the accountants had correctly warned, the fearful toll had come from not just hitting the target C2 market, but large numbers of penniless hardcore Ds and Es who had long since given up hope of obtaining credit anywhere. The doorstep hard sell had still pressed it on them regardless of their lowly socio-economic status. 'Go on – just take it free for a couple of weeks. You can always say no and it will be ages before they come and take it away,' the young salesmen had gabbled before getting a signature and rushing off to claim their commission. No one had been safe, and dishes had even started appearing on caravans.

Now, just as building societies hit the front page for repossessing houses, Sky started getting things straight, setting some sort of repossessions record by taking back 17,000 dishes in August. Before things settled down all manner of innocents were swept along in the rush, with tales of unsuspecting pensioners being hounded for money when they had never asked for a dish and frustrated customers who had complained for weeks about a problem, but received no joy. Their plight was helpfully highlighted by the non-Murdoch press.

A parallel series of noisy internal disputes then erupted within the trade. In cases where the free trials had not worked out Sky tried to reclaim the commission from the companies, but this frequently failed as the directors had already taken out the funds. It then tried deducting money from the new contracts, until the more fly by night operators shut down the companies and simply walked away, leaving the Sky accountants tearing their hair out. Further down the line hordes of spotty youths angrily claimed they had not received the commission they were due. More cash-flow had been gobbled up by increasing the supply of dishes from Alan Sugar, which had been bought and stored in warehouses.

But despite all this, maverick and unconventional though it had been, Project X was pronounced to have worked. Backed by a huge advertising campaign run in News International papers to promote the deal, the salesmen on the streets and sometimes the phone had worked wonders in pushing up sales. Although the total fallout was costed at just under £40 million Sky was still convinced it was cheap at the price. The same amount spent on advertising would not have brought such sensational results.

Writing off bad debts was one thing, but the inevitable corollary was to cut costs, both back in the office and on programming. To achieve that Murdoch now took a step backwards to hand over the post of chief executive of Sky to a man already a legend in his own country rivalling Kelvin MacKenzie, the dreaded editor of the *Sun*, in Britain.

Samuel Hewlings Chisholm had come a long way from being a brush and floor wax salesman in New Zealand, where he had been born the son of a farmer. There is a saying in Australia: 'All New Zealanders are perfectly balanced – they have a chip on each shoulder,' and Chisholm was the epitome of the competitive and aggressive New Zealanders who populated the Australian media business, determined to show their home country contained more than sheep. The Australian press, in some awe, had dubbed him the Most Feared Man in Television. Murdoch had been trying to hire him for years.

It was not just Chisholm's ethnic origins that made him aggressive. At little over five foot he was also the classic small man with a big ego, a TV Napoleon needing to prove himself. Famously described in Australia as a compressed package of energy, like a ping-pong player on amphetamines, who was also known as the Jimmy Cagney of Australian Television, with a strut straight out of Yankee Doodle Dandee. Chisholm had started his TV career selling airtime for Kerry Packer's brother on a local station in Melbourne before joining Channel Nine and rising to become managing director. Under Chisholm, Nine was the most successful station in Australia, with ratings far ahead of its rivals. And he remained in charge when ownership switched in 1987 from Kerry Packer to BSB share-holder Alan Bond.

During the 80s the Australian television industry had degenerated into an extraordinary spectacle reminiscent of the Last Days of Pompeii, with limitless spending in every sphere from mega-stars' contracts to ordinary salaries and expenses. Chisholm had fuelled the trend by outbidding the opposition to build up such an impressive stable of highly-paid talent that Channel Nine became known as the Bollinger Channel. Apart from his image as a spendthrift, who bought not just expensive stars but legendary lunches, Chisholm's management style demonstrated his belief in fierce internal as well as external competition. Ben Hawke still had fond memories of his Sixty Minutes days when what were known as 'Sam's Friday Night Follies' were held in Chisholm's lurid green office, based round an industrial freezer ten deep in bottles of Chardonnay. At these events select staff were encouraged to criticise and argue with each other while Chisholm eagerly provoked disputes, waiting patiently until the early hours when some legless drunk would go over the top and say what he or she really thought. The next day Chisholm would quote their remarks back to them, word for word.

But by the end of the 80s the world of Australian television had changed just like everywhere else and the commercial networks had hit serious problems. On his fiftieth birthday Chisholm had been presented with a Harley Davidson motorbike, which was lifted into the Channel Nine boardroom by a crane, but the celebrations for some of the staff were short-lived. The same day over 100 of them were made redundant. Alan Bond, as BSB knew only too well, had been teetering on the edge, and Chisholm had travelled the world attempting to raise money for his beleagured boss until the Australian Broadcasting Tribunal had ruled Bond unfit to hold a broadcasting licence. With no choice but to relinquish custodianship, Bond had sold the station back to Kerry Packer and on the first day of the new regime long lunches were abolished and the bar fridges emptied. When a team of men in suits from the consultants Coopers and Lybrand were unleashed into the building Chisholm had known the Bollinger days were over and this time he had been ripe for Murdoch's picking.

When news of the incoming boss reached Osterley a shudder went through the Australian execs all of whom knew his reputation. Many had come from Channel Nine themselves and one unfortunate had already stretched the limits of even Australian management style by taking a swing at Chisholm when he had been there. Fortunately Chisholm's tiny stature had meant he had missed, but the exec had still had no choice but to leave and seek sanctuary in Britain. Now his past was about to catch up with him. Even David Hill, the boss of Eurosport, who was regarded as the ultimate aggressive Aussie, was alarmed. 'Just you wait for Sam's Monday morning meetings,' he warned his British colleagues. 'The only way I could handle them at Channel Nine was by playing The Ride of the Valkyries, like in Apocalypse Now, on the car cassette player when I was ten minutes from the office. If I didn't psyche myself up for the confrontation I'd be pulverised.' Sky's Brits were taken aback by this. As a toughie from the Kerry Packer mould Hill had a sign on his desk proclaiming 'Assumption is the Mother of all Fuck-ups' and it was quite worrying to think of him being intimidated by anyone.

Chisholm had already gained some knowledge of British satellite TV world through a little informal snooping he had carried out on behalf of Alan Bond when he had owned Nine. In June 1989, just after the announcement of the BSB launch delay, ASG had received a call from him, saying he was passing through London. As the emissary of BSB's largest shareholder ASG had invited him to Brompton Road where he spent a friendly hour in the office, with ASG showing him prototype squarials and a promotional video and describing the programming plans. Chisholm had returned the compliment by inviting ASG to join him in the Bond hospitality tent at Wimbledon, where they made an unlikely pair as they sat at the bar, the diminutive, stubby Chisholm dwarfed by the large flamboyant figure of ASG. Chisholm drank several cans of his employer's XXXX lager and, despite his asthma, smoked what seemed to ASG like 50 cigarettes, reeled off some of his endless fund of dirty jokes, said 'G'day', and disappeared. Now he was back in London working for the other side, with the additional irony – given his free-spending reputation at

Nine – that Murdoch had hired him to take care of the bottom line.

Chisholm installed himself in the luxurious Hyde Park Hotel, where ASG and John Gau had met for their working breakfast before Gau had joined, and immediately set to work with the first of his Monday morning meetings. If anything these turned out to be even worse than David Hill had warned they would be. Previously the exec meetings had been casual fortnightly affairs starting at 9.30 am but Chisholm changed them to a weekly start-time of 8.30 am and turned them into terrifying ordeals. At the first he announced that the sales director had handed in her notice. She would be leaving that day. 'The company wishes to take this opportunity to thank and pay tribute to . . .' he intoned briefly in standard corporate-speak before moving on to the next item. When the meeting had finished a colleague rang to commiserate, only to find Chisholm had not yet bothered to inform her of the immediacy of her fate. The marketing director was next.

None of the execs had ever experienced anything like it before. When Murdoch had run the meetings he had expected results, but there had been a civilised atmosphere which encouraged frank and open debate. Chisholm wanted none of that. He never set an agenda, as that would have given participants a chance to prepare, and instead at 8.30 am precisely would stride into the boardroom and take a look round the table while everyone held their breath, wondering whose turn it would be today. Then he would pick his topic. 'That fucking promo last night . . . who the bloody hell put that together?' he would snarl and an exec would cringe as he became the first jockeyed into the firing line. Chisholm would then dive in, effing and blinding and saying it was all fucking useless.

The only comfort was in numbers when the rant turned on them all. 'You bastards are draining the group's reserves. This can't bloody well go on. This bloody operation has got to come under control,' he would shout. Hammer, hammer, hammer, it went. The next week it would be the news department's turn. 'Fucking costing us so much. You sit around here losing a million a week, you useless fuckers.' On occasions Chisholm would get up from his chair, draw himself up to his full height and lean across table to emphasise his point as he bellowed at his victim. Any head that rose above the parapet was shot off. When the personnel chief tried to argue on a staffing issue Chisholm retorted: 'I don't give a fuck about anything. I can't afford to get involved with people's personal feelings and lives.' The personnel man himself soon had his marching orders.

With the exception of the Monday morning and other occasional meetings Chisholm rarely left his office and weeks after he had arrived many of the staff still had no idea what he even looked like. Murdoch always delighted in going on walkabouts round the station chatting to staff, as well as eating in the canteen. At night, on his frequent journeys to Heathrow, he would invariably stop off at Osterley for a wander round the newsroom. But Chisholm, shut away in his office, showed no interest in having anything to do with the staff, the viewers, or apparently any of the rest of the human race. 'You don't sit down and measure your achievements in life by citing a list of your friends,' he once remarked grimly.

In Australia Chisholm's idea of weekend relaxation on his yacht had been poring over the viewer complaint and response logs at Channel Nine. At Sky, for obvious reasons, these made pretty thin reading, so he substituted a viewing rota. Senior management had to take turns in watching the Sky output across four channels for the entire evening, summarise their reaction and hand the report in to Chisholm the next morning.

One unfortunate, settling down for his first duty evening, found to his horror that none of the Sky channels was working. As he fiddled with the set his wife came in from the garden to tell him it looked as though someone had tried to tear their dish off the wall, so he spent the evening Skyless. The next morning he went in to face Chisholm, terrified he would get his ears ripped off. Not for nothing did Chisholm have a sign on his desk reading: 'To err is human, to forgive is not my policy'. But quite unexpectedly Chisholm saw the funny side of a thief being after the dish. The exec congratulated himself on a lucky escape, at the same time thinking it was this unpredictability which made Chisholm hardest of all to deal with. One minute it was all antipodean jocularity, the next a grenade would go off without warning. After a while some of the execs began to suspect the endless aggression was all part of a big act by which he felt he had to

DISHED!

prove himself, almost like a deliberate management technique. On one occasion Chisholm responded to a Sky legal adviser: 'Why should I bother listening to your advice?' But when the brave soul quipped back, 'You don't have to listen Mr Chisholm, you just have to pay the bills,' there was a roar of laughter and it was all taken in good part.

Meanwhile Chisholm spent days poring over figures with the accountants as he settled down to the real business of wielding the axe and tried to work out ways of reducing the losses of nearly £3 million a week. Murdoch's maxim was always that it is easier to take a million out of costs than add a million to your revenue and the target was to cut costs by a third, to £100 million a year. Some three weeks after Chisholm had started he was discussing the various options in the office of the managing director, Gary Davey, when Murdoch joined them. It was clear what needed to be done, Chisholm announced – the only solution was to shut down the expensive luxury of Sky News. Murdoch disagreed. Not only was he pleased with its achievements but he told Chisholm there were overriding reasons of prestige and politics for keeping it. The final hurdle of the Broadcasting Bill had still to be overcome and the case being mounted in the Lords for the acceptability of Sky would collapse if suddenly there was no News Channel.

Chisholm retaliated by saying he wanted to halve the News budget, saving £20 million a year. Murdoch told him that was not possible either and then left the room to make a phone call. Chisholm turned laconically to the others. 'I don't care what the kid says,' he declared in his Jimmy Cagney mode. 'I'm shutting it down.' There was a sharp intake of breath as execs silently speculated about how long the Rottweiler, as he was now far from fondly known, would last. Eventually, though, Chisholm backed off. The News Channel cost £40 million a year, plus another £10 million share of the overheads and Chisholm, persuaded a £20 million cut was unrealistic, after much wrangling tried for cuts of £10 million and finally retreated to £4 million. This 10% reduction was accompanied by a similar 10% cut across the board on all the channels.

How this was to be achieved was left to each channel head, leading to endless negotiations with the finance department as they struggled to find ways of cutting back. In an already lean and mean operation it was not easy, but Chisholm was always willing to help. Before one meeting he remarked to the finance director: 'Are any of these people giving you trouble with the cuts? If so just let me know and I'll fire a couple of them.' To emphasise the point he then walked into the boardroom and looked round the table. 'If any of you bastards aren't prepared to cut, let me know and I'll replace you,' he told them. There was silence.

The impact of the economy drive soon reached the lowest level of the factory floor. Even in the good times the Sky stationery cupboard had always been tight. Now it was unlocked for less than an hour every morning and complicated requisition forms, countersigned by senior execs, had to be handed to the glowering minions, who only cheered up if requested items were unavailable. As a double check the Securitate guards outside periodically carried out spot-checks on cars leaving the site, searching, amongst other things, for unauthorised sheets of blank paper.

Of more concern to the journalists was the new edict on video tapes. Normally in television stations all programmes and news stories are shot on tape and then kept in the library to fulfil the frequent demand for archive material. But Chisholm ordered that no new tapes were to be purchased. Instead some of the tape library was to be junked and the old tapes recycled for future use. Minicab accounts, already tightly controlled and requiring endless authorisations, were cut back even further. Chisholm took this aspect of the operation particularly seriously and if ever he looked out of the window and saw a minicab waiting outside would clench his fists and leap up and down with fury at the waste. Telephone bills were targeted and detailed print-outs of each individual's calls sent to their head of department. The unfortunate Irish clerk who was discovered to have called home to Mother 16 times in a month got a bollocking to end them all.

Naturally Chisholm's own highly animated phone calls to Sydney, did not come under the same financial scrutiny, and in a personal capacity he had also managed to resume some of the traditions of the Bollinger Channel. The bills from the Hyde Park Hotel were staggering, and the finance department, issuing payments, marvelled at the amounts of alcohol consumed. The department also had to act creatively on Chisholm's behalf when, after having instituted a freeze on new recruitment, he demanded a chauffeur. The driver had to be employed as a freelance, submitting invoices, which although it was more expensive, did not officially add an extra member of staff. Chisholm meanwhile continued to display his own special brand of humour, as on the occasion when he announced to Murdoch he would be moving out of the Hyde Park Hotel to a flat which he had found. The rent, he said, would be £2,000 a week. The Boss swallowed hard, whereupon Chisholm beamed happily and added: 'Don't worry, mate – I'm only joking.'

At Osterley the Murdoch dry rule meant Chisholm was unable to repeat his Friday Night Follies, getting his staff blind drunk to find out what they were thinking, so he devised other means. After inheriting a secretary from another exec he posed as an outside caller and rang her replacement, asking for her. The reply came that she had moved offices and was now working for Sam Chisholm. What kind of a person had the new secretary heard Chisholm was? the caller asked. She said enough to hang herself before Chisholm revealed his identity and slammed the phone down, leaving her mortified. It wasn't a sacking offence to have a low opinion of him. It just seemed he took a delight in knowing that his act succeeded.

As the staff giggled at this story they agreed that he might be awful, but his Anzac bluntness was sometimes quite appealing. And those who did encounter him often suspected his manner was all part of an elaborate game. He would fire off a few salvos and wait for a reaction, and if anyone fought back it was often taken in good part. Some even maintained he did have a more attractive side, such as the occasion he went to an advertising presentation and afterwards insisted on seeking out the catering staff to thank them for his lunch.

Chisholm's various savings in the office were ultimately pretty marginal and more for cosmetic and psychological reasons. But his programming cuts produced a sense of real gloom amongst the staff. Everyone knew this was the only way to save serious money, and Ben Hawke had feared the worst from the beginning. His features shows were perceived as the glossy end of the Sky

News output and therefore likely candidates. There was an obvious saving to be made through replacing original material with foreign shows that could be bought in. And at the beginning of October, when Chisholm struck with a night of the long knives, the news was as bad as Hawke had feared. Target was to be reduced to once a week and The Editors, Challenge, and the Frank Bough Interview all to be axed entirely and, in true Sky style, immediately.

Hawke smiled wryly as he remembered Anthony Howard's closing line at the end of the previous week's The Editors: 'See you again in a month's time on the twenty-eighth of October.' The producer of the religious programme Challenge mused that 'morality was beaten by Mammon' when he heard his programme would be canned forthwith. Vigorous cross-party lobbying by the formidable Tebbit-Mitchell duo got Target reinstated to twice a week, but Frank Bough was not so lucky. After losing the deal which had been worth £100,000 over two years he commented: 'We have been buried by the accountants.'

John Stapleton had already left on his own initiative. A couple of months before Chisholm arrived he had started to sense a change and realised Sky News could not continue in its present form. No one could lose money like that. It would either be shut or there would be what the Australians called 'major retrench-ments'. Anyhow the need for the Brownie points his programme bestowed was lessening. Stapleton wasn't complaining. He had hugely enjoyed his ride on the Skyship Enterprise, as his riotous leaving party at a Thai restaurant in South Ealing indicated, and in some ways was sorry to be retreating to the relative safety of a presenter's job back in the world of real television.

But at least, he thought, in terrestrial TV he would have a job, whereas in the satellite world such luxuries were about to become in exceedingly short supply.

CHAPTER SEVENTEEN

The Eagle is Landing

For the minions at BSB the taboo word had always been 'merger', even though it had surfaced on many occasions both in public and private. Probably the first time had been in the mind of Richard Branson, when back in June 1988 he had heard Murdoch's Sky announcement while dressing to go to work. At that stage Virgin was still a BSB shareholder and Branson's immediate conclusion was that Murdoch would be such tough competition the only solution would be for the two organisations to merge. He set up a secret meeting with Murdoch at the houseboat in Little Venice from which he still conducted much of his business and tried to persuade him the two systems could never co-exist. But when Branson proposed a merger, Murdoch, with his traditional dislike of working with consortia and unconvinced BSB would ever get its act together, rejected the idea. Sky would be first and therefore it would win. Andrew Neil had then put the boot on the other foot by taunting BSB at the Sky launch, inviting it to join them on the Astra satellite. Three months later James Lee, a media consultant who had himself been involved in one of the unsuccessful franchise applications repeated an idea first floated at the Royal Television Society in 1988 and proposed a merger in the trade paper *Broadcast*.

For the public record BSB had always scoffed at the suggestion, maintaining the stance that as it was the quality system, with superior prospects, what reason was there for it to compromise? But inside the company senior executives had seen things rather differently. Only a couple of months after he had joined in the spring of 1989, the down to earth Ian Clubb had written to ASG suggesting the idea. Later in the year Peter Bell had done the same, and then been joined at the BSB launch by John Gau. He had proposed both satellites and transmission systems should continue while the two companies and some of the channels merged, with the two entertainment channels, Sky One and Galaxy, joining up to offer their combined best output. The public would still have a choice, but the battle for movie or sporting rights would stop and, most important of all, the crazy marketing war would be terminated. Instead a service would emerge incorporating the best of both satellite worlds which could turn its combined talents to fighting the terrestrial opposition, solving the problem which had always troubled Nigel Bogle of who the real enemy was supposed to be, and whether the advertising was supposed to be anti-Sky or pro-BSB.

The only alternative to merger was obviously a fight to the death, and this was the line traditionally peddled by both sides. But in February 1990, just after the huge gales which compounded Sky's problems by knocking some dishes askew, Murdoch was interviewed on the Thames Television City Programme, much-valued for its high AB viewing figure. For the first time he admitted BSB had made an impact and said Sky might now cost as much as £400 million before it went into profit. He had changed his viewpoint, he said, and accepted there was room in the market for both companies. ASG, after his previous uncompromising statements, joined him in the change of heart by adding: 'I used to say there wasn't [room for both] and now I've changed my tune and the reason is I've become, over the last ten months or so, increasingly convinced that the British consumer is going to take to satellite in an enormous way.'

By the autumn of 1990 the British consumer had clearly not done that. Instead the position was the one ASG had referred to in an interview with *Broadcast* in August 1989. 'From a business textbook point of view a merger makes sense,' he had said. 'But I can't quite see it in practical terms. The issue might become more potent if there is more blood-letting and things get tricky for both of us without a merger. But it must be a merger and not a takeover.'

If the logic of a merger was not lost on members of the BSB management and sections of the press, it was doubly obvious to the shareholders, although they kept it to themselves. 'The BSB project is gathering momentum and we are meeting the financial targets,' the Reed interim statement for the benefit of its own shareholders chirruped in September 1990. Meanwhile, to the annoyance of City analysts, the full horror of the BSB losses was kept off the shareholders' balance sheets by skilful use of accounting practices. Rather than a consolidation of a share of the BSB losses the money put into the company was written into the accounts as a one line investment, which minimised the damage on paper. In each case shareholders were allowed to do this as their investment represented less than 50% of the total, but it certanly obscured matters. One City analyst grumbled: 'They sure would have consolidated their share of any profits.'

Away from the niceties of accounting, the scale of the conflict was more obvious as the two companies slugged it out on the doorsteps and billboards like a pair of exhausted heavyweight boxers. BSB swept Marcopolo for Sky bugging equipment while ad agencies, lobbying firms and lawyers looked on in glee as the battle continued to rage, leading to further skirmishes in the law courts. A number of comparative studies had been published assessing the merits of the two satellite contenders, with the City giants of Kleinwort Benson and Citicorp duly making their assessments in thick volumes. They predicted that there might well be room for two in the market, although further funding would probably be needed before BSB could reach the magical breakeven point. Citicorp saw Sky going into profit in 1992, and BSB following by 1994. But it was the third report on the contest which caused the trouble. It was published by Technology Advisory Services, which despite its grand title was a one man band run from a lock-up in South London. The author, John Anderson who had been involved in a rival consortium to BSB originally, took a different line from the City's. He was extremely gloomy about the prospects, adjudging the Good Ship BSB to be 'financially dead in the water'.

BSB was outraged, while Sky gleefully seized on the 'dead in the water' quote to run in an advert, portrayed as a Public

Warning to anyone contemplating the purchase of a squarial. The day the report was published, around lunchtime Edward Bickham received word on the grapevine that Sky was trying to place the ads. When he rang the papers he found several had been approached and were now considering their position. The *Independent* had told Sky it would require an indemnity, while the *Financial Times* was consulting the Advertisers' Code of Practice. Knowing Sir David English, the editor of the *Mail* and Lord Rothermere, its owner, were having lunch at Marcopolo, Bickham went to enlist their help.

By 7pm the *Mail*, *Express*, *Telegraph*, and *Financial Times* had all declined to run the advert, along with the *Independent* which had been refused its indemnity. The News International papers, however, were still going ahead and that evening Bickham sat with the BSB solicitors and Frank Barlow in the Grays Inn chambers of Charles Gray QC, trying to raise the duty judge on the phone to seek an injunction. They had discovered he had disappeared for his evening sherry when a call came from the Sky lawyers. They offered an undertaking not to use the ad for 24 hours. The next day they extended it to a week.

But the same afternoon a fax arrived at Marcopolo from Los Angeles where the offending ad had appeared in the daily media paper, *Variety*. Sky, caught red-handed, pleaded that it was a genuine mistake. They had simply forgotten to pull it in America. But there was a real poison pin in *Variety*'s being owned by the key BSB shareholder Reed, which was furious. BSB rushed back to the lawyers for more expensive late night sessions, and a few more tens of thousand pounds disappeared in fees, while John Anderson of Technology Advisory Services joined in the fun by sueing Sky for breach of copyright in using quotes from his report. When tempers had died down three days later ASG phoned Andrew Knight, the Chief Executive of News International, to tell him BSB had decided not to pursue the matter. All this public fighting gave satellite television a bad name, he told him. Knight agreed, pointing out if they wanted to stop fighting BSB should call off the cross-media battle as well. It was an outrageous campaign, he said.

But the cross-media side of the business was not something Sky had to worry about much longer. On 9 October the Sallingbury

Casey targeted lobbying paid off as BSB's final attempt at a cross-media ownership clause fell in the House of Lords. Lord Whitelaw, well briefed and carrying out a request from on high, stood up to accuse the proposers of the clause of mounting a 'Sky witchhunt'. Whitelaw himself had had a dish kindly arranged for him by Norman Tebbit, and the former deputy Prime Minister now informed his fellow peers Sky News had 'a very high reputation . . . I admire it, as do many other people,' he went on. 'It will certainly waken up both the BBC and ITN and ensure that they compete with what is a very important news service.' Whitelaw's powerful influence swayed a number of undecideds and the final tally was the substantial majority of 50 in favour of Sky.

Jonathan Miller, jubilant his hard work had been so successful, bumped into a less than jubilant Edward Bickham as they crossed the Central Lobby that night, only for Bickham defiantly to declare: 'The war continues', and inform him BSB's next aim was mounting a challenge at European level under EEC anti-competition laws. But the crucial victory had been in the Lords and a great sense of relief was felt throughout Osterley. Otherwise things were grimmer than ever. Despite the fearsome Sam Chisholm's costcutting the outlook was bleak. Every morning the finance department at Osterley had to call the office of the News International finance director at Wapping. It was then informed how much advertising revenue had come into the coffers of the News International papers the day before, which in turn determined how much Sky could spend. The station was banging right up against its overdraft limits and operating a kind of Pay As You Earn. If there was not sufficient revenue allocated to Sky to cover all the cheques to be sent that day, they were put back in the drawer to be reconsidered the next.

There were financial problems with allies as well as enemies. As part of Project X Sky had placed huge orders with Amstrad for receiving equipment. Now the market was slowing down it wanted to reduce that requirement, but Alan Sugar had already done his deals in the Far East to boost the volume. He was in any case angry at Sky's increasingly sluggish payments and rang Osterley screaming abuse at whoever would listen and demanding to speak to Rupert or Sam. When he got no satisfaction he sent abusive semi-literate faxes demanding prompt payment. Young secretaries receiving them blushed at the language.

Thanks to Chisholm's abrasive influence Sky's losses had been cut down to close to £2 million a week, but the problem was still the same. There was no doubt Sky was slowly working and getting close to 1 million dishes sold. Subscription take-up for the Movie Channel had been extremely good and there were now 750,000 homes paying for it, but income from advertising was still small. Project X, with its 30% bad debts, had left a heavy hangover and along the High Streets the confusion over the two systems was continuing in the recession-hit shops.

In normal circumstances Sky, now so far ahead in the game, would have sat tight and waited for the opposition to crumble. But these were not normal times for the Empire. In his McTaggart lecture in Edinburgh back in 1989 Murdoch had spelt out that it was the strength of News Corporation as a whole which had enabled him to start the station. Close observers of Murdoch thought this typical of the man, as they knew he had the nerve to both take the long view and absorb the punishing losses whilst sticking to his guns. But this time he was not to be allowed to do so. The old equation in which Sky's losses and difficulties could be swallowed and sustained until breakeven by the parent company no longer applied. Worldwide the clouds were gathering over the Empire, with its billions of dollars of debt.

From his start in business, when he inherited two Adelaide newspapers from his father in 1952, Murdoch had held to his strategy of keeping control and in 1990 his family still owned 43% of the Empire's global parent company of News Corporation, making it effectively takeover proof. Compared with most multi-national conglomerates Murdoch's style was to run the company as a one-man band, endlessly roaming the globe as he kept up his close and personal interest in everything that was going on and constantly searched for new opportunities. The hallmark of the business, which after Time Warner was the world's biggest in the communications field, was his ingrained dislike of committees, bureaucracy and red tape. The worldwide headquarters in midtown Manhattan employed barely 60 people, with hardly a memo in sight and internal communication kept to a bare necessity. Not for him endless paperwork and an organisation top heavy with executives but, as one aide put it, 'an emotionally driven and bonded company, where executives don't spend time guarding territories because nobody has one nailed down.'

Murdoch's style was to take a hands-on approach to every aspect of his far flung operation and it had been typical that when Sky had been facing its greatest challenge with the launch of its rival he had temporarily moved to live in London and be chief executive for the duration. His obvious love of the business, in which he displayed an extraordinary synthesis of the editorial and corporate functions, was in particularly sharp contrast to the BSB shareholders' belief that managers should be left to manage and editors to edit. Murdoch's highly personal sense of his business showed itself in the way he liked to address the Sky execs. 'You guys are wasting my money,' he would often say when complaining about something like a poor programme or a perceived extravagance in the way a particular channel was using resources.

Murdoch's key to running his Empire was a weekly document known as the 'Flash', for which each constituent part had to provide a summary of its operating results. These had to show the budgeted figures for every aspect of its affairs, set against the actual figures for the week, and then compared with the same week in the previous year. At Sky alone ten employees had almost the sole purpose of collating this information, channel by channel. Each Thursday it was passed to HQ, where it was assembled into a bound document along with the figures from every other company in the group. Murdoch studied it over the weekend and woe betide any manager who was not properly briefed by Monday, when the Boss might casually ring to query a figure. The call might come only for one week in a year, but it kept everyone on their toes for the other fifty-one.

To preserve control of his equity Murdoch had sought bank debt in preference to diluting his holdings. It was very much as if one of his C2 Sky customers, starting with his original house, had then proceeded to build an entire estate as well as financing a timeshare in Benidorm by borrowing on the back of it. Now, just as their mortgages had soared, so had the interest rates on

Murdoch's borrowings, which at $8 billion were equivalent to the debt of the entire country of Ecuador in South America. The scale of the borrowing had been enhanced by Murdoch's ability to exploit the opportunities offered by the different tax and accounting laws in the UK, the USA and Australia. Most international operators did the same thing. Murdoch just did it better. 'I can show you the balance sheets of the same company – one for Great Britain and the other for the US – and you would think you were looking at the finance of two different companies,' is how one analyst described it. In Murdoch's case it had been the lax Australian accounting rules that had been of particular use in enabling him to revalue his assets.

At the end of the 1989/90 fiscal year News Corporation had revised the valuation of its mastheads and television licences upwards by $2.2 billion, revising its decision on what they were worth and writing the sums into its books, thereby correspondingly increasing the amount of borrowing that could be done on the back of them. By late 1990 his colossal debt included borrowings from 146 different banks all over the world, as in some cases large banks had passed on the exposure to smaller banks, and his annual interest bill totalled over $800 million.

Although Murdoch had always believed in using leverage to finance his expansion this time things were getting a little uncomfortable and during 1990 the financial community had slowly been becoming aware of News Corporation's increasingly vulnerable position which, combined with worldwide recession, started having a downward pressure on its share price. In particular it was the balance between short- and long-term borrowing which was becoming out of kilter. In the late 80s Murdoch had used comparatively short-term borrowing to finance both ambitious capital investment, such as new printing presses in the UK and Australia and finance new acquisitions, whilst not paying much attention to cash flow. In 1988 he had paid $3 billion for the US magazine group Triangle, which included the popular *TV Guide*, and with hindsight there were mutterings he had paid up to $1 billion too much. The Empire, dangerously over-extended, needed to restructure its debt at the very time interest rates were high and the banks, once delighted to lend, were turning increasingly cautious. In particular they were pointing the finger at Sky as representing a continuing black financial hole and putting pressure on Murdoch both to sell assets and to stop up gaps. And in Sky's case the obvious way to reduce News International's exposure was to do a deal with its rival. It was now a question of who would make the first move.

The self-appointed marriage broker who likes to claim he brought the two sides together was John Veronis, who ran the New York investment bank Veronis Suhler. He knew both sides well and as a former publisher of the *Ladies Home Journal* and later on a founder of publications like *Psychology Today*, had become a specialist in media acquisitions, with his bank having brokered some $11 billion in media deals. The Triangle magazine acquisition, for which Murdoch was now receiving criticism for paying too much, had come through him.

On the BSB side Veronis had also done deals for Reed, which was the most wobbly BSB shareholder and the keenest to press for a deal, and knew its chairman Peter Davis. Earlier in the year Veronis had toured Osterley at Murdoch's invitation, and like most other sane observers seen the craziness of the current situation where two satellite television services were battling it out at a time when it was questionable whether the nation, falling into recession, even wanted one. Without some form of truce, he observed, the biggest asset each of them had was the ability to destroy each other. Veronis had invited Murdoch and Davis to dine with him in his suite at Claridges on 24 July, but the meeting had been inconclusive. With Sky so far ahead in the game, and his habitual dislike of working in consortia, Murdoch was still not prepared to deal. Sky could almost see the light. It just had to wait for BSB to crumble, and given the present dire position of squarial penetration that could only be a matter of months.

Sky had had a strong pointer to the sort of future which could be awaiting it through its exclusive cricketing coverage of the West Indies test series earlier in the year. The deal had been brokered by Mark McCormack, who had first offered it to BSB. John Gau had been forced reluctantly to turn it down because of the uncertainty of the wretched launch date and McCormack had immediately sold it to Sky. It had been shown on Sky One, as it was thought Eurosport's continental audience would not appreciate viewing at such length the subtleties of the cricket field, and had had an astonishing impact. Sky dishes had been sought out by anyone even vaguely interested in cricket and the standard of the Sky coverage had also been widely praised. Now the cricket was over it was scoring another hit with the Fox TV show The Simpsons, which had started life as an insert on the Tracey Ullman Show. Tales of this unappealing cartoon family had reached cult status in the US and the same was now happening in the UK, with children and the youth audience putting pressure on parents to buy. One or two more successes like that, reasoned the optimistic view, and Sky would be out of the woods. All it needed was for the bankers to give it that period of grace.

But instead, over the next few weeks the pressure increased. Poor News Corporation and particularly News International results in August did not help and during September the markets were so jittery about Murdoch's position that the value of News Corporation's shares in the US halved. In the UK the share price of News International fell by 22% in a single week. Veronis, continuing to act as an intermediary, believed Murdoch would shift. But Peter Davis of Reed, while increasingly keen for a deal as the BSB banking targets loomed, was not prepared to try again without a gesture of good faith from the Murdoch camp.

Between September and June 1991 nearly $3 billion of Murdoch's debt was due to mature, a situation considered 'somewhat terminal' by one of the bankers. Unable to meet the repayments, News Corporation now started seeking short-term financing to cover them, only to be alarmed to find it drying up. A massive restructuring job would therefore be required to spread the repayments in a similar manner to a South American country rescheduling its debts. The bankers, increasingly agitated at the overextended nature of the company, now hardened their demands that any further credit lines required a steady commitment to sell off assets and reduce exposure. For the bigger ones Murdoch's debt crisis was turning into a huge article of faith and they started to fear smaller lenders might flinch and demand repayment on time, which would mean their having to take up the slack. It was vital, they insisted, that the Empire began giving signals which would restore confidence.

By the start of October a special team from Citibank and Samuel Montagu had been appointed to sort out the debt repayments under the code-name of Operation Dolphin. Citibank put Bill Rhodes, the man who had done the big Latin American debt reschedulings for them earlier in the decade, on the job and a roadshow started through which the lead Murdoch banks met to agree on the deal for easing his immediate problems and restructuring his borrowing. It moved across the world between London, Sydney and New York as they began a process of sorting out the complicated debt structure and persuading all the participants to roll over the debt to stretch it out over three years.

The deal took three months to put together and the eventual agreement was to lengthen the repayment time in exchange for an upfront 1% fee and an increase of 1% on the loan – the equivalent of £76m for each extra year of interest payments. If the plan worked there would be a further success fee of 1% on the outstanding amount after three years. Finally the banks were persuaded to agree to $600 million of new money to keep the operation going, some of which was secured against the assets of the Sun and the News of the World. For this bridging loan they demanded the high price of an average of 2.25% above money market rates, plus a $9 million front-end fee. They also insisted on quarterly meetings with News Corporation to discuss its progress.

Against this background, and knowing he had to keep his bankers on his side, Murdoch then made the move Peter Davis of Reed required by calling him back on 27 September to say he was now willing to talk. Davis was immediately anxious not to lose momentum. He had the imminent worry of BSB's missing its own banking targets, meaning the project loan going into default and the shareholders, Reed amongst them, being left to carry the can. But there was a problem: Murdoch would not be coming to Europe for several weeks as he was now in Australia for the impending News Corporation AGM in his home base of Adelaide, where he had a major job to do soothing the nerves of his own shareholders. As he could not come to them, they would have to go to him, and Davis promptly sent his portly deputy, Ian Irvine, on the long haul to Australia to get things going.

Irvine had risen to prominence in the media business as the chief executive of the *Daily Express*, from where he had moved across to publishing, which he had combined with his part-time role at TV-am. An accountant by training, he had smoothed his northern accent into the nasal anonymity of downmarket media folk from Down Under, but lost none of his bluffness which manifested itself in a forthright suspicion of what he saw as 'arty imprecision'. Short, podgy and balding, with horn-rimmed specs, he had an unlikely passion for scuba diving in pursuit of which he had spent many happy hours trawling the Great Barrier reef, but on this trip there would be no time for that sort of excursion.

On 14 October Irvine set off along with a Pearson representative, having told the BSB management that he was going to the US. Instead he met up with Murdoch at Cavan, the Murdoch ranch 50 miles outside Canberra, where over two days of talking they stitched together the outline of a deal. Really it was no contest. Although BSB had an inkling of the scale of Murdoch's debt crisis Irvine had little room to manoeuvre. His job was to come back with something which would take the strain of their massive liability in BSB off Reed and the other shareholders. The mere fact that Murdoch would consider talking had come as a welcome relief after the various fund-raising exercises had proved conclusively that there was no other company in the world interested in getting involved.

Ian Irvine returned to London feeling bullish and on Sunday 21 October called a 10am meeting at the Reed offices in Mayfair to brief the other shareholders and their advisers. ASG, on holiday in Ireland, was blissfully unaware of any merger talks and no one thought to enlighten him. The only representative of the BSB management was Ian Clubb, the man who had admired Murdoch when he took over *The Times* and had now been detailed to provide backup information for the talks, with the quid pro quo that his efforts would no doubt be rewarded in the satellite life hereafter. Irvine explained that negotiations for merger would start at once. The basic framework had already been agreed in Australia and Murdoch had instructed his English lawyers, Farrer's, to make the necessary arrangements to take them forward. Irvine informed the others there would be a roughly 50% split in the new company, a recognition of Sky's superior position in dish sales, and a merging of some channels. Most crucially, Sky would have both operational and editorial control in the new company.

Both sides knew that embarking on full-blown merger talks was a high risk strategy. Once the process had started the momentum would have to be unstoppable, for if it ever leaked out that talks had begun and then failed both participants would suffer a major setback, and there would be mayhem with the share prices of all involved. But after successfully combining the role of being Her Majesty the Queen's solicitors together with acting for Murdoch, Farrer's were well suited to tackle negotiations demanding the strictest confidentiality, and some of the team which had co-ordinated the secret arrangements for the move of the News International's papers to Wapping was now reconstituted to set up the merger talks.

The Farrer's lawyer who had attended the meeting at Murdoch's Australian ranch had instructed his office to find a suitably discrete location for the further negotiations. The answer had been found in the delightful country house hotel, Lucknam Park, in the rolling Wiltshire countryside near Bath where, according to its promotional blurb, 'tranquillity becomes one's natural state, born from a sense that everything is well ordered'. The choice was cheeky but unoriginal, as it was also where the BBC governors and management had held their annual weekend away and the Georgian mansion befitted the BBC at its most lavish. Dating from the early-eighteenth century, it was set in its own park and consisted of a series of stone buildings round a central courtyard, combining the best of traditional style with every convenience, fax and whirlpool of modern life. Farrer's had booked all available rooms for the key participants to go and hammer out their agreement.

When the BBC hierarchy used Lucknam Park it made tireless preparations, with advance parties checking out the various facilities and discussing their many requirements. Possible camera angles into various rooms were even worked out to ensure the great and the good could deliberate in due privacy. Farrer's, requiring even greater discretion, had no time for any of this as they were working under strict instructions from Down Under to proceed immediately, so to cover their tracks booked under the name Melloward, an off the shelf company they used for the provision of office services. The talks were then to proceed under the codename of 'Operation Eagle', with, in even more Boys' Own fashion, the two sides being referred to as 'Box' and 'Sox' respectively.

Straight after the Sunday meeting at Reed the BSB shareholders and their key advisers made their way down the M4 to Lucknam Park as the News International team also assembled at the hotel. Farrer's set up their base in the elegant, £295 a night Juliet Suite, named after the charming stone balcony off its drawing room, with the theme continued by a crimson four-poster in the bedroom. They brought with them their own fax and photocopier to ensure secure communications, as did BSB, with only Eric Guilly of Chargeurs who now came in on the talks trusting the hotel fax, chauvinistically confident the hotel staff would not understand French.

With the Murdoch lawyers came the key Sky negotiators of Andrew Knight, the News International finance director Peter Stehrenberger, and Sam Chisholm, slipping incognito into the hotel just as the regular Sunday opera evening was commencing. None showed much interest in The Marriage of Figaro, preferring to get straight to work, while the other guests filing into their seats for the performance ignored the convention of grey-suited lawyers from some unknown company called Melloward. They might not have blended perfectly into the opera crowd, but Sam Chisholm and his colleagues were hardly household faces.

CHAPTER EIGHTEEN

To BSkyB or not to BSkyB

As Monday 22 October dawned at Marcopolo House the Christmas schedule was uppermost in people's minds and Edward Bickham had his hands full briefing the press. He had felt momentary unease when he arrived early that morning to see Ian Clubb loading files into his car and driving off. Puzzled that Clubb was driving his own car, he had thought that maybe his chauffeur was sick. But when he finished dealing with the hacks and went to pump Clubb's secretary she replied firmly that it was Ian himself who was sick. So sick, in fact, he would definitely be off ill for the whole week. Ian's determination to take so many files home to bed was commendable, Bickham thought.

At Osterley there was puzzlement in Sky's finance department. As they paused between demands from irate creditors, some of the brighter souls were wondering about the increasingly frequent calls from the News International Finance Director. For the past weeks Peter Stehrenberger had repeatedly rung, insisting on highly detailed information – forecasts, cash flow projections, updates to the business plan . . . They all had to be found within the hour, when he would ring back. He never left a number and nobody had any idea whether he was in the next room or on the other side of the world. Trying to trace his movements by ringing the company travel agent they then found he had covered his tracks by making his arrangements on his personal credit card.

When first Sam Chisholm and then Gary Davey and the inevitable lawyer also disappeared without trace the rumour factory began working overtime. The whispers went round that

Sky was being bought by Kerry Packer or the Italian media mogul Berlusconi, while Ben Hawke had his own private notion Sky News was being sold to Reuters. In any case his thoughts were turning back to Bondi Beach. His old mates had told him Channel Nine was looking for a new deputy editor for 60 minutes.

Eighty miles down the M4 Chisholm and his colleagues were locked away with their former adversaries. In the press, on the billboards, on the doorsteps, and along the High Street the marketing battle raged towards Christmas, but behind the chintz drapes of Lucknam Park the two protagonists were staggering into each others arms. They worked night and day, stopping only for four star meal breaks. In the Methuen Room, the Juliet Suite and throughout the hotel the two sides were locked in debate. First there was the whole question of how the merger would be achieved. Then the newly merged entity would require yet more funds, so who was going to pay what? Even agreeing on the new name of BSkyB, which although clever was immediately shortened to Sky, took hours of haggling. And one day – at least according to the business plans – satellite television would make a profit, so the two sides had to agree who would be entitled to what when the moment came.

These issues were only the start. There were all the contractual problems involving Hollywood, rights to sporting events, and the multiple agreements with the various manufacturers and retailers. Above all there was the major decision of choosing between the two transmission standards of D-MAC and PAL. D-MAC might have been an albatross for much of BSB's existence, but now it finally worked and was the superior standard it seemed crazy to give it up. But the Sky team was adamant. Astra and PAL had to win or there would be no deal. Twenty three thousand miles up in the Clarke Belt Marcopolos I and II sat in all their pristine splendour. They had cost the BSB shareholders over £200 million. Now Ian Irvine and his team were forced to contemplate turning them into celestial scrap.

Quite apart from the satellites themselves BSB had the small matter of the direct infringement of its original IBA licence to consider. Throughout its short life it had always diligently obeyed the regulatory authority's commands. Questions like the use of four letter words had duly been referred to Brompton Road, with profuse apologies for any transgressions. There had been endless agonising about the VIP chat show, which went out around 10 pm and was repeated the next morning at 9 am, when it was to interview the man who had created the Wicked Willie cartoon. Could they show an erect penis at the repeat time of 10 am? The regulations stipulated no erect penises before the 9 pm watershed, when it was assumed responsible parents had put their children to bed and 'adult' material could therefore be screened. But this was not a real penis, just a cartoon one. So did it count? After about 20 phone calls and many meetings it had been decided to brave the regulators' wrath by displaying the upright member and the programme-makers had awaited the fallout with bated breath. When there was no comeback they concluded the authorities hadn't been watching.

There was less luck with Sex, Lies and Love, a chat show about intimate relations made by New Era which was first screened on the NOW channel at 10 pm, and then repeated for housewives at 3 pm the next day. Unsurprisingly in view of its subject matter, it included the phrase 'having a fuck'. New Era had warned about this beforehand but the channel editors had decided it would be OK. It hadn't been, the regulators had seen it and knuckles had been rapped. Now BSB's shareholders were planning to tell the IBA to four letter off without so much as a by your leave.

Once the prospect of merger became increasingly likely Granada Chairman Alex Bernstein had done what seemed instinctively right. Granada was one of the oldest ITV companies, and had dealt with the IBA over many years. Telling it about a possible merger would not be easy, but it had to be done. The week before the Lucknam Park talks Bernstein had arranged for himself and Lord Blakenham, the Pearson chairman, to go to Brompton Road and explain why they were dealing with Murdoch to George Russell, the no-nonsense boss of Marley Tiles who had taken over as chairman from Lord Thomson. But when Bernstein told the other shareholders what he was going to do they disagreed completely. As far as the Reed representatives of Ian Irvine and Peter Davis were concerned the merger was a question of hard commercial reality. The IBA would only prove obstructive. BSB should get on and do the deal and worry about the authorities later. They could always plead confidentiality as the reason for leaving it in the dark.

Bernstein was still uneasy. Granada had a great deal at stake, especially with the forthcoming ITV franchise rounds coming up. But he was outnumbered and reluctantly bowed to the majority voice, calling George Russell's office to cancel the meeting. He said he would come back to rearrange, but never did. Bernstein was also preoccupied with the other awkward task he had been detailed to handle: the BSB management. For nearly two years the shareholders and senior executives had met, first monthly and then weekly, supposedly jointly to run BSB. Now the shareholders were on their own, independently negotiating a deal which would result in most of the management being swept aside.

Bernstein started with ASG, who was still on holiday at his parents' home in Ireland. He gave him only the barest of details, but John Gau was a trickier case. Most of the shareholders still had great respect for him and apart from his wider reputation in television perceived he had done a good job at BSB. There were one or two howlers, but overall across the five channels BSB's programmes were not at all bad – and certainly a great deal better than the opposition's. If only the same had been achieved in other areas of the company, they groaned.

On the second day of the merger talks at Lucknam Park Bernstein called Gau to Granada's offices in Golden Square, explained the position and said how sorry he was. Gau was puzzled. He was not surprised at the prospect of merger talks. It seemed a perfectly logical development, as he had outlined in his own comprehensive plan only six months previously. But it was the note of apology in Bernstein's voice which concerned him. Later that day Ian Irvine rang him to instruct him to come to Lucknam Park, and Gau set off after work with a sense of unease. When he arrived this turned to gloom. There was a curious atmosphere in the hotel and his worries increased through Mark Burrell, the Pearson director who had been involved in BSB from the start and although effectively replaced by Frank Barlow was still on the scene. Like Bernstein, Burrell kept saying to him: 'I'm really sorry about this, John.'

Gau was then taken aside by Irvine, who told him he was

required to assist in explaining the Hollywood deals. First he had to brief the BSB shareholders and lawyers, and then meet with the Sky team, where he had his first encounter with the legendary Sam Chisholm. How ironic it was, Gau thought as he plodded through the figures, that he should be giving chapter and verse on the very deals he himself had so heavily criticised.

Late in the evening the party, which numbered over 30 altogether, was ushered into the dining room for dinner and all seated together at three large tables. Gau made small talk with some of the News International team before spending the next day doing more explaining to the lawyers. Then he was left hanging around amidst the antique furniture in the hotel lounge, watching the lawyers and merchant bankers as they scooted between the various meeting rooms, until eventually he sought out Irvine and was told he could leave. He climbed back into his car and headed for London feeling depressed. No one had thought to ask him his views on achieving a merger and he had been treated as a bearer of information – a mere messenger. He arrived back at Marcopolo House with no doubt in his mind that if the talks did succeed the merger would not be the kind he had envisaged. Even more depressingly, as he had been sworn to secrecy he could not even discuss his fears with anyone.

At Lucknam Park so many men in suits had now arrived that an overflow party had to be accommodated at the neighbouring Bath Spa Hotel, but even though fleets of chauffeur-driven Daimlers purred backwards and forwards ferrying the many participants the negotiations still remained a well-kept secret. To make doubly sure nothing leaked the Farrer's team ordered a paper shredder, which two porters then tried to heave up to the Juliet Suite via the back stairs. When it wouldn't fit there was a nasty potential security breach as the bulky machine was humped past reception and up the grand staircase used by the other unwitting guests.

There was another minor panic on day four when it was discovered Lucknam Park was hosting one of its regular gourmet lunches for the local press. Frank Barlow was especially alarmed. He had spent much of his career in local newspapers and a sharp-eyed hack might well recognise him and start asking questions. The hotel offered a solution: the 'Melloward' party would be put in a small private room, where food would be brought to them.

Barlow, still nervous, sat it out in his bedroom. After a leisurely three hours the hacks departed none the wiser, blithely unaware of the scoop which had been sitting under their noses, whilst the impatient execs were released from their temporary captivity to get on with the main business.

The one character in the drama in severe danger of recognition was Romeo himself, Rupert Murdoch, still detained at his News Corporation AGM in Adelaide. His calls to henchman Andrew Knight became increasingly frequent and for two nights he threatened to join his team in the Juliet Suite and beef it up by taking control. The splendid Camellia Suite, overlooking Lucknam Park's mile long avenue of magnificent beech trees, was prepared for him. But no Mr Murdoch arrived and on Friday, after five days of talking, the Melloward party abruptly packed its bags and returned to London. That evening Murdoch, his Australian commitments out of the way, met the BSB shareholders over an uneasy dinner at the Stafford Hotel in Mayfair, just around the corner from Murdoch's flat. The BSB team sat on one side facing the key News International people, now backed up by their accountants from Arthur Andersen, and both sides took stock.

At the weekend the talks shifted to Reed's offices as the circle of participants widened and negotiations became more detailed. Murdoch wandered around in his sports jacket and the chairmen of the other shareholders' companies showed their faces, but it was far from plain sailing. The major headaches were over sorting out the immediate funding needed to keep the merged company afloat in the short term. For the BSB shareholders it would mean another embarrassing trip back to their parent boards for yet more money. Murdoch, on the other hand, had to find precious liquidity at the very time he was hopelessly overstretched. By Sunday night the process ground to a halt as both sides dug in their heels. Ultimately it was to turn out to be only a stage in the posturing and ultimatums accompanying any such negotiations, but when news that the talks had broken down filtered through to Gau and ASG, who had belatedly returned from Ireland, they chose to believe it, largely because it was what they wanted to hear.

On Monday Rupert Murdoch had other things on his mind. He was expected in Downing Street where Bernard Ingham, the Prime Minister's formidable press secretary, had set up an appointment a couple of weeks earlier for him to drop in and see Mrs Thatcher. Ingham had observed it was some time since Murdoch had last been to call on the the Prime Minister for one of his regular chats. The conversation in Mrs Thatcher's study lasted about 40 minutes with Murdoch especially keen to talk about Eastern Europe, where he had recently been looking for fresh opportunities to expand the Empire further. He told Mrs Thatcher how struck he had been, especially in Romania, by how appalling things still were a year after the revolution. There was huge scope for the West to move in, yet disappointingly he had found Britain hardly in evidence and he wanted to impress on her the role Britain and British business should be playing. Mrs Thatcher listened as carefully as ever to his remarks.

Then, just as he was leaving, Murdoch dropped an aside. Sky, he informed her, was losing too much money and so was the opposition. They had little choice but to merge with each other, which they were now seeking to do. Mrs Thatcher made a note but said nothing, and Murdoch left the room. In Number 10 they regularly watched Sky News, along with CNN, and there was great admiration for Murdoch's commercial bravery. In the view of one of Mrs Thatcher's close associates Rupert Murdoch was one of nature's chief executives, combining flair plus management of the bottom line – an opinion he did not extend to ASG who was a brilliant marketing man, which was different. The government attitude was already clear. Mrs Thatcher's Broadcasting Minister, David Mellor, had said some months previously: 'A vast amount of money has gone into getting this thing [SKY] off the ground. These [four] satellite stations are in the public interest and it is not for the government to pull the plugs on it . . .' Ingham, when he heard the latest news, assumed the merger announcement would be the next day.

By the Monday afternoon the temporary glitch which had deadlocked the two sides had been eradicated and they were back on speaking terms. The venue now changed again, from Reed's headquarters to the codename of 'Greenacres', the smart offices of the BSB solicitors, Freshfields, with a BSB-style atrium and a location ironically on the corner of Fleet Street and Bouverie Street, which had been the home of the Sun until Murdoch had whisked it off to Wapping in his last great conjuring trick. Ian Irvine and his team, anxious to do any deal, had got the negotiations over their major hurdle by crumbling and agreeing to stump up the major tranche of initial working capital needed to cash-flow the new company. Now the pace became even more intense. Some members of the team, especially lawyers drafting the various decisions into binding documents, were putting in 20-hour days, not even bothering to go home but working all night as they pulled together the key documents. The fees, they consoled themselves, were going to be astronomical.

Back at Marcopolo ASG slowly became aware the talks had resumed and realised the rejoicing had been premature. Clubb had remained off for a second week with his mystery illness and now the company secretary, Peter Clarke, had also done a disappearing act. In the middle of the week the two key operations people, Andy Coleman and Ellis Griffiths, were urgently summoned to Freshfields and vigorously pumped for information. Told nothing about the merger, they assumed the interrogation concerned the eternal refinancing requirement which had dominated their lives for so many weeks. ASG wondered otherwise, but still held on to the hope that as the talks had broken down once, they could always collapse again. Still, as a precaution, he asked to see the shareholders, only to find most of them very unavailable. Eventually he managed to call on Alex Bernstein, the Granada chairman, and a few days later saw Mark Burrell of Pearson.

He gave them each a note on how he believed the merger should be handled, arguing for the best of both companies and keeping both transmission systems to avoid the inevitable claims from manufacturers if one was dropped. He recommended Ian Clubb as chief executive and then listed some of the key operations and engineering people whose input would be crucial to make the systems work. For himself, he accepted he would not have a part in the post-merged company. But nevertheless, he urged, he should be allowed to help smooth the transition and – most crucially – must be the one to break the news to his staff of boys and girls. But instead of the merger's organ-grinders he was merely talking to its monkeys. Bernstein and Burrell both nodded at his suggestions, saying very little. They had been meeting each other for over three years and Mark Burrell had been one of the people who had urged ASG to take the job. Now he seemed a man in a hurry and there was a slight feeling of embarrassment as he ushered ASG out.

Back at Marcopolo House the lower echelons still had no inkling anything was untoward as they continued to beaver away at their Christmas promotions and the new budgets for the future. It was on the Third Floor that there was not enough to do. A strange air of unreality had begun to permeate the atmosphere as senior execs drifted from office to office, speculating on what was up. On Thursday Hugh Williams had an afternoon meeting with the New Era team and as they finished up someone remarked on the black November clouds gathering outside. 'It's going to get a lot darker yet,' Williams remarked grimly. 'Either we'll shut by Christmas or there's going to be a massive retrenchment'.

But on the following morning of Friday, 2 November it was not all bad news. For a start it was the end of the week and Chris McLaughlin was in an especially buoyant mood as he scanned the papers. The previous day the Department of the Environment had finally managed to pronounce on the vexed question of two dishes. Henceforth, it had ruled magnanimously, a household did not require planning permission to erect a second satellite dish, which was welcome good news for both sides after they had been anxiously lobbying Whitehall on this point for so many months. All the prospective purchasers who had been held back by this worry could now hopefully go and splash out for Christmas!

Royal Assent had finally been given for the Broadcasting Bill, which was now Statute, and there was even better news for McLaughlin personally. A regional promotion he had overseen in some of Pearson's local papers had gone extremely well and the evening paper in York had given away 1,000 squarials. He put a call through to Frank Barlow's office to ask whether BSB should continue the promotion in Pearson's Brighton paper. Yes indeed! the message came back and McLaughlin felt chuffed. At last things were beginning to take off. Later in the morning came even better news. BSB had achieved its best-ever sales figures! He knew the technology was being produced smoothly at last and they would definitely have over 300,000 sets in the shops in time for Christmas. With so much good news about, and given it was his birthday, McLaughlin thought it high time he took some of his press office chums out to lunch.

At Osterley Ben Hawke was also planning a good lunch. That morning he had finally made up his mind to accept the 60 Minutes offer and return to Sydney. But when he had gone to hand in his notice he had been puzzled, not to say a little miffed, by the lack of reaction to his impending departure. The authorities seemed distracted and unconcerned and when he thought about it, it had been hard to find anyone even to inform. He had then found out Sky had booked a nearby hall for a big party that night. Clearly there was something going on he didn't know about.

Back in Bouverie Street the laser printers at Freshfields were humming as sheaves of merger documents underwent continuous final rewrites. Men in suits dashed frenetically round, looking red-eyed but increasingly relieved that the two-week marathon was entering its final lap. There had been an extraordinary amount to do, but now it was all coming together. BSB and its merchant bankers had informed the Takeover Panel, made provision for the smaller shareholders who had not been involved, and were arranging the various board meetings of their companies who were needed formally to approve the merger.

The activity at Freshfields was paralleled by a sense of lassitude creeping across the Third Floor at Marcopolo. That morning there had been no usual weekly 8 am Standing Committee and now other parts of ASG's diary had started to evaporate. Calls were not being returned and for once there were no meetings to arrange. He paced around his office and sat drumming his fingers on the polished surface of his desk until by 4.30 pm he could stand the tension no longer. He told his PA Carol Goddard he was leaving for the weekend. If she needed him she knew where to find him. Shortly afterwards John Gau and Hugh Williams met up in the car park. They too were leaving to go home, agreeing the inactivity on the third floor was unbearable. They arranged to speak later if there was any news.

Within minutes of ASG leaving his PA Carol's phone rang. She picked it up to hear Frank Barlow demanding to speak to him. 'I'll try and find him for you,' she replied, immediately calling ASG in his car. He decided against returning the call. An hour later from his adjoining office Edward Bickham heard ASG's phone ringing once more and went to answer it. It was Frank Barlow again, wanting to know why ASG had not returned his call and demanding his number in the country. Bickham gave it to him. At 6.15 pm ASG walked into Dorking to find the phone ringing peremptorily. The subsequent conversation lasted less than 30 seconds. Barlow informed him BSB had merged with Sky and he was being replaced. Meanwhile he would be offered a three-month consultancy. Then the phone went down.

ASG felt pole-axed. It was just over three years since his first day at BSB on Black Monday, and the company had been his life ever since. But, he reminded himself briskly, this was no time for idle reflection. The immediate worry was that his boys and girls would hear the bad news from their television screens as they sat at home with their loved ones. He must personally work fast to let as many of them know as possible. He started by trying to get hold of Ian Clubb at Freshfields to discuss exactly how the crew of the Good Ship BSB should be informed, but Clubb was instructed not to take the call. The only person who would speak to him was Richard Baker, Reed's business development manager, who just said he could give no details or information. After a deep breath ASG, taking it from the top, dialled John Gau's number.

Meanwhile John Stapleton and his wife, Lynn Faulds-Wood, sat in a Delta cab travelling along the Embankment towards Marcopolo House, where they were expected to do a turn on the nightly entertainment show 31 West, one of the JGP productions produced by former BBC chums which was named after the Marcopolo satellites' position in the celestial orbit. They would do their familiar number about what it was like both living and working together co-presenting Watchdog and were looking forward to a reunion afterwards with Stapleton's old Nationwide colleagues who produced the programme. The driver chatted away about BSB as they made their way through the traffic. 'What a place it is, eh? We've never known an account like it – have you ever seen their building, eh? Cor! You're in for a nice surprise!'

The car swung past The Rock and stopped outside the entrance. As they walked through the glass doors, like so many before them they marvelled at the atrium and Stapleton thought back briefly to his arrival at the mud bath that was Osterley. 'It's just like entering Buckingham Palace,' they joked to each other as Lynn tested the white lilies on the reception desk to see if they were real. They were. Not only did it feel a long way from Osterley but from anywhere else in television.

After being escorted into the studio and doing their bit they retired to the Green Room with two old chums as they had anticipated. The first drink was just being poured when the phone rang. One of their friends, an amiable New Zealander, joked about a grumbling viewer as he lifted the receiver but as he listened the smile was abruptly wiped off his face. 'That was John Gau,' he said quietly as he put down the instrument. 'We've been merged.'

The atmosphere froze and Stapleton felt uncomfortable. What had been intended as a pleasant reunion with old friends had suddenly become an intrusion into private grief. It was difficult to know what to say. To fill the gap he suggested they look at Sky News to see how it was reporting this item about itself. But when they tuned in, to their amazement there was no mention of it. Stapleton, as an old employee, therefore gave Ben Hawke a ring at Osterley, only to discover it was the first anyone there had heard about it. Hawke went into a state of shock. No wonder his resignation hadn't provoked any reaction earlier! He rushed into the newsroom and told the duty editor so the story could be in the evening's next bulletin, before passing the news on to all the journalists he could see.

Later Hawke joined his colleagues in the boardroom where, against all the rules, drinks had been brought out for the senior staff. Gary Davey and Sam Chisholm, whom no one had seen for a fortnight, looked tired but jubilant and there was plenty of good-natured joking and toasting of Chisholm, who was now managing director of the new five channel combined company which, it was revealed to them, had been named BSkyB. Already there was much chortling at the thought of the the Rottweiler being let loose in Marcopolo, although as civilising influences Gary Davey and Ian Clubb were to be his joint deputies. Beyond that it was to be 'the best person for the job' – whatever that meant.

DISHED!

As John Stapleton and his wife tried to make a tactful exit, two
floors above them the BSB press office was in a state of imminent
nervous collapse. Bickham had called up Chris McLaughlin, still
reeling from his birthday lunch, to come and help man the phones
and they both sat there with the other press officers hour after
hour busking the answers as every available line rang constantly.
With no instructions they helplessly watched the BBC's Nine
O'Clock News for guidance, learning, if it was to be believed,
that BSB had abandoned D-MAC and the Marcopolo satellites
in favour of Astra and PAL. As McLaughlin reflected grimly
on the battles he had fought on behalf of D-MAC, it was
impossible to find clarification although calls kept pouring
in from all parts of the globe. At midnight he exercised his
authority and opened the executive drinks cupboard for the
press officers to help themselves. They sat drinking beer in
ASG's office until at 2.30 am McLaughlin took his final call
from *Variety* in Los Angeles, put the drinks away and they left
for a few hour's sleep.

At the offices of Freshfields the drinking had not even begun.
The various merger documents were so complex just signing
them had taken hours and it was 3am before the trolley of
champagne was wheeled into the room and the exhausted
participants stood around drinking their bubbly. At around
4am the brief party died and Rupert Murdoch emerged into
Bouverie Street with his son Lachlan, whom he had brought
along to witness the historic moment which would be such a
major factor in shaping the future of the Empire. As they walked
along Fleet Street on the brief journey back to their flat the very
silence bore eloquent testimony to the past which Murdoch had
helped to obliterate. Four years previously it would have been
alive with scurrying newspaper vans and the rumbling presses
would have made the pavement tremble. Now it was as silent as
the grave.

The weekend brought no respite as the BSB press officers
manned their post, still without any instructions on what to
tell the world. At Osterley Chisholm held a meeting to map out
the future, while Murdoch welcomed Ian Irvine, now chairman
of BSkyB, and showed him round. When they reached the
newsroom Irvine, playing the hard man, grunted: 'It looks like

292

TV-am before we got rid of all the people.' Murdoch smiled tolerantly.

Meanwhile the finance directors and chief executives at Granada, Pearson and Reed were designing the slides for the Monday morning presentation to the City, where share prices were expected to perk up in response to the merger. As they carefully rehearsed the arguments that would demonstrate to the analysts what a stunning coup they had brought off PR advisers warned of the odd tricky issue, such as someone raising the matter of the imminent wrath of the IBA. Keep the questions session to a minimum, they were advised.

Telling the IBA had indeed been a little sticky. The shareholders had left it until Friday evening, but Ian Irvine had then failed to reach the chairman, George Russell, and instead informed David Glencross, the director of television, at his home. Commercial pressures had forced the shareholders into seeking a deal, Irvine explained, and unfortunately they had been obliged to concede that Astra and PAL would, after a transition period, be the primary system. The news had anyhow already reached Brompton Road through the IBA engineers who had picked up word on the grapevine from their engineering colleagues at BSB.

That Saturday Glencross, who had spent a lifetime in TV regulation, was furious. Phoning his old friend John Gau at home he demanded to know exactly what was going on. Why had the IBA not been consulted? The DBS licence was not the shareholders' to dispose of. Most disgraceful of all was the behaviour of the oldest ITV contractor of Granada. It especially should have known better. It had been a very different matter, he reminded Gau, when it had looked to the IBA for protection against a threatened takeover by Rank. When Glencross rang Gau was preoccupied with showing his young son how to poach an egg, but in any case there was little he could say. His involvement in the merger had been as a simple functionary, he replied. It had never even occurred to him that the shareholders would not have informed the regulatory authority about the negotiations.

The reason Irvine had been unable to get hold of George Russell, the IBA chairman, was that he was at his secluded country retreat in Northumberland, relishing one of his periodic returns to his Geordie roots well away from both telephones and television. The IBA had still not succeeded in getting him by Saturday night and he had been continuing to enjoy his weekend until he arrived at a local bonfire night party. There, over the toffee apples and parkin, he fell into conversation with a neighbour who asked him what he thought of the news. Russell's weekend never recovered.

ASG was having a pretty rum weekend too. The phone at Dorking was constantly ringing as anxious members of staff tried to find out what was happening, while in between the calls he sat slumped in his tracksuit watching Sky News. As the weekend progressed he saw the interpretations of the merger were becoming increasingly bloody and an interview with Murdoch left viewers in no doubt about the major 'retrenchments' which were about to take place in the merged organisation. ASG sensed Monday morning was going to demand every ounce of leadership he could muster. More than ever he felt a deep sense of responsibility to the young people he had hired and built into a team. He started to work out what he would need to say when he called them all together. It was not going to be easy.

But late on Sunday evening the phone rang yet again. This time it was Jennifer Haigh, BSB's director of personnel. She spoke hesitantly. This was not an easy thing to say, she told him, but Anthony would not be required any longer. In fact, he was not to come to Marcopolo House again. She would make sure his personal belongings were returned to his home. That was all. There was no further mention of three-month consultancy. As Haigh's call had made clear, ASG, unlike the captain of the *Titanic*, would not be allowed to go down with his ship.

CHAPTER NINETEEN

Ninja Mutant Hero Television

The Sky troops entering Marcopolo House early on Monday morning goggled in sheer disbelief. Legendary tales had circulated at utilitarian Osterley about this fabulous place, but few had actually been there and for once reality measured up to the gossip. They all had their different points of comparison. Nick Carrington, Sky's deputy finance director, thought it like walking into a merchant bank, and in many ways it was hard for all of them to come to terms with. But there was one aspect they could handle immediately. Amazingly, Marcopolo was officially a no-smoking building. That was soon dealt with by ripping the No Smoking signs off the walls and implementing the first executive decision of despatching a secretary to buy 20 ashtrays. Both Sam Chisholm, now managing director and chief executive, and Gary Davey, his deputy, were smokers, as were many other Sky people.

The previous evening when John Gau had called him Chisholm had demanded to see the executive board at 8 am. Meanwhile ASG had called Carol Goddard to tell her he wasn't being allowed into the building. He had debated long and hard about defying the ban and going in to help his boys and girls but, deciding against it, had asked his faithful PA to pack his belongings. Arriving early, she had begun laying out boxes on the table in his office when a small bull-necked figure walked in. 'G'day,' he said, 'I'm Sam Chisholm. Do you remember I came to Brompton Road?' With that he went and sat down at ASG's desk. He was joined by Gary Davey and the two went to the Board Room for the executive board meeting.

Compared with the normal Monday morning meeting at Sky it was very mild, with Chisholm doing most of the talking and using relatively moderate language. But although there was little of his normal shouting the BSB people, used to a gentler style, still found him very loud. Chisholm effectively gave them a sermon, haranguing them on the scale of the losses and spewing forth lots of stuff about the corporate insanity that had prevailed until then. The shareholders of both companies had been remarkably accommodating in giving the backing they had, he told them. Now it was time to sort it out. There would be cuts and all sorts of changes would happen very quickly, and unpredictably. Although none of them said anything, they all knew that meant the actual executive board itself was to go.

The pattern then changed to a variation on ASG's meet-the-staff lunches, with each person in turn around the table giving their name and a summary of their responsibilities. The execs all tried to be cool, rational and totally unhysterical, despite their almost palpable alarm and anxiety as they worried about their individual futures. Chisholm was gruff, and there were glimpses of the cavalier attitude to people they were expecting. His mercurial temperament flashed occasionally, as when Andy Birchall raised a point then mentioned he was leaving at the end of the year. 'Why should I listen to you when you're leaving?' Chisholm barked back at him and everyone got the point. They would almost certainly all be leaving in the near future. When Bob Hunter started writing things down, Chisholm yelled: 'Why are you taking notes?'

He closed the meeting after about an hour and a half – never, as they had suspected, to call another one. Afterwards, sitting in ASG's old office working through events, he kept asking: 'Who's this?' and 'What's that?' but when it was suggested he found out for himself by going round and meeting the rest of the staff, he replied he didn't want to. Neither did he want to hold a staff meeting. In ASG's absence John Gau stepped into the breach. He called the staff into the windowless War Room and told them to the best of his knowledge what was happening. Many of the more junior people were very upset and some were crying. Hugh

Williams, the head of the NOW channel, appeared shattered. Gau stayed calm, reminded them it wasn't their fault and told them how well and hard they had all worked together. Whatever they thought about Sky, he advised them, they shouldn't be silly, but carry on doing their jobs properly as: 'Who knows where we'll end up?'

BSB hadn't been the only organisation to assemble that morning in a state of shock. At Brompton Road the IBA regulators were feeling badly let down. It was inexcusable that they had not been consulted. After all, they had been as helpful as possible, on a number of occasions waiving the rules – from the trouble over the ITN news coverage at the very start to the whole drama about Bond. The suggestion there would have been a leak if they had been let in on the talks was just insulting. Ian Irvine, when he was asked to come and explain matters, turned up the next day to inform them he had done the best deal for the shareholders. The outcome had reflected the respective bargaining power of the two sides. The IBA was not appeased. Granada then tried to imply the meeting which Alex Bernstein had set up with the chairman and then cancelled should have been a strong enough hint to Brompton Road something was afoot, but the IBA remained stony-faced. Just because the chairman of Granada arranged a meeting, how were they supposed to know he was concerned about BSB? Their assumption had been that Bernstein wanted to talk about Granada itself, or some other ITV matter.

The shareholders had an easier ride in the City, where Ian Irvine, Frank Barlow, Derek Lewis and their company finance directors gave a 10.30 am presentation on Monday to analysts at Cazenove's. The share prices of Reed, Pearson and Granada had risen that morning by small amounts and there was a smug atmosphere as they all congratulated each other. There was a cheerful slide-show with projections showing the new company would be making £400 million a year profit by the end of the decade. Details were now revealed of the carve-up between the two sides for when this happened. The first £400 million profit would be split 80/20 in Sky's favour, to compensate it for being closer to breakeven at the merger point. The second £400 million would be split equally and looking even further into the future the third £400 million of profit would then be split 80/20 in favour of the BSB shareholders. After that it would be 50/50.

Despite this impressive number-crunching Chris Akers, the Citicorp analyst, sensed a feeling of great relief at the gathering. It felt more like a parole meeting, with the shareholders' representatives very much giving the impression they were glad to have survived that one. And although they were happy to parrot their point of view, Akers also noticed they were not so keen to answer questions. When queries were raised about the new company's liabilities, as well as relations with the IBA, they fobbed them off and were obviously keen to cut the session short.

Back at Marcopolo after the meeting with John Gau a sinking feeling permeated the staff. Despite his advice to be sensible and carry on with their work nobody could do any. Some juniors went to the kitchen and got some wine, which by force of habit they took to the now-redundant smoking room. They then proceeded to get drunk. In general the more junior the staff, the greater the shock. Most of them had been wrapped up in their own little part of the organisation as they knew changes would be inevitable the way things were going and were expecting a major rationalisation, with perhaps their individual jobs being lost as a result.

Zoe Grimwood, a young production secretary on the Movie Channel, was preoccupied with the crisis caused by Andy Birchall's imminent departure and the prospect of John Gau muscling in and looking closely at the channel structure. They had all been extremely conscious of the political situation and were expecting heads to roll, when from nowhere their little sub-plot had been blown into oblivion. The merger was the only thing in the world that Zoe hadn't thought would happen. On the Friday night, when she had gone to dinner at Le Bouchon and met various BSB secretaries, they had been just as flabbergasted at the news.

At first, as they sat swigging the wine, they were almost too dumbfounded by what had happened to speak. But after a while with the aid of the alcohol their mood changed and they began feeling almost high on the newness and unexpectedness of the whole situation. Suddenly everyone started talking to people they had never spoken to before, belatedly becoming the one big family ASG had always striven for. Even though by then people had started to smoke all over the building, the smoking room now became its common room.

Whilst the juniors were drowning their sorrows, Chisholm started acting in the way stories filtering into Marcopolo had led them to expect. Edward Bickham, in his next door office, was talking to the marketing man from Sky when Chisholm walked in and shouted: 'The phones aren't working!' Bickham proffered a mobile, but Chisholm just screamed. Bickham went out to find Jennifer Haigh, the personnel director, and see whether she could activate something. He returned to find Chisholm waving his clenched fists about as he jumped up and down. The fact that he couldn't 'phone out had made him like someone possessed. 'If the 'phones aren't working in an hour, I'm going to sack everyone in this building,' he screamed.

The switchboard had frozen through the sheer weight of incoming calls, which had happened before when it had become overloaded. BSB was being besieged by an army of creditors, retailers, and endless hapless squarial owners. 'If I'd wanted to watch the Sun, I'd have bought Sky', one of them commented bitterly. When the switchboard girls told them to speak to the customer service girls in Leeds, they phoned back to say the Leeds girls could not talk as they were in tears. There were tears on the Marcopolo switchboard as well as senior staff tried to soothe 19 year olds in their first job, who had never come across anything remotely like this before.

As they recovered from the shock people began to leave the building. Equipment started leaving with them. Most of the execs had not brought their company cars to work that morning for fear they would be taken away, and now people started walking out with anything that wasn't screwed down, from portable computers which mysteriously disappeared from various offices to the last dregs of freebie goods from the merchandising cupboard. A person from graphics received summary retribution when he was caught and instantly dismissed.

Then Rupert Murdoch arrived, sweeping past The Rock in a gold Mercedes – a typically vulgar vehicle as the BSB staff instantly noted. He grinned broadly from the front passenger seat for the benefit of the waiting press cameras and then entered the building, politely asking the way at reception. John Gau, requested to give him a conducted tour, found him very affable and apparently interested in everything, including the studios in which the daily JGP movie show was being recorded.

A meeting with him was called for that evening at 6 pm. By then a lot of other Sky people had arrived and as they got down to business the execs were struck by how different the new Boss's style was from the way BSB had previously been run. The main issue under discussion was working out a letter to retailers informing them what they were going to do with the BSB dishes and how the whole thing was going to be sold. Murdoch was very involved, encouraging lots of debate, and Hugh Williams found it very interesting despite the circumstances. Here was a man whose personal fortune was estimated to be £500 million sitting in Battersea on a Monday evening actually taking charge of strategy in a highly detailed way. He was obviously a man with a concern for his various companies which was ingrained and endemic. It proved to Williams, in contrast to what had gone before, that if you wanted to run a broadcasting operation or a newspaper successfully, you had to be someone who really knew about it and liked the media.

The meeting was much less tense than the one with Chisholm that had started the day. Williams thought the BSB executives were being jolly British. They were constructive, supportive, and helpful – even though they realised it was unlikely any of them would be wanted in BSkyB. They simply weren't needed. It made commercial sense to get rid of them, although contracts were to be honoured. Most of them were looking forward to fifteen months' salary as a pay-off, which would take them well into six figures. But there was still a degree of humiliation involved, as all decision-making was effectively being made by the Sky people. If, like Williams, you had been called MD of your own channel you had been used to being somebody who commanded respect and attention, it was undeniably galling to go from that to being totally ignored, in reality only waiting for the axe to fall. For some it did not take long. Andy Birchall left the same day, along with sales director Mike Vanderkar, who made the decision of his own accord. With them went Bob Hunter, who had ended up running Sport and Galaxy and was not on the staff but had remained on a consultant's contract.

Hugh Williams could not help thinking what a shame and terrible pity it all was. The way the shareholders had completely bypassed and ignored all the people they had employed and built up relationships with struck him as extraordinary. How contemptuous some of them must have been of BSB's executives. Not having been on the strategy committee he had never really known the shareholders, but there had been lengthy discussion in-house about whether or not they were too remote from the executive board. Williams thought back to how he had always argued they were not – they had to trust their senior execs. The way they had been ignored in the merger talks showed how fragmented the structure had become. But at the same time he was philosophical. Media people could become terribly self-important and for those BSB staff who had been prone to delusions of grandeur this was a salutary lesson in deflation.

After the way things had eased out on Monday evening, Day Two had a harder edge. Murdoch and his henchmen, as the BSB people now tended to called them, no longer entered the building politely asking the way. Now they knew it they just walked straight past reception, giving BSB staff a feeling of being under enemy occupation. It was like the fall of Berlin, some muttered, whilst others hissed back it was more like the arrival of the Barbarians in Rome. Chisholm was certainly living up to his Hunnish reputation – even more terse, abrupt and, most felt, unnecessarily abrasive.

The new company had previously announced Astra and PAL would be the 'primary system' but now it had been decided all sale and rental agreements should be for Astra equipment only, with squarials being withdrawn from sale forthwith. The letter drawn up the previous evening was faxed to all retailers, telling them BSB customers should be reassured they would be supplied with Astra equipment on 'favourable terms'. But the retailers were warned any new BSB system sold after that day would not qualify for the exchange. Their worst fears confirmed, they were furious – as were the manufacturers, who had also been kept in the dark. A senior director of Philips had predicted earlier in the year that D-MAC was the future of satellite, and Thomson was getting close to a widescreen advanced definition TV costing £3,000, which had a 16" by 9" widescreen format like a cinema screen. This would work with D-MAC, but required PAL pictures to be squeezed.

As a fresh wave of outraged calls battered the switchboard more Sky people started pouring into Marcopolo. Screeds of lawyers came asking for files and the dreaded Securitate guards were brought across from Osterley to take charge, immediately upsetting junior secretaries by demanding they turn out the contents of their handbags. Reporters – including, of all papers, those from the *Daily Mail* – chased people in the car park while inside the atmosphere was threatening to get out of control. Ian Clubb told some distressed members of staff not to listen to orders from Sky people before seeking out Ian Irvine and informing him people were in uproar all over the building. Irvine told Clubb to leave it to him, and Murdoch's sidekick Andrew Knight showed up for half a day. To everyone's immense satisfaction word shot round that Chisholm had been chewed up by Murdoch personally.

After that Clubb found that the Rottweiler behaved himself better for a while – a pattern that was to be repeated. Following his key role in providing information for the merger talks, Clubb's reward on paper was his new appointment as deputy chief executive jointly with Gary Davey. But in reality there was no chance of his being treated as Davey's equal and much of the time he was just left hanging around. When he felt Chisholm was going over the top again, he left. The Barclay's project loan had been terminated upon the merger, so Clubb had started trying to raise more money, which he offered to continue to do as a consultant. The agreement was that in order to do this he would be kept fully informed, but Chisholm failed to honour this. So Clubb developed a programme and timetable for the business plan, issued instructions to managers, and finally departed for good.

There was no longer any feeling within the building that this could be the bloodless merger they had been promised. It was a takeover, as they knew full well at the Centaurs Business Park, where the latest joke in the newsroom was 'Is merger a new word for rape?'

Chris McLaughlin, negotiating on behalf of the 19 people in

the press department, was summoned to a meeting at which Chisholm asked why they needed two PR departments. Why didn't they just get rid of all the BSB people? he suggested. Edward Bickham went purple with outrage, parroting the assurances that had been made about the best man for the job, but McLaughlin saw they were on a hiding to nothing. The BSB people simply weren't wanted.

Sitting down with Jane Reed, News International's Director of Corporate Affairs, he told her the two PR sides had fought 'an honourable draw' and people should now be treated in a decent way, to which she agreed. Between them they then hammered out a redundancy package which was adopted for much of the rest of the staff. The terms for the minions below exec level were not particularly generous. Most people were on three months' notice, plus another month for each year of service, although McLaughlin was later mortified to find that the equivalent marketing people who were also going were on six months.

When the package was offered to the staff of the press office only two out of the 19 expressed an interest in working for Sky. One visited Osterley to see the place for himself but came back depressed, saying they all seemed to feel over there that they'd won. He wouldn't be comfortable in that environment, even in the unlikely event of his being offered a job. In the end, after a period of hanging about with nothing to do, they all left, just as the Thatcher leadership crisis broke. Edward Bickham fortuitously transferred back to his old political stamping ground as he helped run Douglas Hurd's doomed campaign for the premiership.

Throughout the first week at Marcopolo the same message was relayed to BSB staff throughout the organisation. On the Movie Channel a meeting was held by Sky's deputy managing director, Stewart Till, with the BSB people sitting on one side and the Sky people on the other, while he asked them all what they did. When he told them that as far as he was concerned Sky was taking over, one of the senior producers got very annoyed and replied: 'It's my understanding that this is a merger and we are working together.' Till replied he was sorry, but that was not what he had been told.

Murdoch himself stayed in the building all day on the Tuesday, providing a moment of light relief when one of the transparent lifts stopped yet again, this time freeze-framing the new Boss. All the staff who could see him simply sniggered and turned away, doing nothing to help, and he kept pushing the button until eventually the lift re-started. On Wednesday he went back to New York, keeping in regular contact on the telephone with Sam Chisholm, who stayed in ASG's old office all week.

Carol Goddard found him very strange. He didn't use the buzzer, but just shrieked at her instead. Get me this person . . . I want them now! he would bark, and then wait for a reaction – seemingly with no respect for other people's feelings. When he remarked to her: 'I suppose everybody hates me,' she just replied: 'What do you expect?'. What was her salary?, Chisholm asked her and when she told him, informed her Sky secretaries earnt four grand less – and that he himself had to share one. ASG on the other hand had had both a PA and a secretary all to himself. 'You don't really like me,' he added 'I'm common compared to Anthony.' 'Well, you certainly are different,' she replied diplomatically. The reaction amongst the rest of the staff was much the same. They found Chisholm loud, brash and unpleasant, and shuddered at his swearing. They did not like the way he winked at the girls. He was not, they decided, a real gent like ASG.

There were faint flickers of the old egalitarian lifestyle when on Day One Chisholm said he would get his coffee from the machines like the rest of the staff, but by the afternoon he had already given up that idea and was demanding it be served from the kitchen. The 'flowers in the loo' culture vanished as he snarled: 'I don't want any flowers in my office' and a Sky-style economy drive started across the board. The habit everyone had got into of having all the newspapers was stopped as they were cut to one copy of each for the entire building. Chisholm was continuously furious about Marcopolo and everything in it. The cost of the furniture and fittings alone would pay for the entire Osterley site, he kept informing anyone who would listen. ASG might be very nice, but couldn't have run a TV company, he told Carol Goddard.

Until the merger BSB had always been a very good payer. But Chisholm's arrival changed all that. Creditors were screaming abuse down the phone as various companies caught up in the mix, from programmers to merchandisers and producers of print and art work, demanded immediate payment. More demands poured out of the fax machines, with mail coming in so fast and furiously it seemed the whole world was writing. Chisholm, unmoved, just said to ignore them all and the letters remained unopened, the faxes unanswered, and all calls to the Third Floor were routed through one secretary.

Chisholm had a rule that all letters being sent out had to be seen by him, but he often left them sitting on the desk for days, along with the redundancy cheques being written for the many leaving, which he had not got round to signing. He insisted that every cheque had to be signed by him and that first they had to be talked through by the accountants. At Sky there was anyway a standard rule that all cheques over £10,000 had to be signed by the MD, but there had been no such controls at BSB. When a cheque appeared on Chisholm's desk already co-signed by two programme accountants, which under the BSB system could technically have gone out to be honoured, he went berserk.

The creditors besieging the company were ignored except for a young representative from a production company, supposed to be paid on invoice, who managed to gatecrash the building by penetrating the Securitate cordon and got into Chisholm's office to demand his money. There was screaming from inside and Chisholm came storming out of the door with the creditor in hot pursuit. The cheque he was after had been sitting on the desk.

Over at Wapping there were long meetings on how the business should be turned around. Murdoch had been against a new project loan, saying why should he give money to these parasites, but anyhow having little choice now the Empire was so strapped to raise more money. The bonus for News Corporation was that it looked good in the accounts. BSkyB could now be written in as a single line investment, appearing as an asset, whereas before the Sky losses had been written off in full. As Murdoch was no longer fully funding the operation he had also theoretically halved the scale of his investment.

But looked at from a different perspective he had exchanged a business which was losing £2m a week for half of one losing a total of £10 million, and further down the ranks, as the finance men sat night after night trying to reduce the astronomical costs, they often wondered if they had bitten off more than they could chew. As far as income was concerned, BSB had made only a fraction of its budgeted income in September, with one of its major revenue sources being VAT refunded by the Customs and Excise. There was no way round the problem, they decided, but to bite the bullet and make huge payoffs. The cheques started to be written.

The Sky finance people often had difficulty comprehending the scale of the extravagance under the former management compared to their own organisation. For a start BSB was crawling with consultants. The September management accounts showed over £1 million paid out to them in a single month. Chisholm stopped all that immediately. Then there was the £3 million bill from Lazards for arranging the project loan, and the huge arrangers' fees from Barclay's. Everywhere at BSB someone had been trying to take a piece of the action, from the consultants and merchant banks to the production companies with their copper-bottomed guarantees and fat management fees. The list went on and on. There was the unbelievable marketing budget of £104 million for the year, and the bonus scheme. The Sky people just laughed when members of the BSB staff, puzzled, asked about their own bonus scheme. How could a company which was making a weekly loss of £8 million pay bonuses, especially when it had only launched after a six month delay? the Sky team guffawed.

The programme deals also were incredibly expensive by Sky's standards. Incidents like the auction for TV rights of the Mike Tyson/Buster Douglas boxing championship fight summed it all up. Gary Davey had done the negotiating through an American agent, bidding against BSB on the telephone. When they got up to $400,000 he had seen his career flash in front of his eyes and was just about to say he would match it when the agent said BSB had gone up again – to $700,000! Davey had only temporarily stopped at $400,000, but BSB had been so desperate that when he had delayed they had upped their offer by bidding against themselves! Davey had been flabbergasted. Sky had been going to stop at $450,000 whatever. It was symptomatic of the two approaches – BSB's to get it whatever it cost, while the Sky attitude was they would like to do it, but if they couldn't afford it, they couldn't afford it. At Sky they made many tough decisions and programmes were chopped instantly if they didn't work or were too expensive. Yet all BSB deals were long term, with guaranteed this and guaranteed that ... It was clear BSB had been terrible negotiators, conducting really bad business. Take football matches, for instance, where Sky paid around £28,000 a match whilst BSB had been paying up to £200,000 for some Scottish FA games.

It was the cars that said it all for many people. BSB had a staggering number – four times those at Sky, and all two grades higher for equivalent level execs. At Sky they all had Rovers, and Murdoch had personally to sanction the Jaguar for the deputy managing director, Stewart Till. But at BSB, with its plethora of BMWs and Jaguars, it seemed you could have anything you could imagine. Even more extraordinary for the Sky people was the fact that the cars were leased. But then, nearly all BSB's equipment was leased, whereas Sky's was always bought up front. Leasing was mortgaging your future and BSB had been pushing a huge wave of liabilities ahead of it, while Sky had said it would take the spend now. Murdoch's philosophy, already translated into action in the News International accounts, was that the company must break even on a trading basis. You had to write off all the investment and get it off the books before you had an accurate picture of the day to day trading position. Then you could see if it was really working. BSB's idea, on the other hand, had been to throw costs forward, hoping it would be able to absorb them in due course.

The Sky answer, in line with the 'bite the bullet' approach, was now to scrub the deals it did not approve of, as it did with the cars. But the result of terminating the leasing arrangement was losing the car, together with all the payments so far, and in addition having to pay a penalty, in some cases as high as £5000 per car, for breaking the contract. Chisholm was furious, but when the Sky staff kindly offered to take them over instead, he promptly said no. They should take the buggers back despite the outrageous penalty payment, which he then considered disputing. He didn't want Sky people absorbing the BSB lotus-eating lifestyle. There was an additional irony when it was pointed out to him that Dial, from whom the cars were leased, was part of Mercantile Credit. This in turn was owned by Barclay's, and BSkyB was of course turning to them again for another loan. Stymied, Chisholm then eradicated another piece of BSB transport philosophy by closing the Delta cabs account.

Many of the BSB staff were unable to face up to the big equation, in some cases finding it beyond their comprehension. To them Sky's actions were baffling. All around them, from cars to production companies, they saw contracts being written off without any apparent attempt to recoup losses - especially on programmes. The original Sky plan had been to get rid of all BSB's output except for movies and sport, with the Power Station music channel going in two weeks. But John Gau then began persuading Davey and Chisholm to keep as much BSB output as possible, using the need to placate the IBA to argue for keeping the weekend arts programming on NOW. Gau sensed Chisholm and the others were worried about the IBA, and that switching to go out entirely on Astra, as they had announced they were doing with the letter to the retailers, would increase the likelihood of huge claims from manufacturers. It was better to stay on D-MAC as well, both to keep squarial owners happy and give manufacturers less of an argument, he reasoned. Gau's argument was accepted, the letter to the retailers withdrawn, and a promise made to keep both systems for the present, with squarial owners eventually being offered a swap.

Gau was then asked to stay on as Sky realised an old hand was needed to smooth the path with the IBA, but without a specific title or seat on the Board. It took him about 30 seconds to decide against it, and he left shortly afterwards, moving back to his JG Productions office in Putney. Gau had not begrudged the shareholders trying to merge, but regretted the way that in his opinion they had been outwitted by better players. He thought Ian Irvine put up a poor show against Murdoch and the shareholders had played a bad hand, showing little concern for detail beside the overwhelming need to unload themselves and preserve their commercial stake. On strictly commercial grounds, as Chisholm had already told Murdoch, they should have insisted on shutting Sky News. Instead, by moving with such speed, they had ended up with a barrage of lawsuits from manufacturers and huge contractual pay-offs. While D-MAC was a mistake, having achieved it at great expense it was correct to keep it. The merger could have been a real one which preserved some of BSB's achievements, but by the way it had been conducted it had lost for ever the chance of establishing a genuine third force in British broadcasting against the BBC and ITV. It could have given a huge boost to the British production industry by not relying purely on buy-ins and acquired programmes, and if the shareholders had hung on for another three months Sky would have been in far more trouble. Unless, of course, they had simply lost interest and just wanted out. If that was the case, Gau felt bitterly betrayed.

ASG meanwhile had been kept in the picture by Carol Goddard who rang him in the evenings with regular updates. He had been having a hard time sitting cloistered at home, not that the merger itself had come as any great shock. The shareholders' representatives were fine, determined people, but were tired and nervous and it wasn't surprising they had decided enough was enough. The poor people, running their wonderful companies, had enough difficulties with fighting off the recession. And the merger had left them the legacy of a stake in the future of a business which ASG was certain would be very successful one day.

On the Wednesday after the merger he went to see Frank Barlow to discuss his severance terms and tell him that people at BSB were very frightened, to which Barlow trotted out the old chestnut 'best man for the job'. Barlow skirted round the question of compensation. Privately he had been shocked about what he saw as BSB excesses and the scale of the extravagance. As for the merger, ASG saw there were two ways it could take place. There was the sustaining, healing sort of way, in which the two tribes would be merged together in a calm and intelligent way, with the best boy or girl genuinely getting each job. Then there was the more brutal, single-minded approach, which seemed to be the one Sky was going for. The prizes, he could see, were to go the loyal and there was no question of the two tribes being joined together. It was as if everything that BSB had achieved had to be wiped out. It's culture and personality was to be eradicated by the savage Pol Pot approach of taking no prisoners. This was the right-hand edge of capitalism, with no care for people at all.

As ASG had seen it Sky was picking up the 5% of customers who were the sort of people who would take up satellite TV – what Peter Bell had called 'the early adopters'. But BSB would have reached the other 95% with its wider understanding of the market as part of the hierarchy of British broadcasting. The same sort of thinking applied to the equipment. The D–MAC and PAL systems could be run alongside each other, enabling the commitments to be kept to the manufacturers. The mountain of 200,000 squarials which had been manufactured but not yet sold would be saved and the public would have a genuine choice. The market could then decide which it wanted. Mind you, he thought, it was fair enough Murdoch should be having the biggest say. He did have 48% of the new company, while the next biggest shareholders now only had 11%.

There was one consolation. People in the media were quite appalled by what was happening, and BSB's role had changed overnight from whipping boy to object of sympathy. That was apart from the News International papers, of course. ASG had suffered a lengthy and bruising article in the *Sunday Times* headed 'The Man Who Fell to Earth', with a cruel picture showing him slumped disconsolately on the sofa in his tracksuit. It all added to satellite's bad reputation as a slightly murky business.

In the hall of his London house were the boxes holding his belongings which had been returned from Marcopolo and were the only tangible memories of his short time at BSB. Of course he still had the whole-hearted support of Marjorie, who had been outraged at the way he had been treated at the end of his short excursion into the world of television. But then, ASG reflected, most of the things they had been involved with were to do with people – the funding, the shareholders, the market research. In a way it was the same as at many other organisations, or when he had been at Saatchis, where he had 14,000 people under him. BSB, he thought sadly, had never really got to be a broadcaster at all.

CHAPTER TWENTY

Sky's the Limit

As the eventful year drew to its close corporate etiquette demanded there be a BSkyB Christmas party which, if it was to be held on company premises, had to be at Marcopolo because of the Osterley dry rule. By the start of the festive season the fall-out from the merger was still coming down, although official government interest had soon evaporated. In the first week after the merger government officials had let it be known they had no objection as David Mellor, the Broadcasting minister, took the line that market forces should prevail. It was already an open secret that despite the changes at the top with the departure of Rupert's ally Mrs Thatcher, there would be no referral to the Monopolies and Mergers Commission.

Patrick White, the managing director of CIT (Communications and Information Technology Research) commented in a letter to the *Independent* that the merger should not be referred to the Monopoly Commission as 1% of the (falling) UK television audience was hardly a monopoly. White had consistently produced pessimistic forecasts for the satellite industry and now he commented: 'It does remind me of a telegram sent home by the man playing the roulette wheel in Monte Carlo – "System a great success – please send more money".'

The IBA, after much huffing and puffing, had ultimately done nothing. It had issued stern warnings about a 'serious breach' and insisted the DBS contract was not the property of the shareholders to dispose of. But all talk of legal action and severe sanctions ultimately faded away as the regulators reasoned that to remove BSkyB from the Marcopolo satellite would simply punish the unfortunate squarial owners and sound an immediate death knell for the D–MAC system. In any case, it felt, there were only limited sanctions you could take against a company which was now losing £10 million a week.

Instead the IBA resolved to put two independent directors in place to keep an eye on regulatory requirements although they had not yet been appointed. But the BSkyB licence would not be withdrawn until the end of 1992, after which the service would move over completely to the Astra satellite with Marcopolo channels advertised again to see if anyone wanted them. BSkyB would henceforth provide free swaps for BSB households, including installing the new Astra dish, meaning they would not be dispossessed.

Some 550 out of the 1,400 jobs in the two companies had already gone, the vast majority from the old BSB, with people being made redundant, simply not applying for new jobs, or having been on short-term contracts which were not renewed. The BSkyB programming team was now entirely from Sky, with Chisholm confirmed as managing director and chief executive. Of the senior managers only Jennifer Haigh, the director of personnel, Peter Clarke, the company secretary, and Ellis Griffiths on the technical side still remained from BSB, although nobody knew for how long. The job losses had deepened the general gloom in the television industry, where other huge redundancies had paralleled BSB's demise, as terrestrial companies like Yorkshire and Central struggled with a combination of the advertising recession and the slimming down of their operations for the forthcoming franchise battle.

Of BSB's onscreen stars Robin Day remained for the time being, as did Selina Scott. The days when she would complain that Sky was using her image in its advertising were over. Instead she was transferred to a Sky News programme called The Reporters, reading three prepared links which together came to less than five minutes, and later hosting a puffing film entitled: Sky News – Two years on, where she read out boastful lines like 'We brought you this ...' and 'We did that ...'

Crown Communications, which had provided the BSB news

service, had had a bumpy ride-out starting with Chisholm offensively remarking: 'Do you guys pay your presenters to do that? Do you think anyone is interested in news without pictures?' Endless phone calls to the one secretary they were being routed through on the Third Floor had been left unanswered until they at last managed to talk to Gary Davey. The result had been a letter which arrived two days later telling them to stop all programmes the following day. The last bulletin had gone out just before midnight on Friday 30 November. But in the end the compensation, a £3.8 million pay-off, had been handsome. The *Daily Mail*/Yorkshire New Era TV had also gone after a meeting with Chisholm, at which they said they would like to continue making programmes for him. He said he would like that as well – but a lot cheaper. 'How much cheaper? What sort of price?' the New Era person had asked. 'For nothing,' Chisholm had replied.

But the whole question of BSkyB's future was still a matter of debate. Frank Barlow had told *Campaign*: 'Two bad businesses will make one marvellous business', and the advertising trade magazine had noted that the market might settle down, as the video industry had, now the consumer was no longer confused and mistrustful. There was confidence in the company's long-term future in the City, where analysts from Kleinwort Benson had pronounced a verdict that the merger was 'a marriage made in Heaven'. But doubts still remained about how big and how fast the UK satellite market would grow.

David Plowright of Granada Television, who had wanted a broadcaster rather than a marketing man as chief executive, and had not been brought into the merger negotiations, had now resigned. He felt regret in terms of the programme service BSB had represented, coupled with relief as far as the Group was concerned now it had put more of a cap on its finances. But there was anger amongst other programmers at Granada that the company should now be helping finance what was effectively a Murdoch operation when, with programmes like World in Action and worthy documentaries, Granada had always been in the forefront of various campaigns for 'quality' television. And despite the merger Granada, along with Pearson, Chargeurs and Reed – which was still the most nervous – had huge exposure. David McCall of Anglia, was also much relieved at the merger and continued to hold firm to his belief that satellite was a high-risk project. Estimates put the new company as still losing £8 million a week, with the certainty another round of refinancing would be needed in the New Year, and nobody knew how many more stretching into the future. Attempts were now being made to restructure the film deals which in the previous war had meant both sides making such heavy future commitments. There were hopes – but no guarantees – that now there was only one buyer for Hollywood's products the moguls would be prepared to renegotiate. The series of heavy writs from manufacturers and retailers was working its way through the system, meaning more bills to come, while Operation Dolphin was still in the throes of the mammoth task of restructuring the debt of the Empire as a whole. The only person who did have something to smile about was Alan Sugar. Dishes had accounted for a fifth of Amstrad's turnover and half its profits in the last year.

ASG also had his say, going on the radio show On the Ropes to say he was surprised Murdoch, for whom he had great respect, had so many thugs working for him, although he refused to name names. This came to the attention of Sam Chisholm. 'I'm not a thug, am I? I'm a bit hard, but I'm not a thug,' he had remarked in a pained fashion to Jennifer Haigh.

BBH, its advertising canned and the account lost, had the consolation of having neatly picked up the massive NatWest account just before the merger took place. Later Nigel Bogle had gone to a meeting of the Marketing Society to hear ASG giving a talk on his BSB experience. Beforehand he heard people chuckling away as they speculated about how ASG was going to get himself out of this one. But the former chief executive had spoken with such conviction as he systematically went through the catalogue of problems and disasters which had hit the company that Bogle, himself impressed by the charismatic presentation, found the audience's mood changing. Afterwards, as he listened to them recalling in wonderment the multiple hurdles ASG had graphically described, he sensed the mood of most of them had turned around and now they were firmly on ASG's side. ASG had told his peers looking back on it all he could think of nothing that BSB could have done which would have changed the course of events, and most seemed to be agreeing. 'Impossible brief! Impossible brief!' they were saying. ASG's one-word summary for the whole experience, as at Saatchi's, had been 'character-forming'.

There had been various celebrations and many of the old BSB staff had put a date in their diaries to meet up for yet another reunion at the Banqueting Hall, Whitehall, where Sir Trevor Holdsworth, who was an accomplished pianist, was giving a concert. But the real wake for the company had been held at The Legless Ladder in downtown Battersea. This was the office local, situated opposite Body's Health Club which had also been a popular destination, with staff moving seamlessly from one to the other.

Two weeks after the merger a huge crowd had gathered for a karaoke evening which had already been organised by the sports and social club. In a last freebie fling everyone was supplied with Sports Channel baseball caps to round off the BSB T-shirts, sweatshirts and bomber jackets they had already acquired. A stage had been set up for the karaoke singers to perform, and as people got stuck into the bar with a vengeance the animosity towards Sky, starting with a rude version of 'Tie Me Kangaroo Down, Sport', became less and less subtle.

As things really got going, McLaughlin, who had performed a rendition of Marvin Gaye's 'Heard It on the Grapevine' on behalf of the press office, thought what a pleasant bunch of people the BSB staff had been, even though they might not have been in business long enough really to weld into the team ASG had always so desperately sought.

Everything about the evening underlined what a good lot they were. There were no arguments and not a hint of violence, and they had all arranged transport home beforehand so they could get drunk as lords without worrying about it – as they were obviously doing as the evening got wilder and wilder. People were standing on benches and tables belting out the songs and swigging down anything which remotely resembled alcohol. Finally so many were dancing on one of the large refectory tables that it snapped under the strain. Three people promptly rushed forward offering to pay for it, but the owner refused, telling them he was just sorry they were going. The incident said it all for McLaughlin. You could criticise BSB people for being middle-class, but the one word that summed them all up was 'nice' – and there was no harm in that. And they knew how to have fun, as the evening proved when it climaxed with a drunken conga that wound unsteadily in and out of the pub as everyone chanted in unison: 'Sam Chisholm is a wanker . . . Sam Chisholm is a wanker . . . Sam Chisholm is a wanker . . .' The consequent hangovers were epic.

There was another do a fortnight later at Jongleurs restaurant in Lavender Hill were ASG had accepted an invitation to attend and was called on to give a little speech. He asked Chris McLaughlin what he should say, and McLaughlin advised him just to thank everyone, tell them how wonderful they had been, and how sad he was about it all – which ASG said was what he had been intending to say anyhow. Slightly to his surprise he was cheered to the echo and there was rapturous applause as, despite what they thought of the execs in general, the staff responded in an overwhelmingly warm fashion to him personally.

ASG rounded off his final appearance by announcing the winners of the raffle, which included a booby prize of a squarial and a decoder, while his old staff members chanted 'ASG! ASG! ASG!'.

Ten days before Christmas the two sides came together at Marcopolo House, which was also going in the mix with the 25-year lease being abandoned and everything to be gradually shifted over to Osterley. Chisholm's cheery invitation to 'the greatest Christmas party south of the river' had offered 'an unforgettable evening', together with a blunt reminder that the party was for BSkyB staff only. The Securitate were there in force to keep out redundant BSB riff-raff who had been paid off and might come to make a scene. But they all stayed away and only the few ex-BSB employees still on the payroll dutifully attended to gather in a sorry knot on the second floor. Gloomily they surveyed the simple buffet and refreshments of wine and beer laid out in the central atrium below them. This, in a triumph of timing, had been given its finishing touches two days previously.

How times had changed, they commented to each other as they took in their aerial view of the repast and spied drumsticks and sausage rolls. Nothing so naff as that would have been allowed in the good old days – unless the sausage rolls were made by Prue Leith!

After nervously eyeing each other they gathered their courage and descended in the glass lifts to stand around awkwardly, dwarfed by the vast space. It had all the warmth and conviviality of a morgue. Then, shortly after 6 pm the coaches bussing in the Sky contingent from Osterley edged their way past The Rock and the victors walked in. They glanced briefly up at the glories of the atrium before noisily piling into the tubes of lager and tucker. Ellis Griffiths, retreating back to the safety of the gallery, watched in fury as they ground their cigarette butts into the immaculate flooring. There was animosity in the atmosphere until a rock band started up and both sides switched their attention from bristling at each other to boogying, the more elderly trying to conjure up visions of either MTV or the Power Station according to their respective loyalties.

The old BSB people felt left out. Apart from anything else the invitation to a 'joint' BSkyB party had hardly been borne out by the huge Sky banner hanging across the atrium, completely dominating it. The squarial and Astra dish on display in reception had long since been dismantled and taken away. Gary Davey made a short speech, to the accompaniment of heckling, in which he said no one had chosen for what he ascribed as 'the merger' to happen. But as he spoke the BSB people felt it was almost as if they were passé and had never existed. Davey was telling them it was Sky who had grabbed the bull by the horns and there was a distinct sense of shock as he now described BSkyB staff as 'street fighters'. The few ex-BBC people still there took that hardest. Street-fighting was definitely not an activity they wished to be associated with.

When Davey had finished Zoe Grimwood of the Movie Channel was one of the few to grasp the nettle by taking up matters personally. She marched straight up to Gary Davey, poked him in the chest Aussie-style and told him bluntly: 'Thanks a lot, mate, I'm out of a job thanks to you guys.' Davey, who was enjoying himself hugely, looked her straight in the eye. 'You're the only one who's had the nerve to come up and say that to me,' he roared. 'We'll probably want to employ you in a few years' time!' He was still laughing as he strode off.

Some of the Sky employees inspired by Zoe's confrontation decided to have a go themselves. Bob Friend the grizzled ex BBC presenter on Sky towered over Chisolm. 'Was it true – as everybody was saying – that Chisholm had tried to shut down the News Channel.' The response was only a broad grin.

But whatever they thought of his conduct most of the execs and some of those lower down the tree agreed that Chisholm had been given a near impossible job – something a Mr Nice Guy could never do. First of all Chisholm had been told to take £1 million a week off Sky's losses and then, just as he had taken a grip on that, he had been landed with stemming total losses of £10 million. Only someone acting in the way he did could do it and there were already flickering signs his stringent medicine, although it might sometimes be hard to take, was working. And that, after all, was the point of the whole exercise and what was keeping them all in work and giving them something to celebrate this Christmas.

The Securitate were stopping people going beyond the atrium to look round, but two Sky people managed to give them the slip, to pad in awed fascination along the blue-grey carpet through the empty areas of themed grey Olivetti desks and designer waste-baskets. The transmission suites were humming steadily away as they automatically pumped out programme material, which by now were mostly Sky rather than BSB offerings. An enormous amount of energy was being generated, yet there was not a soul in sight and they did not stay long. The atmosphere was eerie and the whole place had a curiously abandoned air. 'It reminds me of the *Marie Celeste*,' one remarked as they made their way back towards the welcome babble of the party below them, which was just warming up.

The evening continued in raucous fashion, finally to end without bloodshed, although there were some raised voices and one particularly acrimonious wrangle at the door after a member of the Sky executive board nabbed a Delta cab ordered by a BSB person, who let off a loud stream of very un-BSBlike language.

Tiring of the din and having achieved her personal encounter, Zoe Grimwood made her way out on to Queenstown Road for the short walk back to her nearby flat. She had been fortunate in living so close to work, as at her lowly level she had never expected the status symbol of a company BMW. Anyhow it was pleasant to walk and she breathed in the cold night air gratefully. The air inside the atrium had been wreathed in smoke from countless cigarettes and smelly pipes and great vulgar wafts of beer.

How different from the delicate wine-sipping of the many parties in the old days she thought. Not that those had not been very jolly affairs, with lots of people letting their hair down after the execs had all left. But on this occasion many of the men had been drinking their beer straight out of the can, whilst others had reversed the equation by drinking wine out of their beer glasses!

As the evening had become more riotous, a number of her fellow BSB colleagues, whilst grudgingly admitting the incomers certainly knew how to enjoy themselves, had still been appalled by the behaviour of what they sniffily called the Sky mob. Zoe herself had taken it personally in terms of losing her job, but otherwise had been more laid back, finding the head-on clash between the two cultures highly amusing.

The cars whizzing by on the still-busy road brought her back to the present. She was being laid off in six weeks and had yet to decide what she would be doing next. But that didn't mean she would accept Gary Davey's offer of a job, even if it ever came up. With all that had happened recently she wasn't even sure if she wanted to continue her career in this particular branch of the media. All those loud, rather stout corporate men in suits, drinking their beer and bawling their rude jokes at each other, were not her sort of scene at all. But then, she reflected as she turned into her doorway, she might have no choice. For what she had just been witnessing – one way or another – was the shape of British television to come. With the demise of the high ideals of the old BSB, the foreign cultural invasion which Sir Harold Wilson had predicted so many years ago had finally taken place.

Index

ACTT 84–5
advertising
 of BSB/Sky 61–4, 144–6, 182–4,
  206–18, 219–20, 237–8,
  246–7, 251
 on satellite TV 69–70, 137–8
aerials, see squarials
Akers, Chris 153, 298
Allen, Rod 224–5
Alwood, John 83
Amstrad 10–12, 44, 138, 270, 314
Anderson, John 268, 269
Andrews, Leighton 216, 217, 218
Anglia Televison 10, 14, 250,
 313–14
Annan, Lord 217
Ariane 4 rocket 77, 154
Arthur Andersen Accountants 285
Arthur D. Little consultancy 188
Aspel, Michael 222
Astra satellite 9, 41, 43–4, 46, 47,
 48, 60, 77, 99, 154, 281, 292, 301,
 308, 312
Australian Broadcasting Tribunal
 258
Australian (newspaper) 87

Baker, Richard 290
Balfour Beatty 16
BARB (Broadcasters' Audience
 Research Board) 255
Barclays Bank 188, 242, 306, 308
Barlow, Frank 243–4, 247, 269,

284–5, 288, 289–90, 297,
 309, 313
Barnett, Steven 236
Bartle, John 61
BBC 6–7, 42, 81–2, 91–2, 96, 97,
 101, 105, 106, 111, 116–18, 156,
 172, 174, 194, 199, 223, 236, 249,
 250–51, 278–9
BBH (Bartle, Bogle and Hegarty)
 61–3, 144–6, 183–4, 212–13,
 225–6, 237–8, 314
Beecham's 137
Bell, Peter 30–32, 34, 44, 58, 63,
 181, 190–91, 224, 246, 247
 also mentioned 61, 63, 75, 127,
  130, 132, 144, 150, 154, 183,
  219, 242, 310
Bellamy QC, Chris 209–10
Benn MP, Tony 62, 200
Bernstein, Alex 243, 244, 282, 283,
 287, 297
BICC 16
Bickham, Edward 46–8, 131, 150,
 155, 166, 207, 212–15, 221, 269,
 270, 280, 290, 292, 299, 303
Bicknell, Marcus 39
Biggins, Christopher 228–9
Birchall, Andy 33, 34, 67–8, 71–4,
 110, 156, 173, 228, 246, 296,
 298, 300
Bird's Eye 21–2
Birk, Baroness 214, 215
Bjelke-Petersen, Sir Jœh 186

Black, Conrad 241
Blackburn, Tony 94, 98, 177
Blakenham, Viscount 9, 282
Bland, Christopher 13
Bogle, Nigel 61, 63–4, 144–50, 181,
   183, 225, 237, 251, 267, 314
Bond, Alan 12, 14, 76–7, 87, 93,
   185–7, 190, 191, 241–2, 243,
   258, 259
Bond Corporation of Australia 12
Bond, Jody 186
Bonham-Carter, Lord Mark 214,
   215, 217
   Border Television 113
Bordes, Pamela 80
Bough, Frank 81, 94, 113, 254, 265
Boulton, Adam 82, 83, 95, 96
Bragg, Melvyn 201, 214
Brandon, Michael 73
Branson, Richard 10, 16, 27, 75,
   76–7, 266
British Aerospace 16
British Board of Film Censors 6
British Board of Film Classification
   202
British and Commonwealth 12
Broadcast magazine 221, 266, 267
Broadcasting Bill (1990) 209–18,
   262, 288
Broadcasting Standards Council 202
Broome, John 158
Brown, Maggie 135, 179
Bruce-Gardyne, Lord 194
BSB (British Satellite Broadcasting)
   formation of company 9–17, 18
   technical problems 55–61,
      122–36
   marketing 61–66, 229–31
   and film rights 67–77
   programming 105–119
   management 120–22, 140–50
      see also Simonds-Gooding,
      Anthony
   Mission Statement and
      image 148–50, 181–5,
      223
   finance 150–55, 185–91, 219–31,
      240–52
   official launch 223–9

merger with Sky 266–71, 278–9,
   280–94
   see also Marcopolo House,
   Marcopolo satellites
BSkyB name 281
Bullmore, Jeremy 28
Burley, Kay 82
Burrell, Mark 9, 13, 243–4, 283,
   287, 288

Cable Television Association 98
Cambridge Electronics 12
Canal Plus channel 70
Capon, Susanna 164–5, 167
Carless company 151
Carlton Communications 12–13,
   50, 241
Carmody, John 199–200
Carr, Alan 171
Carrickmore incident 105–6
Carrington, Nick 295
Casey, Michael 215, 218
CBS 222, 235, 241
Centaurs Business Park 78–9, 86,
   88–9, 92, 93, 96, 192–3
Central Television 10, 312
Channel 4: 6, 81, 106, 156, 217
Channel Nine (Australia) 87–8, 186,
   257–8, 259, 281
Chargeurs SA 14–15, 189–90, 242,
   243, 279, 313
Charles Barker PR company 56, 135
Checkland, Michael 19, 51
Chegwin, Keith 177
Chisholm, Samuel Hewlings 88,
   257–65, 295–6, 299, 301, 302,
   303, 304–5, 306, 307, 308, 312,
   313, 316
   also mentioned 270, 271, 279,
      280, 281, 284, 291, 292
Christian Brann Ltd 181–2
CIT (Communications and
   Information Technology
   Research) 311
Citicorp 153, 268, 276, 298
Clarke, Arthur C./Clarke Belt 99
Clarke, Kenneth 193–4
Clarke, Peter 287, 312
Club of 21: 7, 9, 21

Clubb, Ian 150–54, 160–62, 164,
  183–4, 185, 187–91, 219, 240,
  242, 244–5, 248, 266–7, 277, 280,
  287, 290, 291, 302
CNN (Cable News Network)
  93–4, 195–6
Coleman, Andy 133–4, 140–42,
  146–7, 154, 223, 248, 287
Collett Dickinson Pearce 63
Collins, John 56–8, 146
Colombia Pictures 12, 74
Cook, Sue 113
Coopers and Lybrand 258
Cotton, Bill 106, 108
Cowdray family 9
Cowgill, Brian 19
cross-media ownership/promotion
  47–51, 63–6, 177, 206–18,
  269–70
Crown Communications 112, 227,
  248, 312–13
Curry's 176, 224

Daily Express 3, 95, 101, 135, 221,
  229, 269, 277
Daily Herald 40
Daily Mail 114–15, 117–18, 207,
  228–9, 240, 269, 302, 313
Daily Mirror 15, 40, 49
Daily Telegraph 181, 221, 241, 269
Davey, Gary 83, 262, 280, 291, 295,
  302, 306, 313, 317
Davies, George 15
Davis, Peter 190, 274, 275, 276, 282,
Day, Sir Robin 115, 222–3, 226,
  228, 312
DBS (Direct Broadcast by Satellite)
  6–7
DBS UK 12–13
de Lisle, Tim 208
DER 176, 224–5
Devereux, Robert 10, 11, 12–13, 27,
  33, 68, 75–6
Diamond, Anne 114, 115
Dickens, Chris 75, 129–31, 134,
  143, 152, 172–3, 183, 213,
  227, 246–7
  also mentioned 145, 150, 154,
    190, 225

direct selling 176–81, 224, 238,
  251–2, 256–7, 270–71
Disney Channel (Sky) 138–9
Disney Corporation 74, 138–9, 241
Dixon's 176, 224
D-MAC see under MAC
Dodd, Ken 198
Donahue, Phil 204
Downey, Morton, Jr. 204
Drexel Burnham 188–9
Dunkley, Chris 253, 254

Edelman, Asher 189
Eglise, David 56–8, 128, 133, 141,
  142–3, 246
  also mentioned 121, 124, 126,
    127, 129, 140
EIM (European Institute of the
  Media) 206, 207
encryption ("scrambling") 45–6, 70,
  125, 126–7, 132, 133–4
English, Sir David 114, 207,
  240, 269
Equity trade union 117, 249
European Broadcasting Union 97
European Space Agency 154
Eurosport channel (Sky) 96, 97,
  116, 253
Everett, Kenny 177

Falk, Bernard 113, 223
Farrer's (solicitors) 278, 279
Faulds-Wood, Lynn 290–91, 292
Ferguson 59, 140, 220
Ferranti 12
Ferrari, Nick 83, 197–8
Filmnet 201, 254
films 67–75, 96–7, 115, 143–4, 202,
  228, 241, 250, 254, 314
Financial Times 110, 135, 138, 244,
  253, 269
Ford, Anna 113
Forgan, Liz 125
Fortel 58, 60, 146
Fox channel (US) 200, 203
Fox, Sir Paul 19, 116
French, Gordon 78
Freshfields (solicitors) 286–7,
  289, 292

Frost, David 82, 172, 203

Galaxy channel (BSB) 107, 118, 228
Gardener, Llew 90
Gau, John 105–19, 131, 147–8, 154,
    172, 173, 183, 190–91, 223, 231,
    249, 250, 267, 283–4, 285, 289,
    293, 296–7, 308–9
  also mentioned 150, 225, 244,
    248, 290, 291, 295, 298, 300
Gau, Susie 109
GCHQ 142–3
GI (General Instruments) 125, 134,
    140, 142, 143
GKN 16
GKR agency 20, 26
Glencross, David 293
Goddard, Carol 166, 244, 289, 295,
    304, 309
Goldsmith, Harvey 207
Goldsmith, Sir James 189
Grade, Lord 217
Grade, Michael 50, 214, 217
Granada 9–10, 14, 76, 156, 189–90,
    242, 243, 246, 282–3, 293,
    297, 313
Grant, Russell 114
Gray, Charles 269
Green, Michael 12, 50, 241
Grey, Dame Beryl 214
Griffiths, Ellis 125, 126–7, 129, 134,
    142, 287, 312, 317
Grimwood, Zoë 298, 317–19
Grist, Graham 16–17, 30, 50, 58–9,
    120–30, 133–5, 140–41, 143, 156,
    189–90, 221–2, 245
Guardian 135, 149, 238
Guilly, Eric 243, 279
Guinness 172
Gunn, John 12
Gyngell, Bruce 50, 82, 84

Haigh, Jennifer 294, 299, 312, 314
Hailsham, Lord 217–18
Hambros Bank 12
Harper-Collins 214–15
Hart, Alan 106
Harvey-Jones, Sir John 214

Hawke, Ben 87–95, 97, 101, 195,
    229, 258, 264–5, 281, 289, 291
Hawkshead 113
HBO (Home Box Office) 142
HDTV (High Definition Television)
    7–8
Hearst, William Randolph 212
Hegarty, John 61
Henry, Georgina 135
Heseltine, Michael 216
Hill, David 78, 97, 259
Holdsworth, Sir Trevor 16, 26, 45,
    47, 50, 73, 76, 129, 185, 187, 213,
    242, 243, 315
Hollingsworth, Mike 114–15
Home Box Office channel 67
Howard, Anthony 91, 265
Howard, George 106
Howell, Lis 113
Hughes Aircraft Company 16, 133,
    155, 241
Hume, Cardinal 20
Humphreys, John 222
Hunniford, Gloria 113, 114
Hunter, Bob 33, 34, 107, 110, 150,
    156, 296, 300–301
Hurd, Douglas 46, 303
Hussey, Marmaduke 51

IBA (Independent Broadcasting
    Authority) 7, 8, 13, 35, 47, 51,
    107, 112, 121–3, 142, 154, 185,
    249–50, 281–2, 293–4, 297,
    311–12
IBM 16
IBS 202
Independent 135, 148–9, 179–80,
    269, 311
Industrial Bank of Japan 188
Ingham, Bernard 285–6
Invest International Holdings 15
IRN (Independent Radio News) 112
Irvine, Ian 84, 243, 276–7, 281, 282,
    283, 287, 292–3, 297, 302, 308
Irwin, Chris 9, 14–15, 28, 121–2
Isaacs, Jeremy 19, 50
ITN 34–5, 112, 199
ITT 124–7, 134, 140, 147
ITV 6–7, 81, 111, 250

James Whale Radio Show 255
Jameson, Derek 81, 94, 99
Jessel, David 227
John Gau Productions 106, 108–10, 166, 222
Junke, Manfred 126
Just, Adrian 251

Kasem, Casey 255
Kershaw, Steve 144, 225, 237
Kinnock, Neil 95
Kleinwort Benson 268, 313
Knight, Andrew 269, 279, 285, 302
Korda, John 126, 128

Ladies Home Journal 274
Lawley, Sue 223
Lawson, Hilary 114
Lazards 43, 190, 306
LBC (London radio station) 112
Le Grand, Jean-Pierre 243
Lee, James 266
Lewis, Derek 10, 11, 13, 19, 26, 243, 244, 297
Lifestyle programme (BSB) 107, 113–15, 118
Lineker, Gary 226–7
Lintas 22
Liveing, Chris 136
Liverpool Post and Echo 15
Livingstone MP, Ken 62
Longley, Clifford 203
Lonrho 12, 159, 185
Lucknam Park hotel 278–9, 281, 284–5
Lumen 2000 (Vatican channel) 201
LWT (London Weekend Television) 12, 39, 156–7

MAC (Multiplexed Analogue Component) system 8
C-MAC 8
D-MAC 8, 15, 30, 44, 45, 51, 56, 58–9, 61, 122–7, 131–2, 133, 150, 281, 292, 301–2, 308, 309, 310
D2–MAC 8, 122, 125–6
HD-MAC 8

McCall, David 13, 28, 29, 313–14
McCann-Erickson agency 176
McCormack, Mark 113, 274
McDonnell Douglas Delta Space Systems 154, 155
MacKenzie, Kelvin 49, 99, 197, 257
McLaughlin, Chris 56, 131, 134–6, 155, 163, 171, 183, 226, 227, 288–9, 292, 302–3, 315–16
Macmillan's 214–15
Mandela, Nelson 199
Marcopolo House 156–75, 227, 241, 295, 304, 316–18
Marcopolo satellites 154–5, 220, 248, 281, 292
Mars Electronics 56
Mastandrea, Pat 136, 178
Matsushita 57
Maxwell, Robert 15, 41, 49, 50, 241
Media Futures Group 236
Mellor, David 286, 311
Merrill Lynch 148
Mersey Television 114
MGM/United Artists 74
Milken, Michael 188–9
Miller, Jonathan 65, 95, 215, 217, 270
Milne, Alasdair 19
Mitchell MP, Austin 93, 95, 136, 200, 229, 265
Monopolies and Mergers Commission 200, 311
Movie Channel (BSB) 228, 250
MTV channel (Sky) 253–4
Multi-Broadcast company 176
Murdoch, Anna 215
Murdoch, Lachlan 292
Murdoch, Rupert
  character and philosophy 66, 132, 151, 196, 202–3, 209, 260, 261, 292, 299–300, 303–4
  running of "Empire" 189, 255, 262, 271–8
  and Sky launch 37–46, 77–9, 86, 96, 99–101
  and film rights 69–71, 73, 74–5, 139
  and print unions 83–4
  and direct selling 177

and merger with BSB 266,
    267, 285
relations with Mrs Thatcher
    48–51, 210–11, 215, 285–6, 311
also mentioned 5, 12, 30, 54, 55,
    62, 193, 199, 238, 239, 257, 294,
    301, 305, 314
see also cross-media ownership/
    promotion
National Film School 118
National Westminster Bank 16, 137,
    188, 314
Naughton, John 99
Neil, Andrew 79–82, 86, 95, 101,
    138, 139, 193, 266
NETV (New Era Television) 115,
    207, 240, 282, 313
News Corporation 37, 38, 255–6,
    271–6
News International 12, 37, 47–51,
    63–6, 177, 206–18, 255–6, 274,
    275, 269–70, 310
News on Sunday 62, 63
News of the World 48, 180, 201, 276
Newsweek 203
Next 15, 241
Noel Gay Television 108, 112
Nokia 59
Norman Broadbent agency 20
NOW channel (BSB) 107, 118, 229,
    230–31, 240, 250, 282
NTSC system 7
NUJ 208

Observer 99, 159, 162, 168, 185
O'Loan, John 78, 82–3, 85, 88, 92,
    97, 199
Oyston, Owen 62–3

Packer, Kerry 87, 93, 257–8, 281
PAL system 7, 8, 44–5, 70, 123, 132,
    281, 292, 301–2, 310
Paramount/Universal 71–4
Paxman, Jeremy 81, 193
Pearson company 9, 14, 27, 30, 33,
    43, 76, 135, 189–90, 242, 243–4,
    277, 282, 287, 288, 293, 297, 313
Philips company 123–4, 125, 301–2
Pizza Hut UK 30, 31, 32

Plowright, David 10, 18–19, 26,
    28–9, 76, 108, 161, 313
Pollard, Ian 158–9
Power Station (BSB) 250
Premiere cable TV 33
Pringle, James 180
Prior, Lord 46
Private Eye 208
Project X (direct selling) 176–81,
    224, 238, 251, 256–7, 270–71
Psychology Today 274
Puttnam, David 118

Radio Rentals 176
Raising Kane 212–14, 216, 218
Rank Corporation 293
Rapier company 56, 59
Rather, Dan 222
Rayne, Lord 15
Redmond, Phil 114
Reed International 15, 27, 76,
    189–90, 242, 243, 268, 269, 274,
    275, 276, 277, 282, 293, 297, 313
Reed, Jane 210, 215, 216, 303
Rees-Mogg, Lord 202
Renton, Tim 65
Rhodes, Bill 276
Riley, "Tiger" 20
Rippon, Angela 253
Rivera, Geraldo 204
Robertson, George 194
Ross, Nick 59
Rothermere, Lord 269
Rowland, Tiny 12, 185
Rugheimer, Gunnar 107, 169
Rumbelows 176
Rushdie, Salman 196
Russell, George 282–3, 293–4

Saatchi, Charles and Maurice 25
Saatchi and Saatchi 12, 20, 25,
    27, 240
Sainsbury, Sir John 158
Sallingbury Casey company 215–18,
    269–70
Salora 59, 140
Samuel Montagu 276
Scargill, Arthur 200
Schuller, Reverend 202–3

Scott, Selina 94, 115, 222–3, 226, 229, 240, 312
scrambling *see* encryption
Sears company 12
SECAM system 7, 8
SES (Société Européenne des Satellites) 37, 39, 77
Shah, Eddy 112
Shearson Lehman bank 188–9
Simonds-Gooding, Anthony (ASG)
  character and style 18, 61, 63, 75, 76, 135–6, 152–5, 162–4, 166–7, 169–70, 173, 219, 220–21, 227–8, 229, 259
  background 20–30, 130
  and management of BSB 58, 70–71, 73, 107–10, 114, 124–9, 133, 142–50, 156–7, 184, 206–7, 242–3, 244
  and Graham Grist 120, 140–41
  merger and final days at BSB 277, 283, 285, 287–8, 289–90, 294, 295, 309–10, 314, 315
  quoted 45, 65, 219, 248, 249, 252, 253, 267
  also mentioned 50, 55, 64, 190, 191, 210, 214, 244, 246, 269, 277, 286, 288, 26–36, 51–4
Simonds-Gooding, Major Hamilton 20
Simonds-Gooding, Marjorie 27, 46, 52, 53, 154, 162–4, 167, 227, 310
Skinner MP, Dennis 200
Sky
  formation of company 37–43
  and film rights 69–75, 138–9
  official launch 77–8, 96–101
  organisation and modus operandi 77–86, 87–96, 257–65
  programming 113, 116, 192–205, 253–5
  finance 136–9, 255–6
  direct-selling campaign 176–81
  merger with BSB 271–9, 280–87, 292–3
  see also Astra satellite, Centaurs Business Park, PAL system
Sky Arts channel 138, 207
Sky channel 96, 98, 116

Sky Europe 5, 38, 96
Sky Movie channel 96, 202, 228, 241, 254, 271
Sky News 96, 97–8, 116, 253, 255, 262, 270
Sky One channel 254
Skynet 4 satellite 77
SMATV (satellite master antenna television) 238, 245–6, 247
Smith MP, John 200
Smith, Peter 240
Snoddy, Ray 109–10, 135
Sports channel (BSB) 250
squarials 55–66, 133, 145–7, 236–7, 238, 301, 308
Stack, Robert 255
Stapleton, John 92–3, 113, 192–9, 265, 290–91, 292
STC company 146–7
Stehrenberger, Peter 279, 280
Sterling, Lord 50
Stewart, Will 135
Stock Exchange 14, 187, 189
Stockton, Earl of 214–15
Street-Porter, Janet 208
Stringer, Howard 235
Styles, Jim 79
Sugar, Alan 10–12, 15, 39, 44, 60–61, 101, 138, 270–71, 314
Sun 29, 40, 48, 49, 62, 64, 77, 195–8, 201, 238, 276
Sunday Telegraph 224
Sunday Times 43, 45, 48, 55, 65, 79–80, 94, 159, 193, 200, 206, 310
Sutch, Lord David 239–40
Symes, Peter 246, 251

Target programme (Sky) 94–5, 136, 229, 265
Tarrant, Chris 177
Tatung 59, 140
Tebbit MP, Norman 93, 100, 229, 265, 270
Technology Advisory Services 268, 269
Telesat company 126
Television Entertainment Ltd 224
Tesler, Brian 19
Thames Television 14, 49, 156, 267

Thatcher, Margaret 3, 5, 6, 14, 29, 38, 48–51, 106, 210–11, 215, 285–6, 311
Thomson of France 59
Thomson Group 151, 187, 302
Thomson Holidays 137
Thomson, Lady 154
Thomson, Lord 13, 154, 219, 282
Thynne, Jane 221
Till, Stewart 303, 307
Time magazine 203
Times 48, 49, 64, 151, 180, 200, 206, 208
Today 48, 64, 202, 207
Touchstone Films 74, 241
trade unions 83–6, 200, 208, 211, 244
Trans World International 113
Trethowan, Sir Ian 50
Tri-Star Pictures 74
Triangle magazine group 273, 274
Trillion company 12
Trinity International Holdings 15
TSI company 166
TV Guide (US) 273
TV-am 14, 82–4, 114
TVF company 114
TVS company 201
20th Century Fox 69

Unilever 21, 30–31

Vanderkar, Mike 300
Variety (media paper) 269, 292
Veronis, John 274, 275
Veronis Suhler 274
video industry 5–6, 131
Virgin company 10, 14, 27–8, 47, 75–7, 242, 266
VSAT (very small aperture terminal) 57

W.H.Smith 41
Walke, Eric 180
Wapping, News International papers at 83–4, 200, 211, 244, 278
Warburgs 190
WARC (World Administrative Radio Conference) 6–7
Warner Brothers 69, 73, 74
Washington Post 199–200
Waterman, Pete 255
Waugh, Auberon 239
Whitaker, Frances 113
Whitbread 22–5, 31
Whitbread, Colonel Bill 22
White, Patrick 311
White, Tim 85
Whitehead, Phillip 110
Whitelaw, Lord 270
Whitney, John 50
Whittam-Smith, Andreas 148
Wild West End show (Sky) 90–91
Williams, Hugh 223, 229, 248, 288, 289, 296–7, 300, 301
Willis, Lord 217
Wilson, Sir Harold 3, 5, 319
Winfrey, Oprah 204
Wogan, Alan 240
Wogan, Terry 222
Wonfor, Andrea 113
Woodcock MP, Mike 212
Woodside Petroleum 187
WPP agency 28
Wright, Steve 177

Yorkshire Television 14, 114, 312, 313
Young, Lord 47
Younger, George 194

Zenith company 113

According to most estimates, by the time they merged BSB and Sky had spent a combined total of £1.25 billion. These are some of the other things that you could have done with that amount:

* Paid for 15,625,000 cataract operations, thereby restoring the sight of everybody in the developing world blind for this reason several times over

* Fed 27,274,710 starving people for one year

* Chartered the QE2 for ten years

* Funded the entire Save the Children operation for the financial year 1989/90 twenty-three times over

* Bought 340,905 litres of Chanel No 5 perfume

* Funded the entire BBC operation for one year, thereby saving everyone their annual licence fee

* Travelled round the world 327,276 times with British Airways first class

* Sustained Oxfam's entire overseas aid programme at its present level for more than twenty years

* Paid for 520,826 protected water sources in the Third World

* Bought 160,228 BL Metro 1.1L cars

* Bought 146 Gazzas

* Purchased and shipped 6.25 million tons of grain to Africa

* Paid the basic salaries of all the MPs in the House of Commons since the beginning of the century

* Raised the same amount of money as 52 Live Aid concerts

* Paid for 416 million children to be inoculated against the six killer diseases

* Deposited the money in a building society to produce an income of £2,403,846 per week at 10% interest

* Bought 250 British Airways 125-800 executive jets

* Bought 52 copies of Van Gogh's painting, *Sunflowers*

* Bought 1,000 copies of the Sun newspaper daily for 1,603 years

* Bought 2,049,180,300 loaves of standard white sliced bread